The Hunter-Gatherer Use of Caves and Rockshelters in the American Midsouth

A geoarchaeological and spatial analysis of archaeological features at Dust Cave

Lara K. Homsey

BAR International Series 2129
2010

Published in 2016 by
BAR Publishing, Oxford

BAR International Series 2129

The Hunter-Gatherer Use of Caves and Rockshelters in the American Midsouth

ISBN 978 1 4073 0670 4

© LK Homsey and the Publisher 2010

The author's moral rights under the 1988 UK Copyright,
Designs and Patents Act are hereby expressly asserted.

All rights reserved. No part of this work may be copied, reproduced, stored,
sold, distributed, scanned, saved in any form of digital format or transmitted
in any form digitally, without the written permission of the Publisher.

BAR Publishing is the trading name of British Archaeological Reports (Oxford) Ltd.
British Archaeological Reports was first incorporated in 1974 to publish the BAR
Series, International and British. In 1992 Hadrian Books Ltd became part of the BAR
group. This volume was originally published by Archaeopress in conjunction with
British Archaeological Reports (Oxford) Ltd / Hadrian Books Ltd, the Series principal
publisher, in 2010. This present volume is published by BAR Publishing, 2016.

Printed in England

BAR titles are available from:

	BAR Publishing
	122 Banbury Rd, Oxford, OX2 7BP, UK
EMAIL	info@barpublishing.com
PHONE	+44 (0)1865 310431
FAX	+44 (0)1865 316916
	www.barpublishing.com

Preface

This study investigates the form, function, and organization of features at the Late Paleoindian through Middle Archaic site of Dust Cave, Alabama, using a multidisciplinary approach combining macromorphological, micromorphological, and chemical analyses. Previous studies have relied on observations made at the macroscopic level using morphological and/or content attributes, severely masking the diversity of activities they represent. A more robust method conceptualizes features as sedimentary deposits and reconstructs their depositional history as a means of identifying feature function. At Dust Cave, an integrated method combining micromorphology and geochemistry with more traditional studies of morphology and content highlights the importance of several activities not previously recognized, including broiling, smoking, nut processing, storage, and refuse disposal.

Use of Dust Cave as a place in the hunter-gatherer landscape of the Middle Tennessee Valley did not remain constant through time, but rather changed over the millennia. During the Late Paleoindian and early Early Archaic, Dust Cave functioned as a short term residential camp which was occupied fairly intensively during the late summer through fall. During the late Early Archaic, the site shifted to a residential base camp. During the Middle Archaic, the site shifted again to a logistical extraction camp where groups processed hickory nuts on such a large scale that the copious amounts of refuse generated give one the impression of a longer term base camp. The changes seen at Dust Cave mirror changes at other regional cave and rockshelter sites at which numerous nut processing pits, nutting stones, and enormous quantities of nut charcoal indicate a general shift in site use as plant extraction camps—sites where nuts were boiled and parched for transport to base camps located at lower elevations. The increased reliance on mast resources corresponds to warming and drying associated with the middle Holocene. These vegetation changes played a key role in the increasingly logistical mobility strategy of Middle Archaic hunter-gatherer groups. The changing use of caves and rockshelters during the Middle Archaic is therefore not one of longer occupation as has been argued, but rather one of intensified use as special purpose sites dedicated to the collection and processing of mast resources.

Acknowledgments

This book is a revised version of my 2004 doctoral dissertation submitted to the Department of Anthropology, University of Pittsburgh. The members of my doctoral committee strongly supported me in my interdisciplinary endeavor to investigate the effect of the natural environment in the lives of prehistoric populations. Rosemary Capo helped me to see and decipher the methodological trees. Marc Bermann helped me to see the theoretical trees. Kathleen Allen helped me to see the forest when the trees got too dense. Boyce Driskell planted the seeds that allowed the forest to grow in the first place. Jim Richardson was the sunshine.

My most sincere gratitude and thanks are extended to Dr. Boyce Driskell for the opportunity to work at Dust Cave. Little did I know when I came to the Dust Cave Field School as a student in 1996 that I would spend the next seven summers there. Sarah Sherwood generously and enthusiastically shared her time, talent and microscope in order to teach me the fine art and science of micromorphology. My Dust Cave colleagues Sharon Freeman, Kandi Hollenbach, Asa Randall, Scott Meeks, Meta Pike and Renee Walker provided valuable field assistance and motivation. Joe and Nancy Copeland left their door open and fed me no matter how dirty I was and provided invaluable nurturing for all swamp-weary Dust Cavers. Asa and Kandi I additionally thank for welcoming me to Stanfield-Worley and for patiently taking micromorphology samples and wonderfully detailed field notes. Craig Sheldon graciously provided me with maps and field notes from the original Russell Cave excavations. Finally, many field school students over the years enthusiastically carried out the experimental studies that are the foundation of this study, especially Laura Roskowski, Eddie de la Rosa, Chris Lydick, and the students of the 2002 Skidmore College field school: Abbey Copeland, Fife Harkins, Asa Snyder, Murat Terzioglu, Meg Winchester, and Casey Zivin.

Financial assistance for this project came from several sources. Dr. Boyce Driskell generously provided employment as a graduate research assistant and the equipment necessary to complete my fieldwork from 1999 through 2002. The research and field schools at Dust Cave were supported in part by grants from the National Science Foundation (Grant No. SBR-9619841), National Geographic Society (Grant No. 5023-93 and No. 5260-94), Alabama Historical Commission Preservation Trust Fund, Tennessee Valley Authority, IBM Corporation, and the Alabama Humanities Foundation. The geochemical analysis was partially supported by a NSF grant (EAR-0214212) to Dr. Rosemary Capo, and Brian Games ably assisted me with elemental analysis by ICP-AES. A scholarship from the International Zonta Club of Pittsburgh enabled me to have micromorphology thin sections from Dust Cave prepared. Dr. Mary Malainey of Brandon University conducted lipid analyses, research financially supported by a grant from the Committee for Institutional Studies and Research (CISR) at Murray State University. CISR funding also supported the preparation and analysis of thin sections from the Stanfield-Worley Bluff Shelter.

Last and most importantly, I thank my family for instilling in me a desire to learn and a curiosity about the world around me—both past and present—and David, whose spirit has been the motivation behind my work all along and in whose memory this book is dedicated.

Table of Contents

Preface iii

Acknowledgements iv

Table of Contents v

List of Tables vi

List of Figures vii

Chapter 1. Introduction 1
    Influential Models of Late Paleoindian through Middle Archaic Settlement 2
    The Use of Caves and Rockshelters: Ethnographic and Archaeological Evidence 4

Chapter 2. Theoretical and Methodological Framework for the Study of Features 6
    Deciphering Feature Function 7
    Deciphering Feature Organization 8
    Summary 10

Chapter 3. Reconstructing Activity at Dust Cave 11
    Feature Macromorphology 11
    Feature Geochemistry 13
    Feature Micromorphology 16
    Integrating Macromorphology, Micromorphology and Geochemistry 21
    Summary 40

Chapter 4. Reconstructing Spatial Organization at Dust Cave 42
    Evaluating the Units of Analysis 42
    Component Comparisons 42
    Organization of Space through Time 56
    Summary 53

Chapter 5. Dust Cave in Regional Context 56
    Cave and Rockshelter Sites in the Project Area 56
    Inter-site Comparison 58
    Open Air Sites in the Midsouth 63
    Discussion and Summary 64

Chapter 6. Modeling the Role of Caves and Rockshelters in the American Midsouth 67

Appendices 70
    Appendix A. Attributes for Dust Cave Features 70
    Appendix B. Dust Cave Micromorphology Samples 84
    Appendix C. Descriptions for Common Materials Identified in Dust Cave Thin sections 87

References Cited 89

List of Tables

3.1. Summary of feature counts by type 12

3.2. Cultural geochemical samples 14

3.3. Samples from Column N60W65 14

3.4. Sterile geochemical samples. 14

3.5. Typology of burned deposits at Dust Cave 18

3.6. Typology of unburned deposits at Dust Cave 20

5.1. Radiocarbon dates (uncal) and corresponding components and/or zones for other sites 57

List of Figures

3.1. Location of Dust Cave in Alabama (*modified from Walker et al. 2005:Figure 2*). 11

3.2. Dust Cave map view and cross-section 11

3.3. Scatterplot of Dust Cave features comparing width to depth ratio and volume. 12

3.4. Comparison of the 95% confidence intervals for Dust Cave feature depths (a), width (b), length (c), and volume (d) 13

3.5. Location of geochemical samples. 14

3.6. Scatterplots of K/P to Sr/Ca for all samples (a) and colluvial samples (b). 15

3.7. Concentrations of Ba, Ca, Fe, K, P, and Sr by depth 16

3.8 Field images of superimposed features (#134, 135, 136) from Eva/Morrow Mountain component and inset showing schematic of Feature 134 with charcoal lenses A through D. 21

3.9. Distribution of surface hearths (a), rock pits (b), expedient & prepared surfaces (c), and pit hearths (d). 23

3.10. Comparison of 95% confidence level for hearth (H) and rock basin (RB) dimensions. 24

3.11. Field image of stacked prepared surfaces with close up showing thin section of surface (zone P4) interbedded between P3e and P4a (a); field image of an expedient hearth (Feature 317) overlying prepared surface (zone E3g) (b); and textile impression fragments of prepared surfaces (*modified from Homsey and Sherwood 2010:Figure 2*). 25

3.12. Scatterplots of elemental ratios showing relationship between Dust Cave prepared surfaces and residual cave clay versus soil clay. 26

3.13. Field images of Features 117 (expedient hearth) and 429 (accessory pit) (a) and Feature 445 overlying a prepared surface (b) with scanned thin section of feature fill and unconformable boundary with prepared surface below (c); and photomicrographs (PPL left, XPL right) of burned bird shell (d); layered ash crystals (note spherulite crystals above and lozenge crystals below) (e); and fish bone (f). 28

3.14. Field image of Features 412 and 419 (pit hearths) (a) and photomicrographs (PPL left, XPL right) of nutshell (b), charcoal incompletely combusted to spherulite ash crystals (c), partially combusted organic material (d) and angular fractures in thermally altered limestone (e). 31

3.15. Field image of Feature 301, a charcoal lens (a) and scanned thin section of feature fill illustrating the cross-bedded charcoal grains. 34

3.16. Field image of Feature 381 (stringer) in plan view (a) and cross-section (b); photomicrographs (PPL left, XPL right) of undulatory charcoal grains and fining upward bedding (c), charcoal lined voids (d), and unconformable boundary with underlying zone T2. 36

3.17. Location of human burials and zone P pits (a) and error graphs showing that length does not differ significantly between burials and pits, but depth does (b) 37

3.18. Examples of pit intrusive into Zone P (P8/P8a) at Dust Cave (*modified from Sherwood 2001:Figure 8.8*) 39

3.19. Representative stratigraphy showing the pit features (P) at Modoc Rockshelter (*modified from Styles et al. 1983:Figure 13.4*). 39

4.1. Dust Cave calibrated radiocarbon dates by component and depth. 42

4.2. Feature distribution by type from the Paleoindian through Benton occupations. 43

4.3. Average feature size through time (a), comparison of feature length by component (b), comparison of feature width by component (c), and comparison of feature depth by component (d). 44

4.4. Feature diversity through time 45

4.5. Distribution of features in Paleoindian (Quad/Beaver Lake) Component 46

4.6. Distribution of lithics (a), bone (b) and shell (c), Paleoindian component 47

4.7. Feature distribution for the Early Side Notched Component 48

4.8. Distribution of lithics (a), bone (b) and shell (c), Early Side Notched component 49

4.9. Feature distribution for the Kirk Stemmed Component 50

4.10. Distribution of lithics (a), bone (b) and shell (c), Kirk Stemmed component 51

4.11. Distribution of features in Eva/Morrow Mountain Component 52

4.12. Distribution of lithics (a), bone (b) and shell (c), Eva/Morrow Mountain Component 53

4.13. Distribution of features in Benton Component 54

4.14. Distribution of lithics (a), bone (b) and shell (c), Benton component 55

5.1. Location of cave and rockshelter sites discussed in the text 56

5.2. Scatterplot comparing Dust Cave and Stanfield-Worley Bluff Shelter features 59

5.3. Organization of Dalton features at Stanfield-Worley Bluff Shelter 62

5.4. Organization of Middle through Late Archaic features at Stanfield-Worley Bluff Shelter 62

5.5. Model of Early (a) and Middle (b) Archaic settlement strategies. Site size indicates residence duration and/or frequency of use (*modified from Stafford 1994:Figure 5*) 65

Chapter 1

INTRODUCTION

Traditional models of hunter-gatherer settlement and subsistence economies in the American Midsouth have been informed primarily by open-air sites. Yet we have unequivocal evidence that hunter-gatherers also made use of caves for thousands of years, at least since the Late Paleoindian period. But just how they incorporated caves into their settlement and subsistence strategies is poorly understood (Anderson 1994; Anderson and Sassaman 1996; Straus 1997; Straus et al. 1996; Walthall 1998a). Many questions remain to be answered, such as what activities occurred in caves and when and how long were they occupied?

The activities occurring at archaeological sites are typically discerned through the analysis of lithic materials and—when available—plant and animal resources. Features, *in situ* representations of peoples' cooking and processing activities, remain a largely untapped resource in the archaeological interpretation of activity. This is due in part to a paucity of data—features frequently fall victim to a host of post-depositional processes that make them difficult to study if they preserve at all. Yet where features preserve well, they have greatly enhanced our understanding of site use and settlement-subsistence systems (*e.g.*, Carr 1991; Galanidou 1997, 2000; Hall 1985; Simek 1984; Ingbar 1985; Thoms 2005; Wadley 2000).

Environments that are especially conducive to the preservation of features include caves and rockshelters. Here, fragile ash and charcoal remains are well protected from the elements. Limestone caves in particular neutralize the acidity that typically is responsible for the decay and destruction of most organic remains. Caves and rockshelters are also desirable locals for studying past activity because they are distinct places on the landscape that were frequently and repeatedly visited by prehistoric populations. As such, they are not simply repositories for tools and the remains of dinner. Rather, they are places of residence for the groups that occupied them, for whatever amount of time. Here, people cooked, prepared and ate food, crafted and maintained toolkits, slept, and socialized. These activities leave behind their traces, however ephemeral, in the form of features.

A study of features is important not only because they hold the potential to inform archaeologists about prehistoric peoples' activities, but also because their spatial arrangement contains clues about the ways in which people organize and structure their activities within a site. Unfortunately, spatial analyses of hunter-gatherer sites have traditionally sought to identify individual activity areas and floors (e.g., use of a certain area for hide processing) relating to discrete occupations. Archaeological palimpsests, defined here as the mixed, cumulative products of human occupation accumulating in zones of low deposition, make this endeavor impossible. As palimpsests, caves and rockshelters rarely preserve intact habitation surfaces or activity areas for archaeologists to study. However, we should not abandon such spatial analyses, but rather seek new methodological frameworks in which to interpret the patterning at such sites. Archaeological features are ideally suited to the spatial analysis of palimpsests.

With this in mind, I develop a geoarchaeological and spatial framework to investigate the form, function, and organization of archaeological features which is then applied at the site of Dust Cave (1Lu496), a Late Paleoindian through Middle Archaic archaeological site located in the middle Tennessee River Valley of northwestern Alabama. Dust Cave is one of the few cave sites in the Midsouth with well-preserved deposits and the antiquity to span the Pleistocene-Holocene transition, a period for which very little is known in the Middle Tennessee Valley. Many Southeastern archaeologists have emphasized that the excavation and analysis of such sites is crucial if we are to understand how hunter-gatherer economies in the Midsouth changed during this transitional period (*e.g.*, Anderson 1994; Anderson and Sassaman 1996; Walthall 1998b). In using Dust Cave as a case study for the application of this methodological framework, it is my hope to convince readers that features can provide archaeologists with information that other artifactual remains cannot, and that our understanding of hunter-gather lifeways and their use of space is incomplete without this knowledge.

Like most other Paleoindian and Archaic sites across North America, lithics comprise the most ubiquitous artifact class at Dust Cave (Meeks 1994). However, due to its stratigraphic integrity and excellent preservation of plants, bone and features, Dust Cave has provided unprecedented material remains for the analysis of people's activities, including cooking and food preparation. Remarkable preservation of organic materials includes both charred and uncarbonized plant remains, as well as animal bones, including delicate small bones and fish scales (Hollenbach 2005; Walker 1998; Walker et al. 2001). Similarly, features and intact occupation surfaces are remarkably well-preserved (Homsey 2004; Homsey and Capo 2006; Sherwood 2001). Micromorphological analyses of feature fill have revealed calcitic pseudomorphs of original plant materials, as well as micro-lenses of ashes representing repeated and alternating fuel types (Homsey 2004). While some deposits have been post-depositionally homogenized or destroyed by bioturbation, much of the Dust Cave stratigraphy remains intact, thereby providing excellent context for the artifacts and features uncovered (Walker et al. 2001).

This book is broadly organized into three sections. The first section (chapters 2 and 3) centers on identifying what activities occurred at Dust Cave. Once we know what activities took place, we can better understand the role a site played as a place in the hunter-gatherer landscape (*sensu* Binford 1982). For example, was a cave a stopping point for a logistical foray, with only the coals of an overnight fire left to preserve as an ashy feature? Or was the cave a residential base camp, at which a great variety of domestic activities took place, leaving behind a diverse array of storage pits, earth ovens, and hearths? This goal will be accomplished by first developing a geoarchaeological and spatial framework for investigating the function and organization of archaeological features. Traditional studies of archaeological features have relied on observations made at the macroscopic level using morphological and/or content attributes, severely masking the diversity of activities they represent. A more robust method conceptualizes features as sedimentary deposits and reconstructs their depositional history as a means of identifying feature function. Here I propose an integrated method combining micromorphologic and geochemical attributes of feature fill with the more traditionally used morphologic and content attributes. Such information is crucial to developing holistic models of hunter-gatherer settlement and subsistence in the American Midsouth and elsewhere. The methodological framework proposed here was designed to maximize the information from archaeological palimpsests, though it should be noted that it is equally productive when applied to sites occurring in less vulnerable depositional environments.

The second section (chapter 4) explores the organization of activities within the cave to determine what processes structured the use of space. Spatial organization is examined through the site-structure lens promoted by Galanidou (1997). To varying extents, the organization of space inside a cave depends on the physical constraints of the shelter. As Straus (1997) has put it, if hearths, storage pits, and the like are "site furniture" (*sensu* Binford 1979), then the natural features of caves and rockshelters are the "real estate." Natural constraints include the size and morphology of the cave (Straus 1997), frequency and intensity of roof fall and attrition (Benyon 1980), the microtopography of the cave or rockshelter (Galanidou 1997; Sherwood 2001); and post-depositional disturbance from animals, water, and gravity (Farrand 2001; Schiegl et al. 1996; Sherwood 2001). Any interpretation of archaeological assemblages in caves and rockshelters must take into account these natural processes. While some have argued that cultural variables are a larger constraining force on the organization of cave and rockshelter space (Galanidou 1997), Straus (1997) cautions us not to interpret all apparent trends as resulting from cultural and historical developments. This said, research has shown that cultural factors do influence the organization of space to some degree, including mobility strategies (e.g., logistical versus residential), length of stay, intensity of occupation, cultural perceptions of "home," and the role of a site in its landscape (Binford 1983; Galanidou 2001; Straus 1997; Thomas 1985). This research explores to what extent the use of space at Dust Cave is controlled by geologic variables, whether any underlying cultural processes may account for some of the variation not explained by natural processes, and how the use of space changes through time.

The final section (chapters 5 and 6) takes both a diachronic view and a regional scale of analysis in order to compare the use of Dust Cave to other sites in the region. Previous research has shown that site function does not always remain constant over time. Changes in the ways prehistoric populations used sites occur when other variables change, including climate shifts (Cable 1996; Funk 1989; Mickelson 2002; Straus 1990; Straus and Clark 1986); variations in plant and animal resources (Akoshima 1993; Funk 1989; Stafford 1994; Straus 1997); changes in the configuration of available living space, such as roof fall and dripline recession (Funk 1989; Straus 1997; Rigaud 1982); and the movement of other human populations in a region (Anderson 2001, 1996; Anderson and Sassaman 1996). It will be argued that many of the temporal changes seen at Dust Cave mirror those at other sites in the Midsouth. This information helps us to make inferences about the role caves and rockshelters had as places in the hunter-gatherer landscape. Using this information, and drawing upon the influential models of settlement and mobility (discussed below), we can therefore refine our current models of cave and rockshelter use in hunter-gatherer settlement and subsistence systems in the Midsouth.

INFLUENTIAL MODELS OF LATE PALEOINDIAN THROUGH MIDDLE ARCHAIC SETTLMENT IN THE AMERICAN MIDSOUTH

From the 1950s through the 1970s, studies of the Paleoindian and Archaic periods focused primarily on the development of chronological sequences based on diagnostic artifacts, usually lithic bifaces (Anderson and Sassaman 1996). Many of these sequences were developed from the excavation of multi-component, open-air sites containing the deeply stratified deposits necessary to place artifacts in their chronological context. Early sites which contributed valuable data to this endeavor include the Hardaway and Doerschuk sites in North Carolina (Coe 1964), Koster in Illinois (Asch et al. 1972; Neusius 1982), and numerous sites along the Little Tennessee River, including Icehouse Bottom, Rose Island, Calloway Island, and Bacon Farm (Chapman 1973, 1975, 1976, 1977, 1978). A few cave and rockshelter sites with deeply stratified deposits were also excavated during this time period, such as Stanfield-Worley Bluff Shelter (DeJarnette et al. 1962) and Russell Cave (Griffen 1974) in northern Alabama, Modoc Rockshelter in Illinois (Ahler 1993, 2004; Fowler 1959), and Graham Cave (Logan 1952) and Rodgers Shelter (Wood and McMillan 1976) in Missouri.

Following the development of these important cultural chronologies, researchers in the 1980s began to refocus their efforts towards understanding the relationship between toolkits and site function. These efforts coincide with the emergence of middle-range theories which sought to use ethnographic and ethnoarchaeological observations to empirically link toolkits and site patterning with settlement and subsistence economies (Skibo 2009; Saraydar 2008). Perhaps the most widely used and cited of these middle-range theories is Binford's (1979, 1980, 1982) Forager/Collector model, which was intended to describe the cross-cultural variability in hunter-gatherer settlement systems. Binford envisioned a continuum of mobility strategies with foragers at one end of the continuum and collectors at the other end, each using distinctly different toolkits. *Foragers* are characterized by a high degree of group mobility in which entire camps are moved frequently (i.e., residential mobility), an absence of food storage, and a generalized expedient toolkit in which tools are made as needed. Residential mobility results in two site types (i.e., "places") in the hunter-gatherer landscape: residential base camps, which are seasonal camps for the entire group, and locations, places where extractive tasks are conducted and which may be occupied for only a very short time. *Collectors* are characterized by low group mobility in which individuals or small task groups move back and forth from a residential base camp (i.e., logistical mobility), the use of food storage, and a curated toolkit in which specialized tools are designed for particular tasks. Logistical mobility results in more types of sites than residential mobility: base camps where the entire group lives, field camps where specific resources are extracted and brought back to base camps, stations where observation and information gathering occur, and caches where hunting and/or gathering implements are temporarily stored. While some applications of Binford's model have given the impression that the two groups are mutually exclusive, it is important to note that it exists as a continuum; a single group could display both foraging and collecting behaviors depending on the season or the intended resource (e.g., Anderson and Hanson 1988).

One of the advantages of middle-range theories is that they create material correlates to link hunter-gatherer behavior to artifact and feature assemblages. In this manner, the Forager/Collector model allowed archaeologists to interpret whether sites were used logistically or residentially, by collectors or foragers respectively. In addition, middle-range theories such as these encouraged archaeologists to take a regional perspective and to make use of multiple data sets in comparative studies across regions (Sassaman and Anderson 1996). Such a perspective became increasingly possible with the large-scale survey and full-scale excavation projects resulting from the new cultural resource management legislation passed in the previous decade.

One of the earliest regional settlement models posited specifically for the Early Archaic Midsouth was Morse and Goodyear's Dalton settlement hypothesis (Morse and Goodyear 1983), formulated based on data from northeastern Arkansas and southeastern Missouri, including the Lace (Redfield and Moselage 1970), Brand (Goodyear 1974; Morse 1973, 1975) and Sloan (Morse 1975b, 1997) sites. Based on the function, clustering and density of stone tools, coupled with environmental factors, Morse suggested that bands exploited hexagonally shaped territories oriented within the confines of resource-rich watersheds. Within these territories, base camps, such as the Lace site, tended to be centrally located sites from which they could launch logistic forays to hunt, gather and process plant foods, and quarry rock among other activities (Morse 1975a, b, 1997a, b; Morse and Morse 1983).

Michael Schiffer (1975), using data from both Crowley's Ridge and the Cache River basin, contends that hunter-gatherer mobility varied seasonally and that band territories would have cross-cut river basins. In his view, temporary summer campsites were moved frequently while base camps were established near rivers during the winter and early spring. Gardner used data from the Shenandoah Valley of Virginia to suggest that rather than being oriented around watersheds, camps were tethered to lithic resources. In this model, the movements among base camps, quarries and hunting sites were constrained by the need to replenish toolkits. Based on data from the Carolina piedmont and the Yadkin-Pee Dee drainage, Daniel (1998, 2001) also argues that settlement and band territories were organized around the distribution of lithic raw material, and that band territories cross-cut river drainages rather than being defined by them.

Anderson and Hanson's (1988, 1996) Band-Macroband model for the South Atlantic Coast took a multi-causal approach to Archaic settlement by considering the role of seasonal and geographic variation in food resources, as well as biological interaction, information exchange, and population size and spacing in macroband aggregation. They postulate that territories followed river drainages and that seasonal movements took place within these drainages (as opposed to cross-cutting them in Schiffer's and Daniel's models). During winter—the period of greatest resource unpredictability—bands established logistically provisioned base camps below the Fall Line in the Coastal Plain, where winter temperatures are slightly warmer relative to the Piedmont. From these winter base camps, they made logistical forays to target patchy resources. During spring and early summer, these bands dispersed into seasonal camps above the Fall Line. During autumn, several bands from neighboring drainages aggregated at sites along the Fall Line in order to capitalize on ripening mast resources and rutting deer. This aggregation of several smaller bands into one larger macroband provided an opportunity to not only exchange raw materials and share food resources, but also to share information and find mates. A strength of this model is that it considers multiple decision-making factors that influence hunter-gatherer behavior and recognized needs beyond just food requirements.

Walthall (1998b:15), however, argues that long-term, logistically provisioned over-winter camps do not concord with the ethnographic record in eastern North America. Based on the compilation of a plethora of ethnographic data, he proposes a model which includes aggregation encampments in autumn, as Anderson and Hanson argue, but unlike the latter, he posits dispersed residentially-provisioned camps in winter rather than logistically provisioned base camps. The implication of this model is that winter encampments are likely to be light lithic scatters representing ephemeral occupations, rather than large, diverse base camps as Anderson and Hanson contend. In contrast, autumn encampments are likely to be larger with more diverse artifact assemblages representing these periods of aggregation. Unlike previous models of hunter-gatherer settlement, Walthall specifically considers caves and rockshelters when he suggests that they were occupied as dispersed over-winter encampments.

In the 1980s and 1990s researchers began to incorporate increasingly available climatic and environmental data into their models of Paleoindian and Archaic settlement. Binford's Forager/Collector model had an environmental component, but lacking diachronic climatic data, few archaeologists could address the link between shifts in mobility and climate change. Using effective temperature (ET), a measure based on the average annual temperature and length of the growing season, Binford demonstrated that a systematic relationship exists between climate and mobility strategy. Regions with ETs greater than 15°C, such as equatorial and semi-equatorial zones, are "food-rich," meaning that they have fairly constant and homogeneous food supplies. In these regions, foragers maintain a residential mobility strategy in which they frequently move to new, predictable resource patches as old ones are depleted. Regions with ETs less than 15°C, such as temperate and boreal zones, are "food-poor," meaning that they have patchy resources as well as seasonal incongruities in resource availability. As a result, collectors use a logistical mobility strategy in which they are forced to make logistical forays to distant resource patches to obtain unpredictable and scattered resources.

Revisiting the Haw River site in North Carolina in light of newly available climatic data, Cable (1996) suggests that Late Paleoindian (Hardaway-Dalton) groups may have behaved logistically as collectors during the winter and residentially as foragers during the summer. He contends that as effective temperatures in winter rose during the Early Holocene, generalized foraging strategies may have been employed throughout the year. This view comes from an analysis of the Haw River lithic assemblage, which shows an increase in lithic diversity through time. Cable argues that this increased diversity reflects the shifting use of the site from a short term camp to a longer term residential base camp. Thus, he contends that the low diversity in the Late Paleoindian lithic assemblage is suggestive of a logistical field camp, while the high lithic diversity in the later Archaic strata is suggestive of a residential base camp. While Cable's lithic data shows some contradictory patterns between the expedient and curated tools, his model serves as a good example of viewing settlement through the lens of climate change.

Dye (1996) models settlement during the Early to Middle Archaic transition, noting that around 7,000 B.P. populations in the Midsouth increased their emphasis on aquatic resources and their use of floodplain settlements as a result of environmental changes associated with the middle Holocene warming/drying trend known as the Hypsithermal event. During this time period, stabilizing fluvial regimes led to enhanced shoal habitats which attracted many species of shellfish, waterfowl, fish, invertebrates, mammals, and turtles. The availability of predictable, abundant and nutritional species offered a heterogeneous environment conducive to logistical foraging strategies and larger, longer-term base camps; these base camps are interpreted to represent increasing sedentism. In Dye's view, increased sedentism led to increased interaction and trade among populations, increasing cultural complexity, and large open spaces favorable to seed germination and—ultimately—plant domestication.

Several models of Middle to Late Archaic settlement in the Midsouth (e.g., Dye 1977, 1996; Futato 1983; Jenkins 1974) posit a cool season/warm season dichotomy in which food resources of major river valleys, such as the Tennessee River Valley, were harvested during the warm months, while upland resources were targeted during the cool season. This idea is based on the fact that mast resources, such as oak and hickory, are most abundant in the uplands and would have ripened in the early fall. In contrast, during the warm months, Archaic populations could readily have targeted riverine resources, particularly shellfish that would have been easily accessible as summer water levels dropped, as well as deer and other species of small game that populated the floodplain (Goldman-Finn 1994:214).

Southeastern archaeologists have constructed the above models using stone tool data, raw material distribution, plant and animal resources, and site distributions from open-air sites. Only Walthall (1998a, b) makes explicit reference to the role of caves and rockshelters. Also conspicuously absent is much discussion or use of features to infer activity or site use. As the byproducts of people's activities, features have the potential to greatly expand our knowledge of activities conducted at sites. Since reconstructing site function is crucial to interpreting prehistoric settlement systems, it is therefore imperative that we draw upon *all* aspects of the archaeological record including features. The following section highlights the need to integrate activity inferred from stone tool, animal and plant remains with activity inferred from features in order to model the use of caves and rockshelters by hunter-gatherers.

THE USE OF CAVES AND ROCKSHELTERS: ETHONOGRAPHIC AND ARCHAEOLOGICAL EVIDENCE

As suggested by the settlement models discussed above, the hunter-gatherer landscape is comprised of many kinds of places, including residential base camps, overnight camps, processing sites, hunting sites, and caches, just to name a few (Binford 1980, 1982). Some of these places are open-air sites; others are caves and rockshelters.

Caves and rockshelters have been used for multiple purposes for hundreds of thousands of years, most commonly as sites of habitation. At one end of the spectrum, foraging parties may camp at rockshelters for a night or two, seeking refuge from weather and animals (Nicholson and Crane 1991). On the other end of the spectrum, people in Scotland established residences in caves up through the 1920s (Leitch and Smith 1997). Caves have also been used as storage facilities (Straus 1991), workshops (Branigan 1997), locations for ceremonial and ritual significance (Nicholson and Cane 1991), and forums of artistic expression (Bahn 1997). Finally, caves serve as places where items are cached—both utilitarian items (Thomas 1988), and sacred items, such as human remains (Straus 1997).

Following the publication of Binford's *The Archaeology of Place* in 1982, identifying how caves functioned in the past—i.e., what role they played as "places" in the landscape—became an explicit goal of hunter-gatherer studies. During the 1980s, primarily in Old World studies, researchers focused on how prehistoric foragers used caves, and how that use changed through time. For example, Simek's (1984) study of spatial utilization at Le Flageolet I showed considerable redundancy in the use of Aurignacian space. He concluded that the site was used in the same way over a long period of time—in other words, that La Flageolet I had the same role as a place in the regional settlement system. At La Riera, Straus and Clark (1986) were able to trace shifts in cave use over a twelve thousand year period of human utilization. In contrast to La Flageolet I, La Riera's role as a place in the human landscape changed as the systems for exploiting resources in the region changed during climatic and demographic shifts (Straus 1991).

At L'Abri Dufaure in southwest France, Akoshima (1993) found evidence for two distinct patterns of structured activities during two different time periods. For the first half of the terminal Magdalenian occupation space appears to have been divided into three discrete areas: large fires in the center of the shelter, which Akoshima attributes to the mass roasting of reindeer meat; a dump zone in a depressed topographic area to the south; and a knapping zone at the front of the shelter. During the second half of the terminal Magdalenian occupation, this division broke down, and space became less compartmentalized. This apparent change in site structure correlates with a decline in the importance of reindeer and its steady replacement by red deer (Straus 1997). Thus, Akoshima's research at L'Abri Dufaure demonstrated the existence of structured activity areas and how diachronic changes in that structure highlight changes in subsistence strategies through time.

In the New World, Thomas (1985) demonstrated that caves served as many different kinds of places, ranging from personal cache caves to residential camps. Some Great Basin shelters had multiple purposes. Hidden Cave, for example, served primarily as a site to store personal gear, and secondarily as a burial locus, a resource cache, and a diurnal way station where logistical parties could "lay over" during the summer months (Thomas 1985). The use of Hidden Cave for these three functions varied little until the protohistoric period, when it ceased to be used.

In the Southeastern United States, Walthall (1998a) has proposed that Dalton groups were the first hunter-gatherers to systematically exploit the habitation potential of caves and rockshelters. In his model, the use of caves as temporary camps signals a fundamental reorganization of hunter-gatherer settlement-subsistence systems established with the onset of warmer Holocene conditions. During the Middle Archaic, a second reorganization occurred, causing hunter-gatherer groups to use shelters differently than they had previously. It is during this period that Walthall notes that shelter floors become strewn with storage pits, processing and earth oven features, as well as burial pits (Walthall 1998a:225). He argues that the increased use of caves and rockshelters reflects longer and more intensive periods of use of these sites, perhaps as long-term base camps, but does not speculate as to why this shift took place.

Based on detailed studies of cave sites in both the north and southeast, several researchers have disputed the first half of Walthall's model (Collins 1990; Sherwood 2001; Walker 1998). For example, we now know that Dust Cave was occupied prior to Dalton times (Collins et al. 1994; Sherwood 2001; Sherwood et al. 2004). We also know that many caves were not available for occupation. In the Middle Tennessee River Valley, for example, deep alluvial deposits choked many caves until the Pleistocene-Holocene transition around 14,000 years ago. Only then did regionally lowered base levels increase water flow through caves, flushing out sediments and opening them up to occupation (Sherwood 2001). Pre-Dalton groups could not utilize these caves because they were not yet open cavities.

Walthall's model raises several other questions: how did people use caves and rockshelters, how long did people stay at them, and what activities occurred there? Furthermore, no one has critically evaluated the second half of Walthall's model: what happened during the Middle Archaic that caused people to use caves differently than during the Early Archaic and what prompted these changes? Such questions remain because detailed studies of southeastern caves and rockshelters spanning the Early to Middle Archaic interval have rarely been undertaken. Before models of hunter-gatherer settlement and subsistence can include caves and rockshelters, we must investigate the activities occurring at them, the intensity of occupation, and—ultimately—their roles as places in the hunter-gatherer landscape.

Chapter 2

THEORETCIAL AND METHODOLOGICAL FRAMEWORK FOR THE STUDY OF FEATURES IN ARCHAEOLGOICAL PALIMPSESTS

Feature function has received relatively little attention in traditional North American archaeological research, largely because poor feature preservation often makes such a goal exceedingly difficult, if not impossible. As a result, no precedent has been set for how to study such archaeological remains. In regions amenable to feature preservation, they have usually been studied based solely on morphology and content (*e.g.*, Lowell 1999; Smith and McNees 1999; Ingbar 1985, 1988; Schroedl 1986; Wolynec 1977). Morphology and content analysis is a valid starting point for identifying feature function, but as Moeller (1992:52-54) notes, such analyses make several assumptions, including the following:

- Feature function remains constant over time;
- There exists a positive correlation between shape, size and contents;
- Features having similar contents and/or morphologies functioned similarly;
- Features that look morphologically similar were contemporaneously dug and utilized.

In order to minimize the erroneous effects these assumptions have on the interpretation of human behavior, a more robust approach to studying features is imperative.

Sherwood (2001) argues that the term "feature" is in and of itself an artifact, produced when archaeologists conceptualize the archaeological record as a series of artifacts and special intrusions into a sediment or soil "matrix." To avoid this, I propose following Stein's (1987) advice to consider features to be fundamentally deposits. As such, they should be described and studied as sediments. This is not to suggest that archaeologists stop excavating features separately from the surrounding matrix, but as deposits, we should record and describe them within the same paradigm and using the same nomenclature as we would record and describe any sedimentologic unit (Stein 1987).

Recent research on feature function at archaeological sites has begun to move in this direction by employing high-tech geologic techniques including micromorphology (*e.g.*, Courty et al. 1989; Goldberg 1979a, b; Goldberg and Sherwood 2006; Schuldenrein 2001; Sherwood 2001) and geochemistry (*e.g.*, Homsey 2003a; Manzanilla and Barba 1990; Middleton and Price 1996; Schuldenrein 2001, 1995; Schiegl 1996). This research will follow suit by integrating both of these techniques with the more traditional attributes of morphology and content. In order to study features as deposits, we must begin by thinking of them in terms of their depositional history. In other words, what is the history of any given deposit: Where did it originate? How was it deposited? In what geologic environment was it laid down? Did anything alter it after deposition? These four questions constitute what Stein (1987) calls a deposit's depositional history. This history consists of four aspects: (1) sediment source, (2) transport agent, (3) environment of deposition, and (4) post-depositional activity. I describe features in the present study using this paradigm. Specific questions that I address for each deposit include:

(1.) Is the sediment source anthropogenic or geogenic? It has been argued that some of the "features" at Dust Cave are not anthropogenic at all, but rather geogenic in source, transport, and deposition.

(2.) By what agent are feature sediments transported? Are they transported by people (e.g., through dumping or sweeping), or by a natural agent (e.g., by flowing water)?

(3.) What is the environment of deposition for feature sediments? Are they created *in situ* (e.g., through burning), or are they re-deposited (e.g., through discard)? If they are burned, at what temperature did they burn, and what was the fuel source used?

(4.) What processes have occurred long after deposition which may have obscured the original sedimentary structures and morphology of the deposit? Post-depositional processes include natural processes such as animal disturbance, bioturbation, water activity, and decalcification, as well as cultural processes, such as trampling.

Studying features in terms of their depositional history promises to be a productive means through which archaeologists can better understand the formation, function, and diagenesis of complex anthropogenic deposits. By thinking of features as deposits, we avoid subjective interpretations of features based on presumed correlations between feature shape, content and function. This is especially important since features may undergo a great deal of post-depositional alteration. If this change is not taken into consideration, gross misinterpretations of function and site use may occur. More often than not, such processes can only be detected at a very fine scale, one at which macroscopic observations are useless. In order to study deposits at this small a scale, high resolution analyses of undisturbed samples must be employed. Micromorphology and geochemical analyses are particularly well-suited to this kind of study (*e.g.*, Gé et al. 1993; Gebhardt and Langhor 1999; Goldberg and Sherwood 2006; Homsey and Capo 2006; Karkansas et al. 2000; Matthews et al. 1997; Macphail and Cruise 2001; Middleton and Price 1996; Sherwood 2001). These analyses are discussed in greater detail below; methodological details are presented in chapter three.

DECIPHERING FEATURE FUNCTION

Micromorphology

Micromorphology, the study of *in situ* soils, sediments, and other archaeological materials (including ceramics, bricks, and floors), is a valuable approach to archaeological inquiry. This technique employs undisturbed, oriented samples in which the original components and their associated relationships can be observed microscopically (Courty et al. 1989). Micromorphological analysis allows for the observation of several attributes, including composition (mineral and organic), texture (size, shape, rounding, and sorting), and fabric (relationship among the constituents), all of which are vital to reconstructing depositional histories. Even within an individual thin section, micro-stratigraphic sequences can be observed which reflect small-scale changes in depositional and post-depositional processes (Sherwood 2001).

Using micromorphology as a means to study the depositional histories of archaeological deposits and to generate information on human activity has been successfully applied to a number of contexts. It has helped archaeologists understand the construction and use of earthworks, hearths, house-floors, and stables (e.g., Gebhardt 1993, 1992; Gebhardt and Lanhogr 1999; Goldberg and Whitbread 1993; Matthews 1995; Macphail et al. 1997; Macphail and Goldberg 1995; Quine 1995); identify and interpret the nature of agricultural soils and the impact of farming and deforestation on them (e.g., Courty et al. 1989; Gebhardt 1993, 1992; Macphail et al. 1997; Sandor 1992); and determine the depositional histories of complex archaeological sites, such as caves and rockshelters (e.g., Bar-Yosef et al. 1992; Goldberg 1979a, b; Goldberg and Bar-Yosef 1998; Goldberg and Arpin 2000; Schuldenrein 2001; Sherwood 2001). Micromorphology's potential to inform on the nature of humanly created and modified sediments is thus well documented (Courty et al. 1989; Goldberg 1980; Macphail and Cruise 2001; Macphail and Goldberg 1995). Questions that micromorphology can help answer include: (1) Is a deposit burned, and if so, was it burned in place or has it been redeposited in a secondary context? (2) If it has been burned, at what temperature did it burn? (3) What is the fuel source? (4) What was burned or cooked? (5) If the deposit represents redeposited materials, what was thrown out? And (6) How have the anthropogenic deposits been modified since their deposition hundreds to thousands of years later?

Experimental studies often play a crucial role in identifying unique sedimentary microstructures related to human activity, such as burning, trampling, and bioturbation. For example, experimental studies conducted during the 2000 field season identified a micromorphological signature for fire-cracked rock and also demonstrated that the occupants of Dust Cave used locally available Tuscumbia limestone, primarily biomicritic varieties, as heating stones (Homsey 2009). Experiments conducted during the 2002 field season demonstrated that the prepared clay surfaces found at Dust Cave (discussed further in chapter 3) served as an important part of prehistoric cooking technology, most likely as roasting or parching surfaces (Homsey and Sherwood 2010; Homsey et al. 2010). Lydick's (1999) experiment demonstrated that organic materials do not fully combust below approximately 200°C, and that ash content increases as fires smolder. Hendrickson (1998) characterized the effects of burning on local cave sediments, including reddening, dessication, and disaggregation of soil particles. A final experiment that played an important role in understanding feature formation is Roskowski's 1999 trampling study in which she identified a sediment signature for human trampling, including the development of channel and planar voids, mixing of burned sediments, dispersion of ash, and splintered charcoal fragments. As will be discussed later, trampling is responsible for the physical appearance of many of Dust Cave's features.

Geochemistry

Chemical analyses have become an increasingly popular application to archaeology (e.g., Cook and Heizer 1965; Eidt 1973, 1985; Holliday and Gartner 2007; Pollard and Heron 1996; Middleton and Price 1996; Schuldenrein 1995) which in more recent years have been applied with greater frequency to caves and rockshelter environments (Farrand 1985, 2001; Schuldenrein 2001; Schleigel et al. 1996; Vento 1985). Such analyses work because human activities, including food preparation, burning and waste disposal, chemically enrich soils and sediments in elements such as phosphorous (P), carbon (C), nitrogen (N), potassium (K), and calcium (Ca). They make their way into the soil via the decomposition of plant residues, animal bones, and human and animal excrement. Some of these elements (e.g., C and N) are mobile and are lost from the soil by both organic and inorganic processes. For example, both form gases (e.g., CO_2) and water soluble compounds that can enter the atmosphere or be carried away in groundwater. Other elements, such as phosphorous, tend to remain in the soil system even over long time intervals by becoming adsorbed onto the colloidal fraction of soil particles, fixed into the lattice structures of clay minerals, or by forming water insoluble compounds, such as calcium and iron phosphates (Hertz and Garrison 1998). As a result, their presence has been used to identify archaeological sites, the activities carried out there, and the intensity of human occupation.

Arrhenius (1931) first demonstrated that areas of ancient occupation had elevated concentrations of phosphate, and by the 1970s phosphate analyses constituted an accepted archaeological technique for site identification (e.g. Eidt 1973, 1985; Hertz and Garrison 1998; Holliday and Gartner 2007). Today, the most common applications of phosphate analyses focus on (1) pre-excavation prospecting to locate and delimit archaeological sites, (2) identifying areas of concentrated activity for full-scale excavation, and, most recently, (3) delineation of features and activity areas (e.g., Cook and Heizer 1965; Lippi 1988; Manzanilla and Barba 1990; Parnell et al. 2001;

Sánchez and Cañabate 1999; Schuldenrein 1995; Terry et al. 1999; Wells et. al. 2000).

Researchers using multi-element analyses have found that different elements correlate with different activities and materials: potassium with *in situ* burning and residual wood ash (Middleton and Price 1996; Schuldenrein 1995); phosphorous with food processing and animal remains (Schuldenrein 1995); calcium with butchering and animal remains (Schuldenrein 1995); magnesium with shellfish processing and mollusks (Vento 1985); strontium with diets rich in plants, fish and nuts (Pearsall 2000; Rosenthal 1981); and zinc with nuts (Pearsall 2000). Other multi-element research focuses on identifying fuel sources (Pierce et al. 1998). Still others focus on sourcing the raw material for feature sediment and artifacts, including clay and chert, by comparing the elemental signature of the cultural material with that of potential sources for the raw material (Lambert 1997; Pollard and Heron 1996; Tykot and Young 1996).

DECIPHERING FEATURE ORGANIZATION

Research regarding the use of hunter-gatherer sites has traditionally focused on identifying activity areas and individual actions on distinct occupational surfaces. Activity area research is most valuable in sites of low density and high resolution where rapid sedimentation rates have preserved intact single-episode living surfaces. While the goals of activity area research are admirable for those seeking to reconstruct specific instances in the past, such a goal is not feasible at sites having less integrity. Such is often the case with caves and rockshelters where intact habitation surfaces or individual activity areas are unlikely to have survived (Galanidou 1997). Most spatial organization models assume the synchronic deposition of archaeological deposits, but this is rarely, if ever, the case in caves and rockshelters. Rather, most cave and rockshelter sites are palimpsests created by the debris from multiple superimposed occupations.

Galanidou (1997) suggests that one approach to studying palimpsests is to describe overall site configurations by analyzing the association between evident and latent structures. Specifically, she proposes to study the relationship between hearths (the "evident" structures) and patterns in their distribution (the "latent" structures). This "site-structure approach" differs from a functional reconstructionist approach (i.e., activity area research) in that it looks for patterning in hearth-related distributions rather than individual activity areas. Specifically, it identifies *redundant patterns* of spatial structure that transcend single behavioral events. Most importantly, it does not assume that any common human principle has directed the organization of space, but instead looks for both cultural and natural variability in site structure.

In order to examine the organization of activity at Dust Cave, I employ a modified version of Galanidou's site-structure approach. This approach consists of five steps: (I) evaluating stratigraphic integrity and identifying the units of analysis; (II) selecting the units of observation appropriate to the question at hand (in this case, how Dust Cave is used through time); (III) describing the habitation features identified during excavation (i.e., the evident structures); (IV) searching for patterns in the spatial distribution of the selected units of observation (i.e., the latent structures); and (V) considering any relationships between the evident and latent structures and the cave's topography. The following sections describe this five-step approach to deciphering the spatial organization of features.

I. Evaluating Stratigraphic Integrity and Identifying the Units of Analysis

Before examining spatial variation, it is first necessary to critically evaluate stratigraphic integrity and decide on the unit of analysis. To make sure that the contextual unit chosen is the smallest one that can be confidently defined, several factors must be carefully evaluated, including microstratigraphy and radiocarbon dates. For the site of Dust Cave, over 40 radiocarbon dates exist (see Figure 4.1). Overall, there is a strong positive correlation between depth below datum and radiocarbon age. Using this data, coupled with detailed microstratigraphic control, I examine spatial variation among cultural components for two reasons. First, thanks to the large number of radiocarbon dates, we can constrain components with acceptable confidence; we do not have this kind of control for smaller ethno-stratigraphic units (*sensu* Stein 1990). Second, studying variation at the cultural component level is intuitively satisfying since previous analyses (*e.g.*, Hollenbach 2007, 2003; Meeks 1998; Randall 2003, 2001; Walker 1998, 2007; Walker et al. 2001) have used this same level as the comparative unit.

II. Selecting the Units of Observation

In the Dust Cave study that follows, I observe features rather than other possible artifact classes, such as lithics or bone, as the main unit of observation. Galanidou (1997) used the latter classes in her assessment of rockshelter use in the Upper Paleolithic. She was able to do so because three-point provenience existed for them. This is common practice in Old World cave studies; however, in the United States, excavators rarely three-point provenience artifacts unless they are diagnostic of a particular time period. Features, on the other hand, always have three-point provenience, giving us much tighter chronological control over their distribution. Moreover, features represent myriad activities that have been sorely overlooked in archaeological studies. Finally, as Galanidou (2000) notes, features (namely, hearths) often serve as a focal point for group activities. Thus, features are an exceptional candidate for use in a site-structure approach to studying site use. I also consider lithic debitage, bone and shell, though these artifacts were not piece plotted. Raw counts for each of these classes per excavation unit are available, however. I convert these counts into densities per unit and graph these using Surfer, a program designed to create isopleth maps for describing changes in one variable (here, density), as a function of two other variables (here, northing and westing).

III. Describing and Interpreting Habitation Features

Traditional studies of archaeological features have relied on observations made at the macroscopic level using morphological and/or content attributes, severely masking the diversity of activities they represent. A more robust method conceptualizes features as sedimentary deposits and reconstructs their depositional history as a means of identifying feature function. Here I propose an integrated method combining micromorphologic and geochemical attributes of feature fill with the more traditionally used morphologic and content attributes. This geoarchaeological methodology is detailed in Homsey (2004) and Homsey and Capo (2006). Such information is crucial to developing holistic models of hunter-gatherer settlement and subsistence in the American Midsouth and elsewhere.

The methodology for describing and interpreting the evident structures (in this case, the features) is based on the integration of four attributes (1) macromorphological, (2) botanical, (3) micromorphological, and (4) geochemical variables for each feature. In the case study of Dust Cave that follows, feature morphology is reconstructed by utilizing feature forms and photographs. Feature forms, completed in the field for every feature encountered, provide detailed information on size, shape (in both map view and cross-section), and the general appearance of the fill (e.g., charcoal-rich, ash-rich, etc.). Attributes used for statistical analyses of morphology include length, width, volume, depth, and shape. Macromorphology profile descriptions follow Moeller (1991, Figure 3). When available, photographs supplemented feature drawings.

The botanical analysis and resulting data are detailed in Hollenbach (2009, 2007, 2005), Detwiler-Hollenbach (2003, 2001) and Pike (2003, see also Pike et al. 2005). The botanical assemblage is derived from flotation of feature fill. The resulting heavy and light fractions are sorted into categories: lithics, shell, bone, and charred plant material. Plant materials are further subdivided into nutshell (e.g., hickory, walnut, acorn), edible seeds, and fruits.

Micromorphological analysis allows for the reconstruction of the depositional history for each deposit, including the sediment source, transport agent, depositional environment, and post-depositional alteration (for a detailed explanation see Homsey 2004). Sediment source is determined by analyzing the fine and coarse fraction for mineralogical and artifact content. Transport agent and depositional environment are determined by looking at the sorting and rounding of individual sediments, as well as sedimentary structures such as graded bedding and cross-bedding. If the deposit is culturally transported and deposited, then several new questions emerge. First is the sample burned? This is determined by looking for combusted materials, oxidation of the substrate, and burned microartifacts. Second, is the deposit burned *in situ*? This is determined by looking at the fabric and orientation of sediment grains, the presence/absence of aggregates typical of re-deposition, and the presence/absence of a burned substrate. Third, at what temperature did the deposit burn? This is determined by looking at the degree of burning in bone and the degree of combustion in plant materials. Fourth, what was the fuel source, which is determined by the type of charcoal present (wood vs. nut), and the type of ash crystals present (lozenge, rhomboid, or spherulite). Finally, post-depositional alteration is examined by looking for evidence of bioturbation, decalcification, fluvial activity, and trampling.

Geochemical data provide complementary and corroborating evidence for many of the trends identified micromorphologically and botanically. Phosphorous concentrations by depth allow for confident determination of occupational intensity through time. Ratios of Sr to Ca and K to P help identify feature content and fuel source. High concentrations of individual elements help identify the activities associated with individual feature types, such as nut processing, animal butchering and intense burning. Finally, elemental ratios help source materials used to construct features, such as prepared surfaces.

IV. Searching for Spatial Patterns in the Selected Variables

Once feature function has been determined, they are mapped two-dimensionally in order to evaluate if, and how, the different feature types distribute relative to one another. Features were mapped using AutoCAD Map. In order to evaluate the relative degree and significance of clustering among different feature types, I used a Nearest Neighbor analysis. The Nearest Neighbor Ratio (NNR) quantitatively characterizes the distribution of points in space by measuring whether a given set of points clusters or distributes evenly across a region by comparing the observed distribution to the expected distribution for a random scatter of points in a given area. The NNR ranges from 0 (extremely clustered) to 2.149 (evenly distributed); a NNR close to 1 represents a random distribution of points.

Other researchers have made use of complex statistical tests, such as K-means nonhierarchical clustering (e.g., Gregg et al. 1991; Rigaud and Simek 1991) and Unconstrained Cluster Analysis (e.g., Galanidou 2000; Gregg et al. 1991; Whallon 1984). Both of these methods entail identification of multiple clusters. After mapping the Dust Cave features, however, it quickly became apparent that there is only one cluster for most feature classes. Initially, it appears that there may be two clusters for some feature classes, but more careful inspection of this "clustering" reveals that the clusters fall on opposite sides of the original test trench, excavated in 1994 (see Figure 3.5). Due to poor lighting and lack of familiarity with site stratigraphy, excavators did not notice many features. Thus, feature density for the Test Trench is inherently lower, and the seemingly bimodal clustering is an artifact of our early excavation.

I also map the spatial distribution of lithic debitage, bone and shell by converting raw counts of each artifact into densities per grid unit within the excavated area (Kintigh 1990; Whallon 1973). The resulting densities are then graphed using Surfer, a high resolution two and three-dimensional graphics software package. The resulting contour maps reveal trends in density peaks and troughs throughout the cave.

Of greater interest than the absolute number of clusters is where in space certain feature types are located relative to other feature types as well as geologic features (e.g., cave walls, dripline, etc.). Ethnoarchaeological studies by Gorecki (1991) and Galanidou (1997) have isolated some typical patterns created by contemporary hunter-gatherer use of caves. For example, the majority of activity tends to occur towards the front of shelters; large cooking ovens are usually located at the cave entrance near the dripline, where they are both closer to daylight and better ventilated; sleeping areas and associated fires tend to occur toward a rear wall; and sleeping areas are often small fires comprised largely of coals, which reflect light and heat off the back wall. Of special interest is whether or not the Dust Cave spatial organization conforms to these ethnographically documented patterns.

V. Determining the Relationship between Evident and Latent Structures

Of final interest is whether the placement of features appears to be constrained by the shape of the cave itself, or whether their placement appears to be independent of physical constraints. To answer this question, I consider several geologic variables, including the dripline, cave ceiling height, roof fall events, horizontality of strata, and water activity through time. These geologic variables change over time: driplines recede, roof fall events increase and decrease with changing climate, and headroom decreases as deposits build up over time. Geologic variables are mapped where possible (i.e., dripline, cave walls, roof fall events). Other variables are discussed with reference to Sherwood (2001), whose dissertation work involved the reconstruction of the geoarchaeology of the site. Her work identified major changes in microtopography and fluvial events over time.

Beynon (1981) conducted a similar exercise in her analysis of feature distribution at Meadowcroft Rockshelter in western Pennsylvania. Beynon found that the distribution of features was contingent upon the physical characteristics of the shelter, namely roof fall. Thus, at Meadowcroft, occupants had little control over their surroundings and therefore little opportunity to manipulate space to their liking and in accordance with their unique cultural perceptions of space. In contrast, Galanidou (1997) minimizes the importance of microtopography in the hunter-gatherer adaptation to caves and rockshelters. She points out that cultural variables also influence the organization of deposits, including mobility strategies, length of stay, and cultural perceptions of domestic space. Given the likelihood that both the natural and the cultural environment affect hunter-gatherer adaptation to caves and rockshelters, it is vital to compare the organization of space to the natural constraints of the shelter before embarking on an uninformed discussion of cultural constraints.

SUMMARY

A true understanding of site function involves not only an understanding of feature function, but also of the organization of the activities the features represent. The organization of space at any given site has much to say about the nature of the activities occurring there, the intensity of occupation through time, the natural controls over site organization, and the diversity of activities—all of which have important implications for mobility and re-use of sites. Using a site-structure approach takes advantage of the processes of redundant patterning. This approach is not supposed to result in snapshots of everyday life at Dust Cave, but rather seeks out redundant patterns in site structure, changes they may have undergone through time, and any clues they may have to offer us concerning site function, intensity of occupation, and other, natural factors accounting for the organization of deposits. Thus, the strength of the site-structure approach is that it allows archaeologists to examine how intra-site spatial variation may be linked to the role of a site within the broader settlement system, without losing sight of the taphonomic overprint of natural formation processes (Galanidou 1997:19).

Chapter 3

RECONSTRUCTING ACTIVITY AT DUST CAVE

Dust Cave lies within a limestone bluff of the Middle Tennessee River Valley, located within the southern Interior Low Plateau physiographic province in the Highland Rim section of northwestern Alabama (Figure 3.1). Here, horizontal Mississippian–age rocks create an undulating karst plateau on either side of the Tennessee River and its floodplain. At the time people first occupied Dust Cave, approximately 10,650 cal. B.C., the entrance spanned approximately 100 m^2 with a ceiling height of 4.5 meters. The cave overlooked a small creek that meandered along the edge of the Tennessee River floodplain whose main channel flowed less than a mile away (Collins et al. 1994). In this landscape, the cave served as an ideal place to collect myriad fish, freshwater shellfish, and plant resources (Driskell 1996; Walker et al. 2001). By 4,000 cal. B.C., after several millennia of periodic human occupation, headroom in the cave decreased to less than one meter, prompting the cave's abandonment (Sherwood et al. 2004). Today the cave vestibule contains over four meters of sediment derived from both natural and cultural sources, with human activity accounting for much of the deposition (Goldberg and Sherwood 1994; Sherwood 2001).

9,000 cal. B.C. and 8,200 to 5,800 cal B.C., respectively. the Eva/Morrow Mountain component and Benton phase comprise the Middle Archaic and spans 6,400 to 4,000 cal. B.C. and 4,500 to 3,600 cal B.C., respectively (Sherwood et al., 2004). After 3,600 cal. B.C., the cave deposits had reached to within two meters of the ceiling and the cave was abandoned (Driskell 1994; Sherwood et al. 2004). Excellent preservation has resulted in numerous anthropogenic deposits not traditionally preserved at open-air sites, and for which function is unknown. Despite this lack of knowledge, the diverse array of feature morphologies, ranging from large circular fired surfaces to flat-bottomed pits to ephemeral charcoal and ash pits, strongly suggest differences in function.

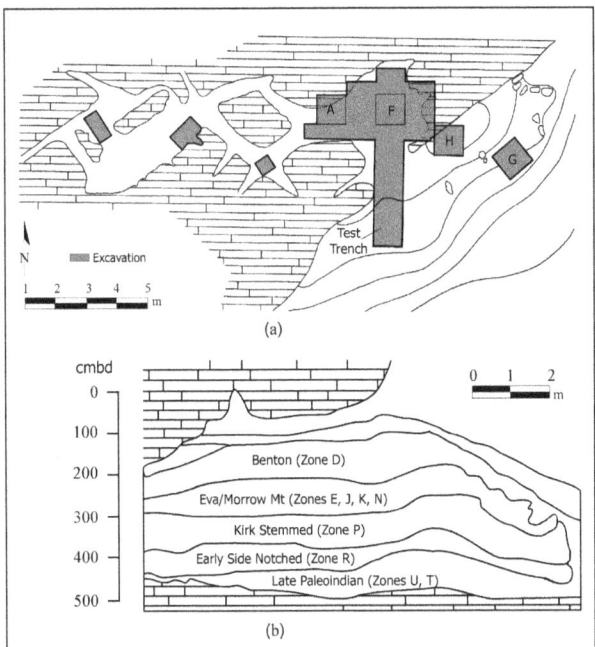

Figure 3.2. Dust Cave map view and cross-section.

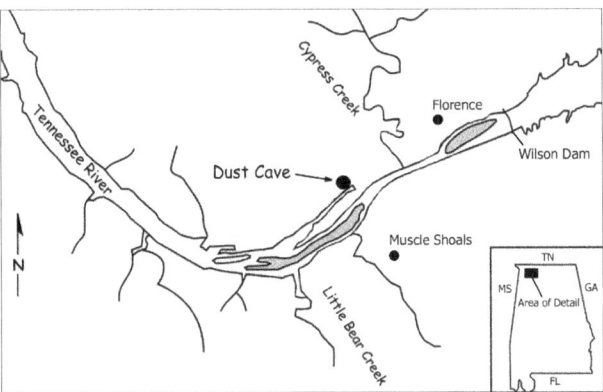

Figure 3.1. Location of Dust in Alabama.

Initially sponsored by the Office of Archaeological Research (OAR) at the University of Alabama, excavations were carried out between 1989 and 2002 under the direction of Dr. Boyce Driskell (Driskell 1996; Sherwood et al. 2004). Over 100 m^2 of cave floor have been exposed within the entrance chamber (Figure 3.2a) (Driskell 1996). These excavations have revealed over five meters of stratified deposits replete with exceptionally well-preserved animal and botanical remains, as well as features and intact occupation surfaces (Sherwood et al. 2004).

A total of five cultural occupations have been documented (Figure 3.2b). The Late Paleoindian occupation spans from 10,650 to 9,200 cal. BC. The Early Side-Notched and Kirk Stemmed components comprise the Early Archaic and date between 10,000 and

FEATURE MACROMORPHOLOGY

Methods

Feature morphology is reconstructed by utilizing feature forms and photographs. Feature forms, filled out for every feature encountered in the field, provide detailed information on size, shape (in both map view and cross-section), and the general appearance of the fill (e.g., charcoal-rich, ash-rich, etc.). Attributes used for statistical analyses of morphology include length, width, volume, depth, and shape. Shape and profile descriptions follow Moeller (1991:Figure 3). When available, photographs supplemented feature drawings. Of the 465 features recorded between 1990 and 2000, 339 remained after eliminating non-features (e.g., root disturbances) and those lacking the requisite data for analyses conducted here (e.g., depth). Features lacking such data often result from partial feature excavation. Whenever possible, excavators retained the same number for features known to cross-cut unit boundaries. Unfortunately, excavating the remaining portion of a feature often happened years later, so they were often given a separate feature number. Whenever possible I correlated feature portions and assigned them one number (the earliest excavated number). Features that could not be correlated were eliminated from statistical analyses.

Results

The 339 features include human burials (n=21), charcoal pits (n=124), ash pits (n=15), charcoal/ash pits (n=15), charcoal concentrations (n=30), ash concentrations (n=10), undifferentiated pits (n=23), and hearths (n=25). The remaining 25 features are charcoal and/or ash stringers (<1 cm thick) (n=34), canine burials (n=2), and unknown (n=24) types. Table 3.1 summarizes feature type, count, and proportion of total assemblage.

Table 3.1. Summary of feature counts by type.

Feature Type	Count	% total
Human burial	21	6.2
Canine burial	2	<0.5
Hearth	25	7.4
Rock pit or cluster	18	5.3
Charcoal pit	124	36.6
Ash pit	15	4.4
Charcoal & Ash pit	15	4.4
Undifferentiated pit	23	6.8
Charcoal concentration	30	8.8
Ash concentration	10	2.9
Charcoal or ash stain	34	10.0
Unknown	22	6.5
TOTAL	**339**	**100**

Graphing feature types by size (depth, length, width, volume) (Figure 3.4) illustrates that most field-identified feature types are significantly different at the 95% confidence level. In particular, charcoal and ash concentrations are significantly shallower than all other feature types, including charcoal and ash pits. This comes as no surprise since the concentrations were differentiated from pits based on depth. This difference is, then, in and of itself an artifact of our excavation protocol. These concentrations occur almost exclusively in the Paleoindian and Early Archaic, both of which are severely impacted by decalcification of sediments (see "feature geochemistry" below).

Burial pits have a greater overall mean depth than other feature types, but note that the 95% confidence interval overlaps that of all the other feature types except charcoal pits. Therefore, the greater depth of burial pits is not significantly greater than other pits. Also note the large confidence interval, between 11 and 25 cm. This most likely reflects not great diversity in burial size, but rather excavation protocol. Since excavators had difficulty discerning pit outlines in the poorly lit cave, we often assigned arbitrary pit boundaries. Over the years, as lighting improved and excavators became more familiar with the burial fill, they improved their ability to recognize the true pit outline. These pits averaged approximately 12 cm in depth, suggesting that researchers dug much too deeply in the early years of excavation.

Both hearths and burials are significantly larger in length, width and volume compared to all other feature types, while charcoal or ash pits are significantly smaller than charcoal/ash pits and undifferentiated pits. That the features types identified in the field differ significantly suggests that they derive from separate populations and therefore functioned differently from one another.

Following Ingbar (1985), I created a scatterplot of volume relative to the width/depth ratio (Figure 3.3). Since overall feature size is smaller in the earlier components, Middle Archaic features were separated from the Early Archaic and Paleoindian features. The scatterplot confirms the trends seen in the error graphs depicted in Figure 3.4; in other words, it too confirms the visual separation of feature types based on morphology. Charcoal and ash stringers have the highest width to depth ratios, followed by charcoal and ash pits, charcoal/ash pits, hearths, burials, and rock pits. Early Archaic and Paleoindian features display the same pattern as Middle Archaic features, except they shift slightly to the left (less volume) and up (shallower).

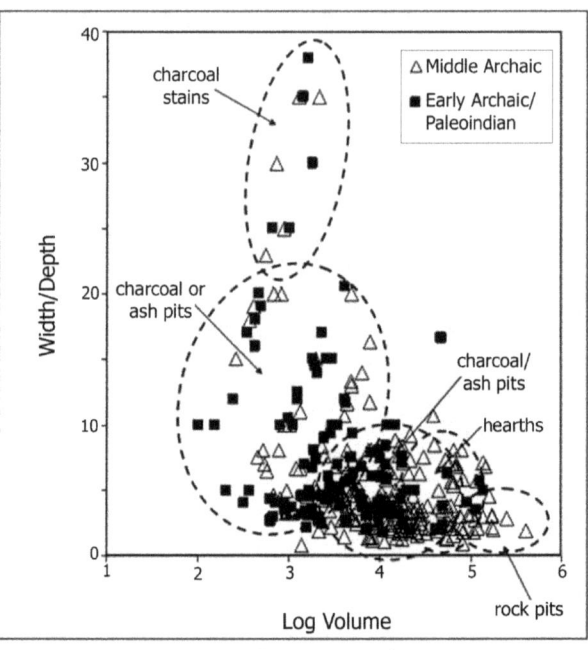

Figure 3.3. Scatterplot of Dust Cave features comparing width to depth ratio and volume.

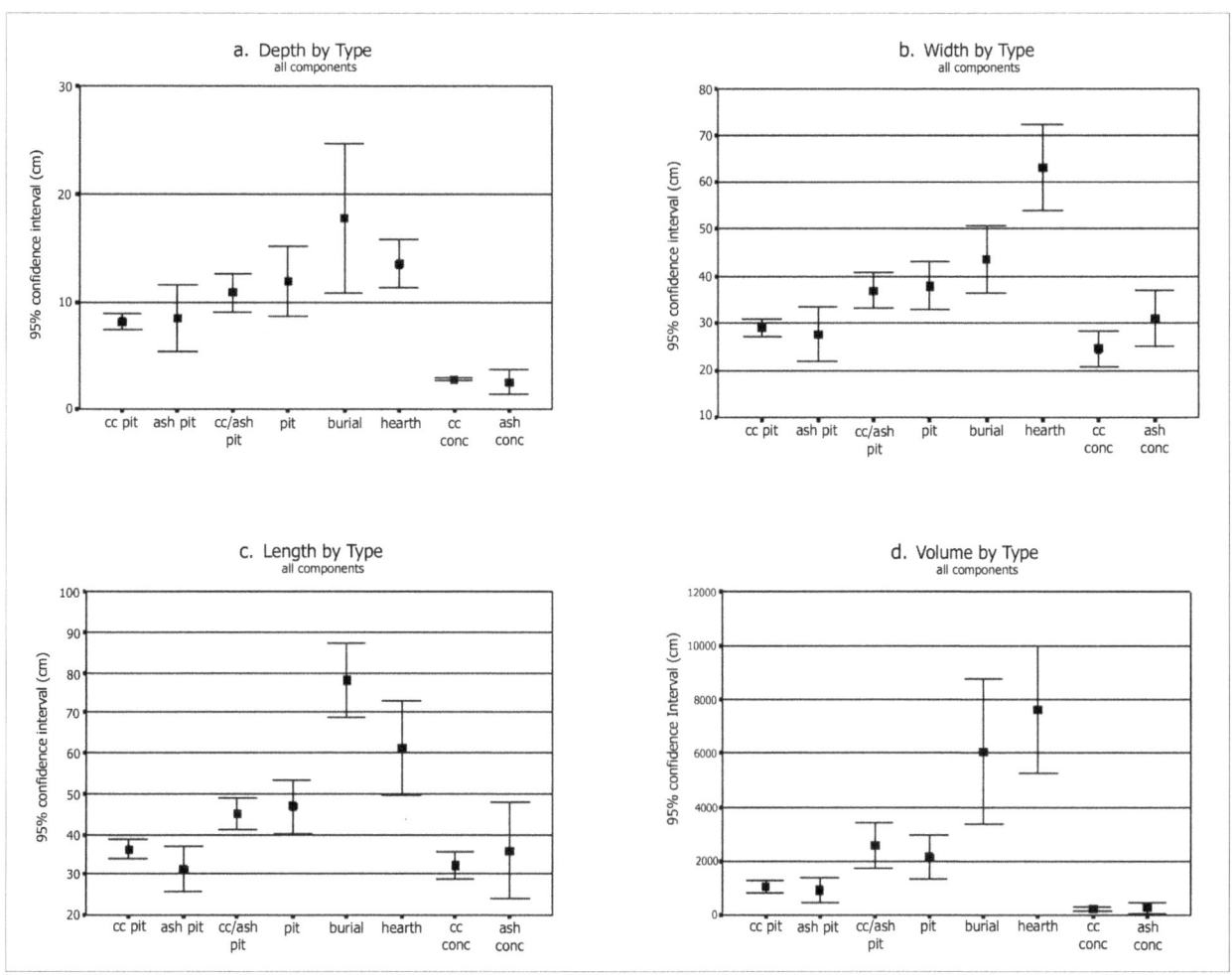

Figure 3.4. Comparison of the 95% confidence intervals for feature depth (a), width (b), length (c) and volume (d).

FEATURE GEOCHEMISTRY

Methods

Geochemical samples fall under one of three categories: (1) anthropogenic features, (2) general "Zone" matrix (i.e., not a feature)[1], and (3) sterile geogenic deposits. Feature samples (Table 3.2) were taken from contexts of both known origin (e.g., burial, hearth) and unknown origin (e.g., charcoal pit, ash pit). In order to investigate occupation intensity through time, samples were additionally selected from a column of sediment in excavation unit N60W65, from 100 cmbd down to bedrock, approximately 460 cmbd (Table 3.3). N60W65 lies in the west-central portion of the entrance chamber, approximately six meters behind the dripline and eight meters from the rear cave wall (Figure 3.5). Based on the concentration of artifacts and features, this area appears to be one of the most highly utilized areas of the cave throughout the cultural sequence (Homsey 2003a). Finally, control samples were collected from known sterile deposits in order to establish a chemical frame of reference for natural, unmodified sediments (Table 3.4).

Sterile samples include Pleistocene alluvium infilling channels in the limestone bedrock, colluvial deposits accumulating after cave abandonment, soil from the unoccupied potion of the talus slope (Test Unit G), Pleistocene alluvium from nearby Basket Cave, soils from the upland plateau, and unaltered Tuscumbia Limestone.

Samples were prepared in the geochemical and clean laboratories at the Department of Geology and Planetary Science, University of Pittsburgh, based on a method adapted from Middleton and Price (1996) and detailed in Homsey (2003a) and Homsey and Capo (2006). Two leachates were used: ammonium acetate (NH_4OHAc) to extract the exchangeable fraction of each element, and 2N hydrochloric acid (HCl) to extract the insoluble fraction tied up in carbonates, such as bone and shell. Concentrations of aluminum (Al), barium (Ba), calcium (Ca), iron (Fe), potassium (K), magnesium (Mg), manganese (Mn), sodium (Na), phosphorus (P), sulfur (S), strontium (Sr), and zinc (Zn) were determined using an inductively coupled plasma atomic emission spectrometer (ICP-AES) (Homsey 2003a). Because of the high concentrations for several elements, NH_4OHAc samples were diluted 1:10; HCl samples were diluted 1:100. Results are reported in ppm and converted to mg/kg for discussion.

---

[1] Major stratigraphic Zones are designated with upper case letters (e.g., A, B etc) while more localized units within major Zones are designated by numbers and lower case letters placed after letters (e.g., A2, B2a etc). Zones at the beginning of the alphabet are younger than those at the end.

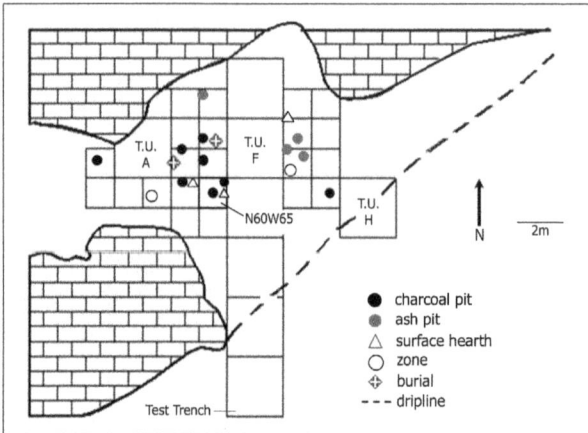

Figure 3.5. Location of geochemical samples.

Table 3.2. Cultural geochemical samples.

Sample	Description
Feature 117	hearth
Feature 120	burial
Feature 301	charcoal lens
Feature 341	ash pit
Feature 342	clay pit
Feature 354	charcoal pit
Feature 405	charcoal pit with fish bones
Feature 410	charcoal pit with gastropods
Feature 420	charcoal pit
Feature 423	possible hearth
Feature 429	charcoal pit,
Feature 438	charcoal pit
Feature 440	ash pit
Feature 443	ash pit
Feature 445	ash pit
Feature 450	hearth
Zone K7	refuse/midden zone
Zone P8/346	possible burial
Zone P3g	unknown
Zone P14	charcoal lens

Table 3.3. Samples from Column N60W65

Zone	Depth (cmbd)	Cultural Affiliation	Date (cal. B.C.)
A2	100	sterile	<3,600 B.P.
D4b	155	Benton	4,500 - 3,600
E4	190	Eva/Morrow Mt.	6,400 - 4,000
J1	210	Eva/Morrow Mt.	6,400 - 4,000
K7	270	Eva/Morrow Mt.	6,400 - 4,000
P3	300	Kirk Stemmed	8,200 - 5,800
R3f	400	Early Side Notched	10,000 - 9,000
U8	440	Paleoindian	10,650 - 9,200
Y3	460	sterile	Pleistocene

Results

A two-tailed Student's t-test of the hydrochloric leachates indicate that cultural sediments are significantly enriched in barium (Ba), potassium (K), manganese (Mn), phosphorous (P), strontium (Sr), and zinc (Zn) at the 99.9% confidence level ($p < 0.001$) when compared to sterile sediments (Homsey 2003a). Cultural sediments are also enriched in calcium (Ca) and magnesium (Mg) relative to all geogenic samples except the carbonate rich Tuscumbia limestone and Pleistocene alluvium (Homsey and Capo 2006). A two-tailed Student's t-test of the ammonium acetate leachates yielded similar results (see Homsey and Capo 2006:247 for discussion). Thus, cultural sediments are significantly enriched in Ba, Ca, K, Mg, Mn, P, Sr, and Zn relative to sterile sediments.

Concentrations of P for all zones exceed 2,500 mg/kg, a value that Schuldenrein (1995) classifies as "intense habitation." Based on the absolute abundance of P, it may be argued that occupation of Dust Cave was high—on the order of "urban living" (Schuldenrein 1995). This is not to say that the occupants of Dust Cave lived there year-round; rather it suggests that they intensively utilized the cave for whatever period of time they stayed there. The abundance of ash and charcoal suggests that burning comprised one of the major activities at Dust Cave. Since P is enriched by both the decomposition of organic and mineral matter as well as burning, it comes as no surprise that P is so abundant at Dust Cave.

A scatterplot of K/P to Sr/Ca reveals two discrete groups: Group 1 consists of Paleoindian and early Early Archaic features (>350 cmbd, alluvial parent material) while Group 2 consists of late Early and Middle Archaic features (<350 cmbd, colluvial parent material) (Figure 3.6a). This grouping reflects the loss of Sr and K via leaching below 350 cmbd, suggesting that features cannot be compared across parent materials. The colluvial samples can be further divided into two sub-groups (Figure 3.6b). Group 2A features have more ash than charcoal, and Sr/Ca >0.005 and K/P >0.10, while Group 2B samples have more charcoal than ash, and Sr/Ca <0.005 and K/P <0.10.

Table 3.4. Sterile geochemical samples.

Sample	Description
Lmst	Tuscumbia Formation
Y3	Pleistocene alluvium, 460 cmbd
T.U. G 80	colluvium from outside cave, 80 cmbd
T.U. G 350	colluvium from outside cave, 350 cmbd
A2	colluvium inside cave, 100 cmbd
Bt	Bt horizon, 60 cmbd
Allv	Tennessee River alluvium, Florence, Al.
BAllv	Basket Cave alluvium, 350 cmbs
BClay	Basket Cave clay from solution dome
Nutmeat	Modern, unburned hickory nutmeat
Nutshell	Modern, unburned hickory nutshell
Pwink	Burned periwinkle shell, Zones K7 and J1

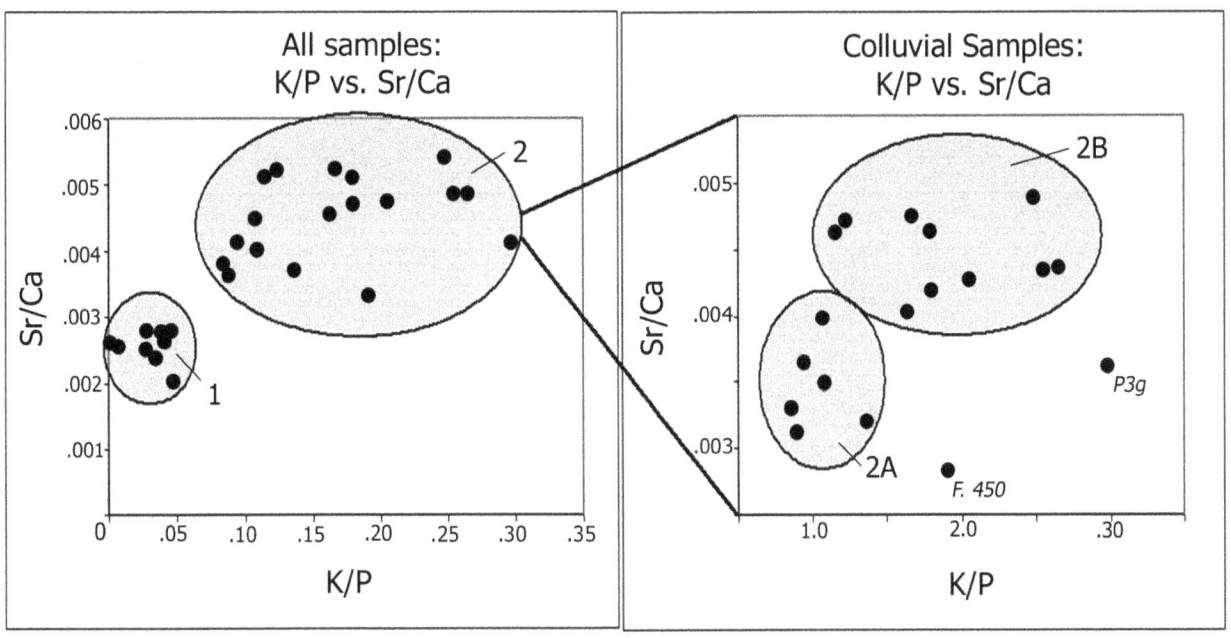

Figure 3.6. Scatterplots of K/P to Sr/Ca for all samples (a) and colluvial samples (b).

Anthropogenic Sources of Elements

Hickory (*Carya sp.*) nutmeat and nutshell yielded the highest K values of all the modern, non-cultural materials tested (see Table 3.4): 107 mg/kg and 2,061 mg/kg respectively. At nearly twenty times the value of nutmeat, nutshell appears to sequester K the most effectively of the two. Given that deposits enriched in ash correlate with high K values (Schuldenrein 1995) and given that sampled nutshell contains nearly 100 times more K than any other substance analyzed (Homsey and Capo 2006:248), then the burning of nutshell likely contributed most of the K to the cave sediments.

Hickory nutshell also contributes Sr to Dust Cave sediments. Some Sr undoubtedly derives from the Tuscumbia Limestone in which Dust Cave formed. However, because cultural sediments are significantly enriched in Sr compared to the sterile samples (also influenced by the Tuscumbia Limestone), then other materials must contribute Sr to the sediments. In a study of common foods eaten by people world-wide, Rosenthal (1981) showed that foods such as red meat, poultry, vegetables, and fruit contain low levels of strontium (<2 mg/kg); grains, legumes, and seafood contain intermediate levels (2-25 mg/kg); and nuts and spices contain the high levels (15-100 mg/kg). Nuts such as pecans (*Carya illinoiensis*) contain approximately 14 mg/kg. Hickory nutmeat and nutshell from Florence, Alabama, yielded values of 14 mg/kg and 17 mg/kg, respectively, values consistent with the high values recorded for pecan nuts. These results lend persuasive, albeit circumstantial, evidence that hickory nuts contribute much Sr to Dust Cave sediments. Future research will examine Sr isotopes in order to determine what proportion of the Sr derives from marine (Tuscumbia Limestone) versus terrestrial (plant) sources.

Strontium can also derive from Hackberry (*Celtis sp.*) seeds, the seed coatings of which are ubiquitous at Dust Cave. Hackberry shells are comprised of aragonite (a low-pressure psuedomorph of calcite), and can be enriched in Sr relative to Ca (Jahren et al. 1998). Most of the hackberries seeds recovered from Dust Cave are burned (Hollenbach, personal communication 2004); aragonite can revert to calcite when heated, expelling Sr. Thus, some of the Sr enrichment of cultural sediments compared to sterile sediments may originate from hackberries in the cave. However, it must be kept in mind that hackberries may not have been intentionally brought into the cave by its occupants; rather, they may have entered the cave via gravity and/or animals and may have been unintentionally burned.

Occupational Intensity

Plots for elemental concentrations by depth were constructed for calcium (Ca), barium (Ba), potassium (K), phosphorus (P), strontium (Sr), and iron (Fe) (Figure 3.7). Interestingly, concentrations of P for all zones exceed 2,500 mg/kg, a value that Schuldenrein (1995:123) suggests represents intensive cultural impact. P concentrations peak at depths of 170, 210, 300, and 400 cmbd, corresponding to the Benton, late Eva/Morrow Mountain, Kirk Stemmed, and Early Side Notched occupations, respectively. The greatest peak occurs at 210 cmbd, corresponding to the late Eva/Morrow Mountain component. Based on the absolute abundance of P, it may be argued that occupation of Dust Cave was high—on the order of "urban living" (Schuldenrein 1995:123). This is not to say that the occupants of Dust Cave lived there year-round; rather it suggests that they intensively utilized the cave for whatever period of time they stayed there.

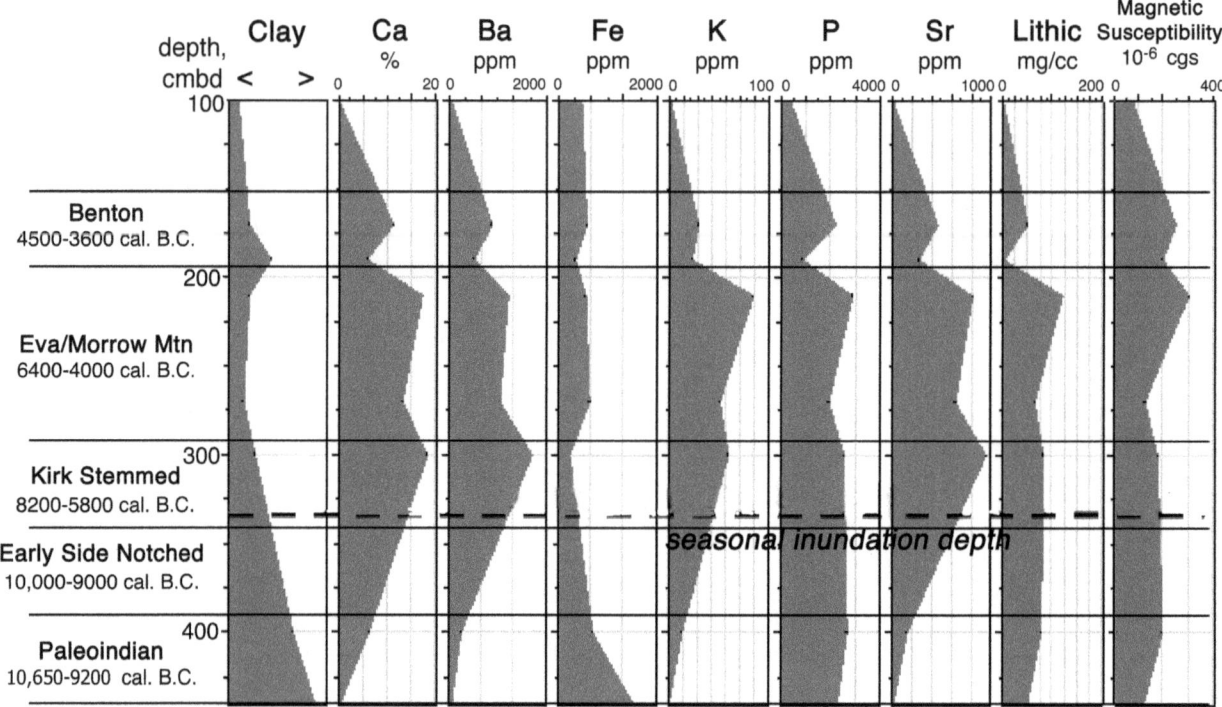

Figure 3.7. Concentrations of Ba, Ca, Fe, K, P and Sr by depth.

We can have confidence in these geochemical data because P concentrations mimic those generated by more traditional occupation proxies, including lithic density and magnetic susceptibility. Statistically, there is a strong positive correlation between P concentration and lithic density[2] ($r=.93$, $p=.05$). The r^2 is .860, meaning that 86% of the variation in lithic density can be accounted for by P concentration (Homsey and Capo 2006). Phosphorous peaks also parallel the pattern seen in a 1993 magnetic susceptibility curve developed by sampling a profile a few meters away in N60W64. Because fire enhances the magnetic susceptibility of iron-rich sediments, it has been used as a relative indicator of burning activity (Collins et al. 1994). As such, it serves as a proxy for human occupation at archaeological sites. Both P and magnetic susceptibility peak at 170, 210, 300, and 400 cmbd before dropping off to sterile levels near bedrock. While there is a weaker positive correlation between P concentration and magnetic susceptibility ($r=.59$, $r^2=.35$, $p=.05$) than there is between P and lithic density, Figure 3.7 clearly demonstrates that they generally follow the same pattern through time.

Concentrations of Ba, Ca, K, and Sr, follow the pattern of P until about 350 cmbd, at which point they drop off to near sterile levels near bedrock. 350 cmbd corresponds closely to the level at which deposits are seasonally inundated[3]. Thus, Ba, Ca, K, and Sr form water soluble compounds that leach out at depth. In particular, the loss of calcium at depth has two important implications for the preservation of features. First, decalcification leads to the dissolution of ash (formed primarily of calcite). This helps explain the prevalence of charcoal pits compared to ash pits in the oldest occupations, as discussed above. Second, decalcification results in the compaction of sediments. The net result is that sediments are compacted and ash is depleted relative to their original volume. As previously discussed, features from older occupations are statistically shallower than the features from younger occupations. Without recognizing and appreciating the compaction and decalcification of ashy features, these size differences could be misinterpreted as simply representing ephemeral occupation of the site, rather than post-depositional processes. Thus, the addition of geochemical analyses to feature studies provides important information for making behavioral interpretations.

FEATURE MICROMORPHOLOGY

Methods

Micromorphology samples (Appendix B) from both feature and zones were collected in the field as intact, fist-sized blocks using precut sections of rectangular vinyl gutter spouting. The gutter spouting sections were carefully pushed into the sediment until full. Prior to their removal, they were examined in the field for provenience, structure and association with other zones and features. Once removed, the blocks were oriented, wrapped in tissue paper and packaging tape, and labeled. After oven-drying the samples to remove all moisture (~60°C), they were impregnated under low vacuum with polyester resin (thinned with styrene to increase viscosity and therefore promote the uptake of resin into pores) and using methyl ethyl ketone peroxide as a hardening catalyst. The

---

[2] Calculated as mass per unit volume for Zones D, E, J, K, P, R, and U in unit N60/W65 (see Homsey 2003a).
[3] Deposits flood seasonally only since impoundment of the Tennessee River in the 1930s.

hardening process took anywhere between a few hours up to several days, depending on the brand of resin, amount of catalyst, and humidity.

Once the blocks finished hardening, they were slabbed using a geologic trim saw. Blocks were then ground and polished into chips approximately 2 x 3 in. They were sent to Quality Thin Sections in Tucson, Arizona, where they were mounted on oversized (2" x 3") glass slides, and ground down to approximately 30 microns. Thin sections were examined at several levels. They were first examined by hand with the aid of a hand lens. This initial step allowed me to compare macroscopic structural observations with field notes and photographs. They were then examined stereoscopically at 2 to 4x and petrographically at 2.5 to 40x under both plane- (PPL) and cross- (XPL) polarized light. Most observations were made at 10x. Photomicrographs were taken using a Nikon Coolpix 990 digital camera attached to a Leitz Laborlux binocular polarizing microscope. Thin sections were described in terms of standard soil micromorphology attributes using standard nomenclature, including coarse and fine fraction, related distribution, void space, microartifacts, microstructure, and post-depositional features (for a detailed discussion see Homsey 2004). Thin section descriptions follow Bullock et al. (1985) and Courty et al. (1989). Appendix C describes common materials, microartifacts, and sedimentary structures identified in the Dust Cave thin sections. Original thin section descriptions can be found in Homsey (2004: Appendix E).

Results

Micromorphological studies proved vital in recognizing and characterizing a number of important variables including the presence, degree, and length of burning; fuel source; transport agent; and depositional environment. Because these vary widely by feature type, they are discussed in greater detail in the following section. Micromorphological analyses also identified a number of post-depositional processes that are responsible for obscuring the archaeological feature assemblage; these processes are briefly summarized below.

Biological Activity

The term bioturbation refers to the reworking of sediments through the burrowing and sediment ingesting activity of soil and sediment dwelling organisms (Blatt 1982:124-125). Their burrowing behavior obscures original bedding and fine laminations, often resulting in the partial or complete homogenization of deposits (Courty et al. 1989:142). In thin section, bioturbation is easily recognized as uniform spherical to ellipsoid fecal pellets measuring between 0.5 and 1mm in diameter (FitzPatrick 1993). Some deposits are so disturbed by bioturbation that feature morphology is unclear and boundaries are nearly impossible to trace.

Plant roots also alter the original fabric of sedimentary deposits by pushing away sediments. Void structures produced by roots include vesicle and channel voids. Micritic coatings of calcium carbonate resulting from the root respiration may coat the insides of these voids (Courty et al. 1989:144). Such coatings are common in vesicles created by rhizomes. These coatings may sometimes be quite heavy or consist of microspar. Root activity is ubiquitous in the Dust Cave sediments, although it appears to be especially prevalent in the soft, porous ashy sediment associated with mixed burned deposits (Sherwood 2001).

Fluvial Activity

Like the geochemical data, which suggest leaching of water-soluble elements, micromorphological observations also suggest a great deal of fluvial activity at Dust Cave. Evidence comes in the form of fluvial laminations of fining upward silts and clay (i.e., graded bedding) (Boggs 1995). Fluvial activity also results in thin, elongated water-deposited charcoal grains oriented parallel to the direction of bedding. These grains have an undulatory appearance such that they often appear to "wrap around" grains and aggregates (Homsey 2004: Plates 6.9 and 6.10). Charcoal may also coat the inside of voids when fluvially redeposited.

Evidence for fluvial activity is restricted primarily to deposits below 400 cmbd (in Zones R through U), though some charcoal pits in Zone P also appear to have been reworked by water. Fluvial activity has altered some hearths below 400 cmbd, obscuring their characteristic traits and making field-identification impossible without the aid of microscopic and geochemical data. Rock basins and charcoal stringers exemplify this problem; the implications it has for their interpretation are discussed further in the next section.

Decalcification

Like the geochemical data, micromorphological data also indicate substantial decalcification of sediments below 350 cmbd. This can be seen in etching of weathered limestone fragments as well as carbonate based shell and bone. In some cases, chamber voids with residual calcitic coatings suggests the near complete dissolution of limestone fragments (Homsey 2004: Plate 6.16). Dissolution occurs as carbonates form water soluble compounds (during seasonal inundation and flooding) and leave the cave system (Homsey and Capo 2006). As previously discussed, decalcification results in the prevalence of shallow, charcoal (versus ash) pits below 350 cmbd.

Some decalcification also occurs at the top of the sediment sequence, in zone D, though to a lesser extent than described above. This occurs most notably toward the front of the entrance chamber and results from phreatic water movement through the front deposits (Sherwood 2001). This decalcification is responsible for poor preservation of discrete anthropogenic lenses in the front and east side of the entrance chamber, and also probably accounts for the low ash content in the two hearths (Features 135 and 136) that I looked at from the front-central portion of the cave.

Table 3.5. Typology of burned deposits at Dust Cave *(prepared & unprepared surfaces adapted from Sherwood 2001)*.

BURNING DEPOSIT TYPE	MACROMORPHOLOGY & CONTENTS	MICROMORPHOLOGICAL & CHEMICAL ATTRIBUTES	POSSIBLE FUNCTION	EXAMPLES
IN SITU FIREPLACE				
Prepared Surfaces	• 1.5-3 cm thick • sharp upper & lower boundaries • cover areas < 1m^2 • two aspects: hard and soft	• aggregated structure, limited void space • packing, channel, planar voids • charcoal/ash articulated to upper surface	• multi-purpose	K3c R6b T2g
Surface Hearths	• ~80 cm in diameter, ~14 cm deep • frequently rock-lined • located centrally • typically oval with basin-shaped profile • often superimposed during Middle Archaic	• red, burned periphery • microartifacts highly burned • articulated ash aggregates • thermally altered rock • variable chemistry	• cooking • light • warmth • social activity	117 450
Pit Hearths	• 40 cm diameter, ~15 cm deep • intrude prepared surfaces • basin to U-shaped profiles • mostly on east side of cave • first appear in Kirk-Stemmed component	• ash > charcoal • burned red clay clasts • nut charcoal; spherulite ash crystals • partially combusted organic matter • Sr/Ca >0.005, K/P >0.20	• nut processing	412 419 440 443
Expedient Hearths	• ~40 cm diameter, <10 cm deep • overlie prepared surface • saucer shaped profile • two aspects: charcoal-rich & ash-rich • may contain thermally altered rock	• microartifacts moderately burned; much fish bone • much partially combusted organic matter • calcitic cellular pseudomorphs • Sr/Ca >0.005, K/P >0.20	• grilling or smoking • nut parching?	377 405 445
Rock Basins	• ~80 cm diameter, ~15 cm deep • little to no ash or charcoal • basin-shaped profile • charcoal lines underside of rocks	• burned microartifacts, mostly bone • thermally altered rock • graded bedding • variable chemistry	• surface hearths altered post-depositionally	384 423

Table 3.5. cont'd.

BURNING DEPOSIT TYPE	MACROMORPHOLOGY & CONTENTS	MICROMORPHOLOGICAL & CHEMICAL ATTRIBUTES	POSSIBLE FUNCTION	EXAMPLES
FIREPLACE RAKE-OUT				
Accessories	• ~30 cm, circular basins, ~5 cm thick • saucer shaped profile • contain FCR • typically associated with hearths	• charcoal > ash • burned microartifacts present • FCR present as sand to gravel fragments • Sr/Ca <0.005, K/P values <0.15	• cooking stone piles	429
Scrape-out	• ~30 cm, circular basins, ~5 cm thick • saucer shaped profile • typically associated with hearths	• charcoal > ash • burned bone, shell present, FCR absent • Sr/Ca <0.005, K/P values <0.15	• rake-out of hearth coals, not dumped elsewhere	83 410? 420
Rake-out	• ~1 m lens <5 cm thick to extensive tabular to lenticular units ~10cm • saucer shaped profile • <30 cm diameter pits, <5 cm deep	• charcoal > ash • >20% porosity • slight orientation of charcoal grains • Sr/Ca <0.005, K/P values <0.15	• redeposited coals, may be swept	301
Rings	• <30 cm diameter pits, <5 cm deep • matrix "ringed" by charcoal • saucer shaped profile	• charcoal > ash • slacking crusts, elongated charcoal • Sr/Ca <0.005, K/P values <0.15	• rake-out altered post-depositionally	374, 375 380
MIXED BURNING				
Midden	• heterogeneous units >10 cm thick • ash > charcoal • burned red clay clasts • bioturbated	• burned microartifacts present • red clay, compound, & mixed clasts • much void space; loose, chaotic fill • Sr/Ca >0.005, K/P >0.25	• dumping of combusted materials	J3(b) K7 P3
Charcoal/Ash Stringer	• <2 cm thick and >1 m^2 • predominately below 400 cmbd	• graded bedding, elongated charcoal • alluvial disconformities • Sr/Ca <0.003, K/P < 0.05	• pits reworked by water	U6/U8 interface; T2c 381

Table 3.6. Typology of unburned deposits at Dust Cave.

DEPOSIT TYPE	MACROMORPHOLOGY & CONTENTS	MICROMORPHOLOGICAL & CHEMICAL ATTRIBUTES	POSSIBLE FUNCTION	EXAMPLES
BURIAL				
Human	<ul><li>~60 cm long; ~20 cm deep</li><li>contain articulated skeletal remains</li><li>flexed, extended or disarticulated</li><li>frequently topped with numerous rocks</li></ul>	<ul><li>high K/P</li><li>loose, porphyritic fill</li><li>unburned microartifacts common</li><li>variable clasts and aggregates</li></ul>	<ul><li>human interment</li></ul>	128 292
Domestic dog	<ul><li>25-50 cm diameter, ~7 cm deep</li><li>some associated with human burial</li></ul>	<ul><li>Not sampled</li></ul>	<ul><li>canine interment</li></ul>	108 202
ROCK CLUSTER	<ul><li>clay matrix</li><li>20-50 cm diameter; 10-20 cm deep</li><li>numerous limestone rocks embedded in clay</li><li>may contain charcoal</li></ul>	<ul><li>low K/P, Sr/Ca</li><li>high Mg, Mn, & Fe</li><li>clay coatings and papules</li><li>rocks not thermally altered</li></ul>	<ul><li>unknown</li></ul>	342
STORAGE PIT	<ul><li>~80 cm diameter, ~40 cm deep</li><li>Somewhat flat-bottomed,</li><li>Bell to U-shaped profile</li><li>originate at Zone N/P interface</li><li>may contain disarticulated skeletal remains</li></ul>	<ul><li>heterogeneous fill</li><li>loose, porphyritic texture</li><li>granular to crumb microstructure</li><li>variable chemistry</li></ul>	<ul><li>storage</li><li>secondary refuse or burial/ cremation?</li></ul>	P11 P8/P8a

INTEGRATING MORPHOLOGY, MICROMORPHOLOGY AND GEOCHEMISTRY TO DETERMINE FEATURE FUNCTION

In Situ Fireplaces

In situ fireplaces involve features that have been burned in place, with no subsequent mixing or re-deposition. These include surface hearths, rock basins, prepared surfaces, expedient hearths, and pit hearths. Each of these is described in detailed, beginning with a description of their macromorphology, microscopic and geochemical attributes, followed by an interpretation of the technology represented, and, lastly, a discussion of their organization with respect to cave morphology and possible underlying cultural patterning.

Surface Hearths (Figure 3.8)

Description. Surface hearths average 78 cm long, 63 cm wide, and 15 cm deep and have basin shaped profiles. Burned red clay underlying the features indicates *in situ* burning (Homsey 2004:148-149). They are characterized by large amounts of charcoal (wood and nut) and ash, and are often rock-lined. Analysis of flotation samples demonstrates that hearths contain abundant artifacts, including burned shell and bone, lithics, and wood charcoal (Pike 2003). Microartifacts of shell and bone, many of them intensely burned, are visible in thin section; the degree of burning in bone suggests temperatures between 400 and 600°C (Homsey 2004). They do not have a consistent chemical signature, but rather exhibit variable chemistries, suggesting that a wide variety of materials was processed in them (Homsey and Capo 2006). Hearths, especially in the Eva/Morrow Mountain component, are often superimposed.

Some hearths appear to have been lined with thin lenses of red clay. In thin section these red lenses exhibit remnant fluvial structures, such as slacking crusts and fining upward silts and clays, oriented parallel to the dip of the lens, about 30 to 40 degrees (Homsey 2004). Since fluvial features are typically deposited horizontally, their dip leads me to believe that the clay was intentionally re-transported and used to line these hearths. This phenomenon was observed in Feature 136 (DC-96-07), a hearth dating to the Eva/Morrow Mountain component. Another example can be seen in sample DUST-93-19, the burned zone K2 surface surrounding Feature 78 (a surface hearth). The surface dips approximately 30 to 40 degrees to the west, as seen in layered lenses of heavy papules (~30% of slide) (Homsey 2004:149). This surface forms an unconformable boundary with the red clay surface below it. If the hearths are indeed lined, this indicates some formality to hearth preparation, rather than a quick fire built just anywhere.

Interpretation. Ethnohistoric accounts of cooking and food preparation describe Southeastern Indians broiling over large fires (Hudson 1976:301). They commonly constructed a rack over an open fire, on which they could cook fish or small mammals such as raccoon, squirrel, opossum, and rabbit. They also impaled meat on sticks which they then stuck in the ground, inclined towards the fire. Regardless of whether the carcasses were placed over the flame, or inclined toward the fire from the side,

Figure 3.8. Field image of superimposed features (#134, 135, and 136) from Eva/Morrow Mountain component and inset showing schematic of Feature 134 with charcoal lenses A through D.

it would be in close proximity to the heat source, thereby allowing the bones to burn. The high percentages of calcined mammal and bird bone seen in the faunal assemblage suggest that occupants may have cooked these species over the hotter and larger surface hearths (Homsey et al. 2010).

Surface hearths differ from earth ovens, which are predominantly used for roasting (Wandsnider 1997). Earth ovens are dug into the ground, burned, rocks added, and dirt piled onto the pit to retain heat. Few features at Dust Cave contain enough rocks to suggest an earth oven. At the most, rocks may completely encircle a hearth, or line the base of the hearth. The only exception to this rule is the presence of two possible earth ovens, one dating to the Eva/Morrow Mountain component, and the other dating to the Kirk Stemmed component. The latter "oven" is the largest feature at the site (Feature 111: length=125 cm, width=78 cm, depth 42 cm). It comes as no surprise that Dust Cave would have few earth ovens, for they tend to be very large and produce a lot of smoke (Homsey 2009; Wilson and DeLyria 1999), neither of which would be conducive to cave dwelling, especially in a cave as small as Dust Cave. Feature 111 occurs directly under the highest point in the ceiling, suggesting that its builders may have intentionally placed it here to maximize ventilation.

A second observation should be made concerning the formation of surface hearths. During excavation of hearths dating to the Benton and Eva/Morrow Mountain, we excavated as many as five separate lenses within individual hearths. The lenses are slightly offset horizontally, but what is most notable is that they are stacked vertically within the same general basin (see Figure 3.8, inset). This stacking gives one the impression of repeated burning events. Ethnographically, hunter-gatherers often reuse hearths from previous occupations. For example, the last thing the Melpa do when leaving a rockshelter is stockpile firewood next to the hearth for use by the next occupants (Galanidou 1997:27). The reuse of hearths is certainly not restricted to prehistory—even at our field school camp about a quarter of a mile from Dust Cave, we reused hearths for several seasons. We used them so often, in fact, that they served in a number of experimental projects for this study from 1997 to 2000. At the beginning of each season, a new, thin layer of sediment covered the coals of the most recent burning event, creating a profile much like that of the inset in Figure 3.8. Unfortunately, no micromorphology samples exist from this our camp fire; if they did, it would be instructive to see if each lens shows evidence of *in situ* burning. Future micromorphological studies of hearths should take samples vertically though hearth basins so as to examine each lens and boundary.

A final question to address is whether or not surface hearths served a single purpose or multiple purposes. I suggest that surface hearths functioned in several capacities based on three observations. First, they contain burned food debris of all kinds—fish bone, mammal bone, and shell. This suggests that, at the very least, several kinds of food were cooked in/over them. The variable chemical signature for hearths corroborates this interpretation. Second, hearth fill contains a large amount of lithic debitage, suggesting that tool maintenance also occurred around them. Ethnographic accounts have shown that lithics may have become incorporated into hearths during refuse disposal or during tool maintenance (Galanidou 1997; Pétrequin and Pétrequin 1988). The Dust Cave surface hearths are clearly in the original burning location and not redeposited, so the lithics most likely represent retooling activity rather than refuse disposal. Either activity represents an additional function in addition to cooking. Third, ethnographic studies have shown that hearths are used not only for cooking, but also for warmth and light, sleeping by, and relaxation and socializing—these activities occur cross-culturally (Galanidou 1997; Gorecki 1988; Pétrequin and Pétrequin 1988). Galanidou further notes that hearths often serve as symbolic dividers of space, such as male vs. female space, domestic vs. refuse space, and individual vs. communal space. Finally, Galanidou (1997) has shown a cross-cultural pattern of multipurpose open hearth use; only closed earth ovens serve a single purpose reserved for cooking.

Organization. Overall, hearths are clustered ($R=.568$, $.001<p<.002$) and focus in the center of the entrance chamber and somewhat to the west (Figure 3.9a). This pattern of centrally placed hearths is consistent with the ethnographic pattern (Galanidou 1997, 2000; Gorecki 1991). Hearths locate nearly equidistantly from the back (northwest) wall and the dripline, approximately two meters from each. This most likely provided ample ventilation for the prehistoric occupants of Dust Cave. Additionally, hearths are located opposite of the west passageway. Anyone who has excavated at Dust Cave has experienced the cool air that blows from the back of the cave along this passageway. Thus fires may have been built in this area due to the additional ventilation the passage afforded.

The average distance between hearth center and the center of the refuse zone located in the rear of the entrance chamber is 2.76 meters. Ethnographically, refuse zones generated by hearth related activities range in their radius from the center of a hearth from two to six meters (Gamble 1991:12). Smaller distances occur when space is constrained, either by nearby structures, other hearths (Gamble 1991). Larger distances occur when space is unconstrained as is often the case with open-air hearth use (Binford 1983:153). The 2.76 meter distance from hearth center to refuse zone at Dust Cave is more consistent with a space conserving strategy (*sensu* Aldenderfer 1998). I suggest that this conservation of space by the inhabitants of Dust Cave was prompted by the geologic constraints of the relatively small living vesibule. The average center-to-center hearth distance is about 65 cm. Gamble (1991) has noted that sleeping hearths have an average center-to-center distance of two meters, whereas cooking hearths average three meters. This extremely small statistic probably reflects neither of these, but rather may reflect the large number of hearths superimposed in the same location. This pattern in and of itself suggests a strong need for space conservation.

One of the most—if not *the* most—important, determinants of the use of space among hunter-gatherers is anticipated length of stay (Aldenderfer 1998; Galanidou 1997, 2000; Kent 1987, 1984). In general, if a group anticipates a long stay at a site, they tend to formally set aside discrete areas for certain activities. Conversely, if a group anticipates a short stay, they give little attention to segregating activities spatially. Rather, space tends to be used for multiple functions. For example, the West Dani horticulturalists of Indonesia go out of their way to segment space. Individual domestic units, each with its own hearth, are dug into the cave floor and are separated by screens constructed from brushwood (Galanidou 1997:25). The individually segregated units are further segregated from communal areas by depressions and screens. In contrast, the highly mobile Pinai, who use shelters for less than a week at a time, have much overlap in activities (Gorecki 1991). The redundant use of hearth space at Dust Cave, coupled with the multipurpose nature of surface hearths, suggests that the anticipated length of stay at Dust Cave was not long, perhaps on the order of a couple of weeks.

Rock Basins
Description. Rock basins occur below 400 cmbd, mostly in Zone T, a zone in which Sherwood (2001) notes extensive fluvial activity and small-scale erosional events. In some cases, the petrographic analysis of the rocks show them to be thermally altered (Homsey 2009). Basins are circular to oval rings of rock averaging 72 cm in length, 66 cm in width, and 15 cm in depth. Usually, the rocks surround the periphery of the deposit. In the field the fill appears to contain little, if any, charcoal or ash and it is not possible to tell if they are burned in place or not. Micromorphological analysis of thin sections taken from feature fill revealed extensive graded bedding, bedded charcoal, and charcoal infillings of voids, all of which point towards extensive reworking of feature fill by water (Homsey 2004).

Interpretation. Rock basin dimensions are reminiscent of the average dimensions for surface hearths: length, 78 cm; width, 63 cm; and depth, 14 cm. The error graphs in Figure 3.10 statistically confirm this visual interpretation, demonstrating that rock basins and surface hearths come from the same population. The question that remains is why do they not contain the charcoal and ash that surface hearths do. I propose that rock basins are surface hearths that have been post-depositionally altered by fluvial activity. Examples of rock basins include Feature 384 and 423 (Homsey 2004: Plate 6.28). Feature 423 appears to have been washed out by repeated sheetwash events, as indicated by the graded bedding and elongated, bedded charcoal grains.

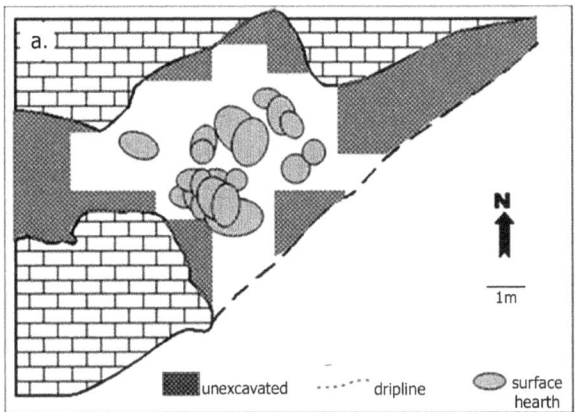
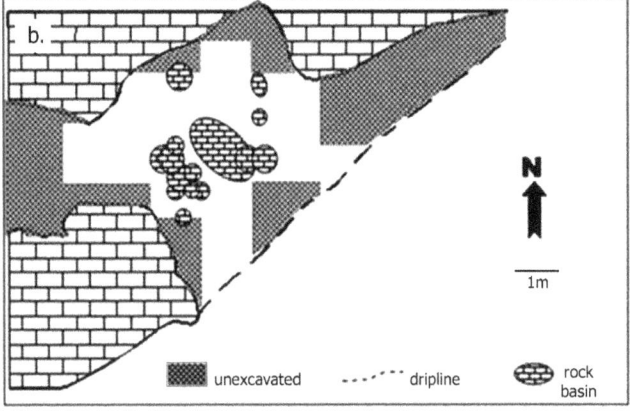
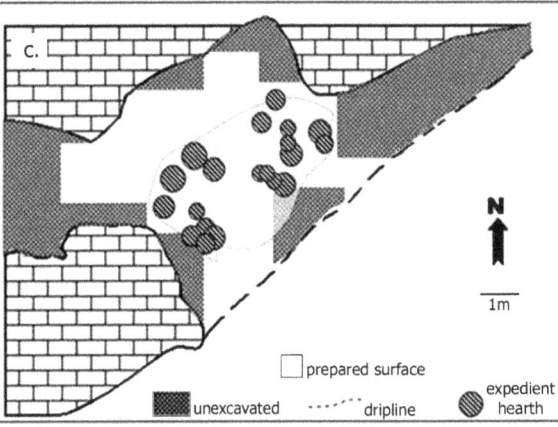
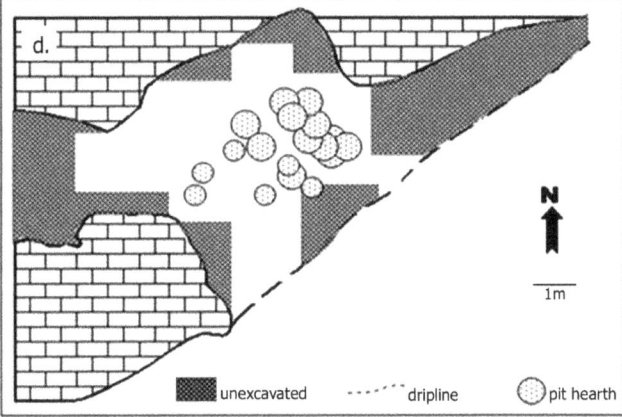

Figure 3.9. Distribution of surface hearths (a), rock basins (b), expedient & prepared surfaces (c), and pit hearths (d).

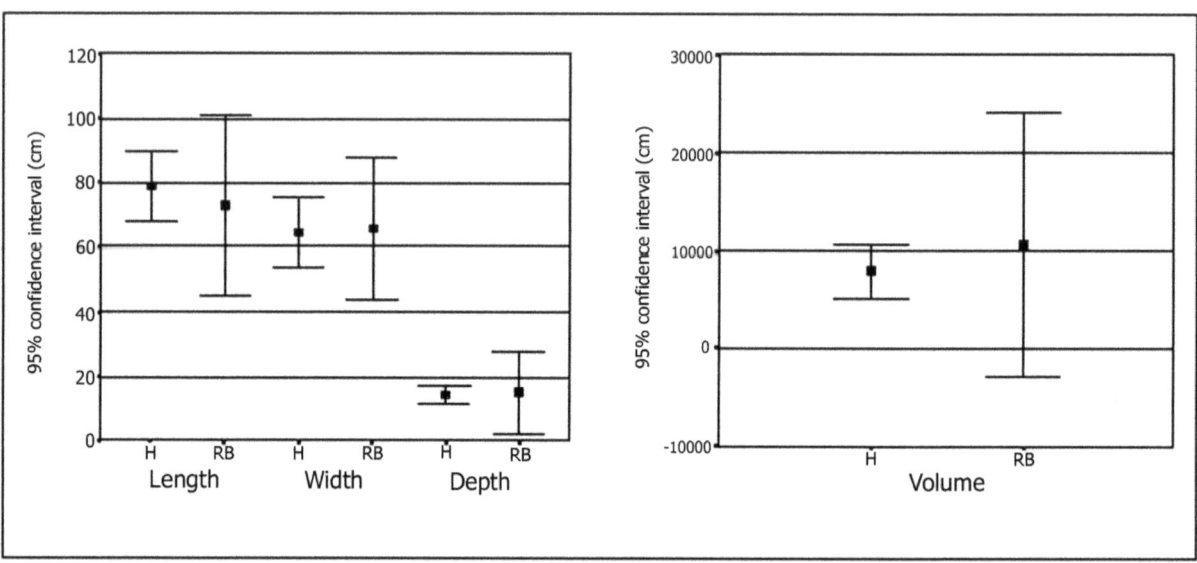

Figure 3.10. Comparison of 95% confidence level for hearth (H) and rock basin (RB) dimensions.

Feature 384 also exhibits graded bedding. Additionally, silt-sized charcoal grains are oriented parallel to bedding (Homsey 2004: plate 6.35). Voids are lightly coated with charcoal. Well preserved cellular structure in the charcoal, as well as the fact that charcoal and ash are preserved at all, suggests a low velocity environment (Homsey 2004).

Organization. The spatial distribution of rock basins adds some support for the interpretation that they are hearths altered post-depositionally. While rock pits are slightly more clustered than hearths ($R=.468$, $p<.001$), with few exceptions, they focus in the central portion of the entrance chamber, somewhat more intensively to the west, just as surface hearths do (Figure 3.9b). The smaller of these pits, which I call rock clusters (discussed later, as unburned features) occur in the same general area around hearths and rock basins. These may represent cooking stone piles. Unfortunately, without detailed micromorphological studies it is impossible to confirm this assertion. The large rock basin in the center is Feature 111, the possible earth oven dating to the Kirk Stemmed component. The pit is about a meter long and 30 cm deep. The basin contained a deep, 25 cm layer of large limestone rocks, with a five cm thick lens of charcoal overlying the rocks. If indeed it does represent an earth oven, it is by far the largest food processing feature represented at the site.

Prepared Surfaces (Figure 3.11)
Description. The excellent preservation at Dust Cave has resulted in anthropogenic deposits not traditionally preserved at open air sites. One of these unique deposits is the prepared clay surface, initially identified by Sherwood (2001) during geoarchaeological investigation of the cave sediments. Since then, researchers have recognized prepared clay surfaces elsewhere in the Midsouth, including Early and Middle Archaic open-air sites such as Icehouse Bottom in Tennessee (Sherwood and Chapman 2005). The prepared surfaces are defined as flat deposits of burned clay creating a hard surface that often includes textile impressions. While their function is unknown, they are hypothesized to have played a significant role in cooking technology and/or food processing (Homsey and Sherwood 2010).

Sherwood and Chapman (2005:70) define prepared surfaces as discrete, localized red (2.5 YR, 5Y) clay, cultural deposits that are fired to a hard consistency. They are characterized by a unique lithology compared to surrounding sediments; a fairly standard size; the inclusion of textile impressions; close proximity to centralized activity areas, a typically hard, "fired" consistency; and a "stacked" appearance, in which later surfaces appear superimposed over earlier surfaces. Recent organic residue analyses of 15 Dust Cave surfaces have identified medium and high chain fatty acids which are representative of foods such as tubers, nuts, fish, terrapin, and snail (Malainey 2007). The presence of organic residues suggests that they functioned in a cooking and/or food processing capacity.

Sherwood and Chapman (2005:72-76) and Homsey and Sherwood (2010) discuss five observations regarding the form, function, and organization of the prepared surfaces. First (1), prepared surfaces are composed of clay that was intentionally selected. Second (2), the clay was transported, dumped and smoothed out, undergoing limited but specific processing. Third (3), surfaces are red and hard due to relatively brief, low-temperature direct heating. Fourth (4), surfaces contain intentional textile impressions relating to their preparation and function. Fifth (5), prepared surfaces did not function simply as traditional hearths (in which foods are cooked by indirect heat on a rack or spit), but rather as a specialized means of direct heating and cooking food directly on the surface.

Figure 3.11. Field image of stacked prepared surfaces with close up showing thin section of surface (zone P4) P4a (a); field image of an expedient hearth (Feature 317) overlying prepared surface (zone E3g) (b); and textile impression fragments of prepared surfaces (modified from Homsey and Sherwood 2010:Figure 2).

Interpretation. Our best evidence thus far for how the surfaces functioned prehistorically comes from experimental studies conducted in 2002; these experiments are detailed and interpreted in Homsey and Sherwood (2010) and Homsey et al. (2010). Based on these experiments, several conclusions can be drawn. First, surfaces can be constructed fairly quickly with the most labor intensive part relating to clay acquisition and transport of clay. Based on micromorphological analysis of the archaeological surfaces, Sherwood and Chapman (2005:72-73) identified several factors that suggest a cave interior source for the material used in surface construction. These include the presence of residual clays, inclusions of weathered limestone and angular chert gravel, the absence of organic matter, and the presence of "ceiling rain" produced inside cave systems. For this reason, we chose nearby Basket Cave as our clay source for the experimental surfaces. During the course of micromorphological analysis of thin sections taken from the experimental surfaces, Homsey (2004, appendix E) noted several of the above attributes, including heavy residual clays and inclusions of weathered limestone and angular chert gravels. Homsey (2004:148) also took geochemical samples of the Dust Cave prepared surfaces and compared them to geochemical samples of Basket Cave residual clay and a Bt horizon from plateau soils directly overlying Dust Cave. Plotting manganese-magnesium ratios against iron-magnesium ratios, and potassium-phosphorus ratios against strontium-calcium ratios demonstrated a distinctly different chemical signature for plateau soils compared to modern residual clay and the archaeological surfaces (Figure 3.12). These geochemical data, coupled with Sherwood's micromorphological observations, strongly support a cave interior source. Thus, it appears that the occupants of Dust Cave chose residual cave clay, the most readily available clay source, as the material for surface construction.

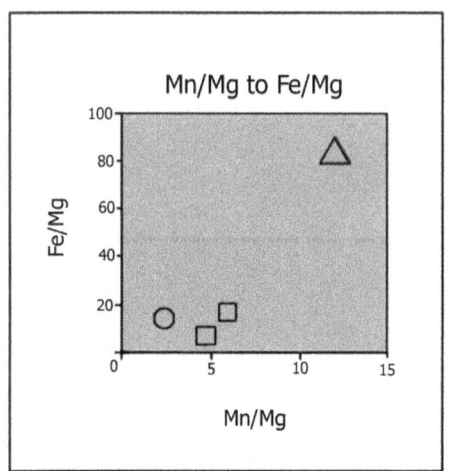 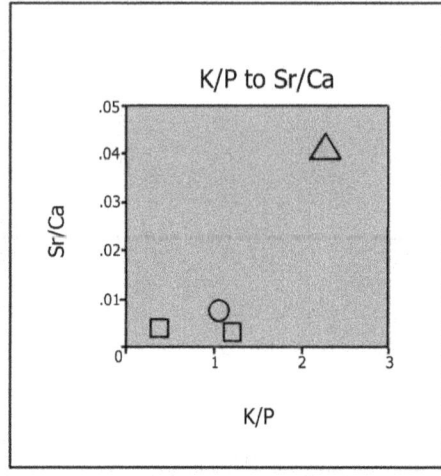 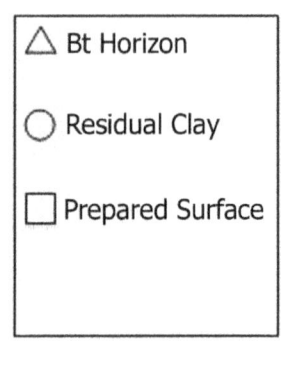

Figure 3.12. Scatterplots of elemental ratios showing relationship between Dust Cave prepared surfaces and residual cave clay versus soil clay.

Secondly, prepared surfaces appear to be red and hard due to relatively brief, low-temperature direct heating. All of the experimental surfaces burned to between 300°C and 500°C hardened, but the one experimental surface which only reached a maximum temperature of 100°C did not harden. Interestingly, the experimental surfaces did not remain permanently hard, but rather disarticulated and rehydrated when placed in water, an observation that Karkansas (2004:520) also noted for Aurignacian clay hearths from Klisoura Cave in southern Greece. These observations are consistent with the firing of low-temperature earthenware (*e.g.,* terra cotta) (Sherwood and Chapman 2005). The structure of the clay molecule changes as water is driven out above 200-300°C; as temperatures exceed 500°C, the clay minerals are altered irreversibly such that the clay will not regain plasticity, even when placed in water (Gibson and Woods 1990; Rice 1987; Sinopoli 1991). That the Dust Cave surfaces are hard suggests that temperatures exceeded 500°C or that repeated firing permanently hardens the clay (Sherwood and Chapman 2005:74). Yet nearly half of the prepared surfaces excavated from Dust Cave do not have this hard aspect and are referred to as "soft" surfaces (Sherwood and Chapman 2005). The absence of hardening suggests that temperatures of the soft surfaces were less than 500°C, thereby allowing the clay minerals to rehydrate. The fact that both hard and soft surfaces occur at Dust Cave make it clear that the firing temperatures of the surfaces varied. Unfortunately, it is not yet possible to say whether this is related to differences in function, or if the harder surfaces resulted from accidentally higher temperatures, repeated firings, or some combination.

Third, the experimental studies support Sherwood and Chapman's (2005:75) hypothesis that prepared surfaces did not function in the same manner as hearths. Historically, Southeastern Indians cooked over open hearths by constructing a rack over an open fire on which small mammals or fish were slowly broiled (Hudson 1979:301). Alternatively, they sometimes impaled meat on sticks which they then stuck into the ground, inclined towards the fire (Hudson 1979). In both these scenarios, food is cooked via a very hot, albeit indirect, heat source. In contrast, the fairly low-temperature prepared surfaces, coupled with their heat retaining properties and the presence of fatty acids, strongly suggest that they functioned as a direct, low-temperature heat source wherein food is placed directly on the surface rather than above or adjacent as in a hearth.

One such type of direct heating involves the use of a griddle—that is, a relatively flat, heated cooking surface. The use of clay griddles has been documented in both archaeological and ethnographic contexts. Formative and Late Prehistoric groups of the Lower Amazon, for example, processed seeds and roasted manioc and other vegetables on flat, clay budare-style griddles (Roosevelt 1995). Griddles are used for this same purpose in south-central Puerto Rico during the Early Ostionoid period (ca. A.D. 650) (Espenshade 2000). The Aztecs used a "comal," a flat clay griddle for roasting of tortillas, chiles, and tomatoes; it is still used today in Taino, southern Mexico (Sherwood and Chapman 2005).

Despite the ethnographic evidence for griddle use, experimental studies demonstrated that prepared surfaces are not effective griddles (Homsey and Sherwood 2010). Despite several tries and different types of foods (e.g., fish, beef), food adhered to the surface when attempting to turn it. Moreover, while the beef cooked to medium rare on some surfaces, the fish did not fully cook on any of them. In contrast, the technique of cooking foods in hot coals proved very effective (Homsey et al. 2010). This technique falls under the method of roasting, in which dry heat circulates around the food on all sides. Foods may be roasted on a rack or a spit elevated above an open flame (*i.e.*, as in a hearth) or placed into an oven. Prehistorically, the latter could have been accomplished in an earth oven dug into the ground, although there is little evidence for earth oven features at Dust Cave. However, using a clay surface satisfactorily cooks food while at the same time eliminating the need to dig a pit, an important advantage in a small cave.

Another possibility is that we may have attempted to replicate cooking the wrong kinds of foods griddle-style. In experiments, we used fish and beef. In contrast, the ethnographic and archaeological examples of griddle-use involve primarily seeds, vegetables, and carbohydrate-rich tubers such as manioc. While manioc was not present in the Midsouth, other tubers were, such as Price's potato bean (*Apios*), cat brier (*Smilax*), and Jerusalem artichoke (*Helianthus*). Starchy seeds, tubers, and roots were probably all important components of the diets of preceramic hunter-gatherers of the Midsouth. Unfortunately, however, these types of foods decay quickly and are therefore archaeologically invisible. One food type which does preserve, however, are protein and fat rich nuts such as acorn (*Quercus*), hickory (*Carya*), and black walnut (*Juglans nigra*); these would have been widely available to Late Holocene groups living in the Middle Tennessee Valley (Hollenbach 2009). Interestingly, both at Dust Cave and Icehouse Bottom, both the number and concentration of prepared surfaces increase with the frequency of charred nuts and nutting stones (Chapman 1977; Hollenbach 2009). Based on the abundance of nutshell recovered from feature fill associated with the prepared surfaces, Homsey et al. (2010) have suggested that the prepared surfaces may have been used to parch (*i.e.*, to make dry via exposure to heat) nuts. Additional evidence for this hypothesis comes from Malainey's (2007) organic residue analysis which identified medium and high chain fatty acids, representative of foods such as tubers, nuts, fish, terrapin, and snail. Based on these results, it is recommended that future experiments focus on evaluating the surfaces' potential for parching nuts, roasting tubers, or a combination of both—so far there is no evidence to suggest that the surfaces were not multi-purpose (Homsey et al. 2010). I will have more to say about nut parching later on.

Finally, the surfaces may have functioned in a capacity that extends beyond cooking and/or food processing. All of the experimental surfaces retained heat (40-50°C) for several hours, especially if the coals are not removed. Even three hours after removing the coals, the coolest surface retained a temperature of 26°C, significantly warmer than the interior of a cave (12-15°C). Whether this was intentional, or a convenient byproduct of cooking is unknown, but it is possible that the prepared surfaces may have doubled as "space heaters" in a cool cave environment (Homsey et al. 2010). The intentional placement of coals close to cave walls to reflect heat and light has been documented for modern cave-dwelling groups living in Papua New Guinea (see Gorecki 1991). Regardless of whether they were used for cooking, heating, or both, prepared surfaces represent some of the earliest manipulations of clay in the Eastern Woodlands and their continued study is crucial to enhancing our understanding of pre-ceramic cooking technologies (Sherwood and Chapman 2005).

Organization. In the field, we often only saw prepared surfaces as patches less than a meter across; when they are mapped, however, it quickly becomes apparent that these surfaces once extended across a good portion of the cave floor (see Figure 3.9c). The question immediately arises: how big were they originally? Earlier (Homsey 2004), I proposed that the inhabitants of Dust Cave may have constructed one or more larger surfaces which were subsequently churned up by pit-digging, burrowing animals, bioturbation, foot-traffic, and later re-use of the site. It may have been more efficient to build one or more larger surfaces, rather than myriad small ones. This would have had two benefits. First, one could cook anywhere that was convenient—without having to construct a new surface every time. Second, a clay "floor" would have provided a fresh, flat surface on which a number of activities could have been more comfortably conducted. Alternatively, based on localized variability in composition and thickness, Sherwood and Chapman (2005:78) have more recently suggested that they are more likely coalescing surfaces. In their view, repeated use of an area resulted in the overlap and linking of surfaces so that they appear as one seemingly large surface.

Viewed from a diachronic perspective, prepared surfaces are often vertically stacked, one on top of the other, with thin lenses of combusted material between them (see Figure 3.11a). The process of preparing and burning new surfaces over the old results in relatively undisturbed sequences of superimposed consecutive burnt layers, similar to what Courty et al. (1989:110) refer to as multi-sequence burnt layers. In thin section, these layers exhibit evidence for trampling in the form of deformation structures (i.e., convoluted and undulatory microlayers of ash and charcoal), splintered charcoal fragments, and compound clasts formed by the compression of two or more clasts into each other (Homsey 2004:183). This pattern of vertical stacking and trampling suggest that that space was used repeatedly over time in the small cave. Moreover, that these sequences occur throughout the cultural sequence at Dust Cave, from the Paleoindian through the Benton occupations, speaks loudly to the consistency in technology and use of space over a period of eight millennia.

Expedient Hearths (Figure 3.13)
Description. Expedient hearths are quite common at Dust Cave. Indeed, they comprise the majority of hearth types during the Kirk Stemmed component. Unlike the larger, deeper surfaces hearths, expedient hearths measure between 30 and 50 cm across and 5 to 10 cm deep, are roughly circular, and have saucer-shaped cross-sections (Figure 3.13a, b). They almost always overlie prepared surfaces—lying right on the surfaces as opposed to being dug into them (Figure 3.13c). They are frequently stratified such that charcoal forms a thin lens at the base. Microlenses of ash preserve, sometimes with different fuel types evident at high magnification (Homsey and Capo 2006) (Figure 3.13e). The layering of charcoal and ash is suggestive of coals that smoldered for a long time and were eventually smothered by ashes. Chemically, these pits have high concentrations of phosphorus. an element associated with burning, and strontium, an element experimentally found to be associated with

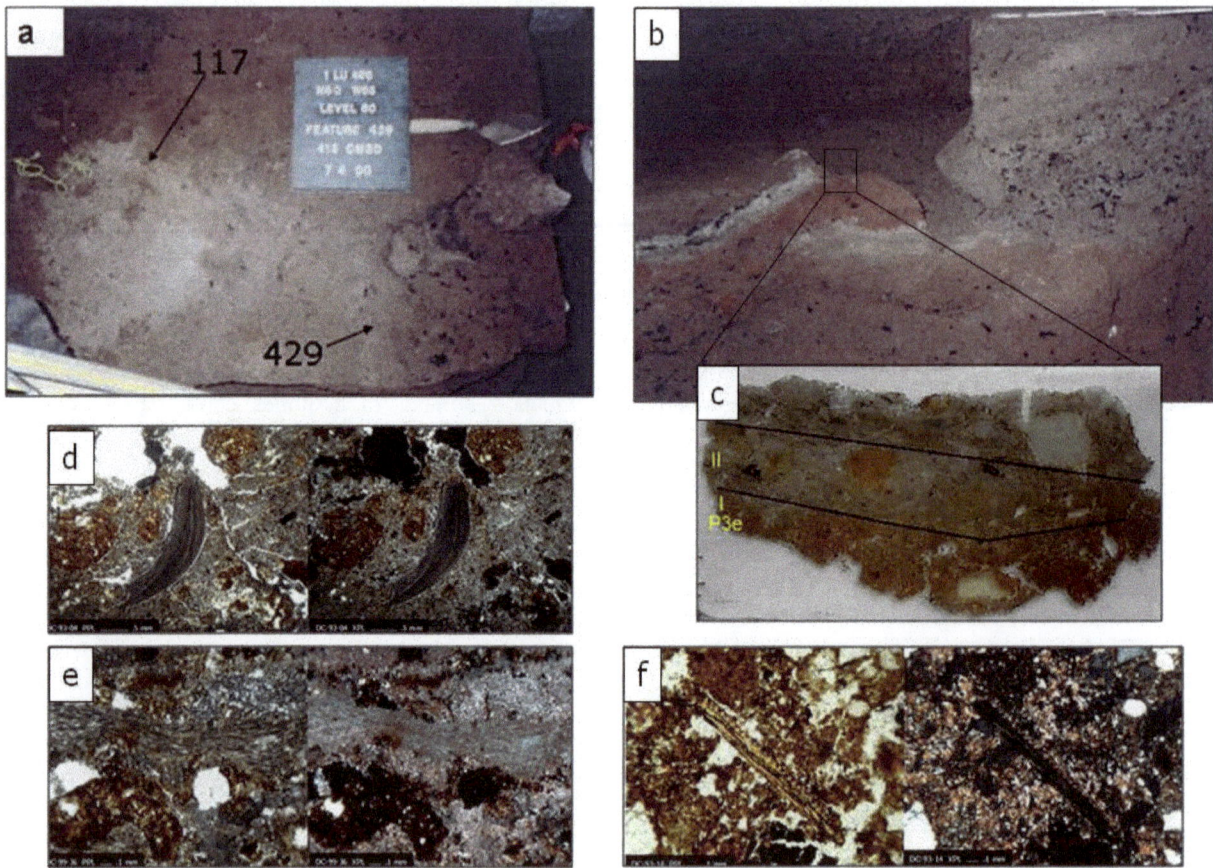

Figure 3.13. Field images of Features 117 (expedient hearth) and 429 (accessory pit) (a) and Feature 445 overlying a prepared surface (b) with scanned thin section of feature fill and unconformable boundary with prepared surface below (c); and photomicrographs (PPL left, XPL right) of burned shell (d); layered ash crystals (note spherulite crystals above and lozenge crystals below) (e); and fish bone (f).

foods such as fish bone, mussel and gastropod shell, and nuts (Homsey 2003a; Rosenthal 1981).

Micromorphological analysis revealed that they frequently contain burned fish bones (See Figure 3.12f), and, sometimes, like Feature 88, burned fish and shell (Figure 3.13d) (Homsey 2004). They may also contain thermally altered rock. They have a large percentage of partially combusted organic materials relative to charcoal, suggestive of low-temperature burning fires. In Features 88, 363, 397 and 445 for example, the organic material has only partially combusted to charcoal (Homsey 2004: Plate 6.40). The presence of intact calcitic pseudomorphs of original plant materials indicate temperatures below 500°C, since temperatures above this will melt calcite, thereby destroying the pseudomorphs (Courty et al. 1989). In addition, the presence of intact pseudomorphs indicates minimal disturbance of these fires since disturbances would tend to disaggregate them (Homsey 2004:158). Feature 445 exhibited calcitic pseudomorphs embedded in a dense matrix of silt-sized ash exhibiting deformation structures possibly formed by trampling (Homsey 2004). These aggregates form preserved "micro-layers" between trampled layers, leading me to believe that the fires were frequently reused and that they underwent trampling and compaction in between burning episodes.

Interpretation. I propose that expedient hearths were used to roast foods, particularly fish, at low temperatures. The experimental studies described earlier (see prepared surfaces above) clearly demonstrate that roasting fish in the coals of a fire built over a prepared clay surface is an effective and simple means of preparing fish. The presence of fish bone in micromorphology samples from nearly every expedient hearth studied corroborates the interpretation that the Dust Cave inhabitants processed and consumed fish in large quantities. Interestingly, in her review of cooking technologies, Wandsnider (1997:13) has noted that coals roasting (vs. pit roasting) is consistent with the optimal thermal processing technique for fish.

One expedient hearth in particular illustrates this pattern. Feature 405 was a dense charcoal/ash concentration overlying a prepared clay surface. The feature fill was so full of fish bones that they could even be seen during excavation in the poorly lit cave. Walker's faunal analysis revealed that most of the fish bones at Dust Cave are not burned, a finding that is consistent with our 2002 experimental studies in which few of the fish bones burned during cooking (Homsey et al. 2010). However, some of the fish bones seen in the micromorphology samples are burned (Homsey 2004). This apparent contradiction may be resolved if people threw the bones of eaten fish back into the cooking fires for discard in the same manner Hollenbach (in Homsey et al. 2010) describes for fruit pits and nutshell.

It is worth reiterating that expedient hearths overlie prepared surfaces—their association with one another is unequivocal, suggesting that the two technologies went hand in hand. Expedient hearths, then, are simply the remnants of the fires built on prepared surfaces. Essentially, these features are hearths, but characterized by their expediency and lack of formally defined positioning (e.g., using clay linings or rocks). As discussed above, it appears that fish and possibly shellfish were roasted or steamed in these quick hearths. In addition, the presence of nutshell in the hearth fill suggests that they are also associated with nut processing. It may be that the nutshell was simply used as a fuel source, but given the high fat and caloric content of nuts, coupled with their known ethnohistoric importance (Hudson 1976), it likely represents the byproducts of food processing[4]. This hypothesis is strengthened by looking at changes in the feature and botanical assemblage through time. Sherwood and Chapman (2003) and Homsey (2004) have noted that the number and concentration of prepared surfaces appears to increase with the frequency of charred hickory nutshell and nutting stones culminating in the Eva/Morrow Mountain component.

This trend begs the question of whether expedient hearths represent the remnants of fires burned to heat the prepared surfaces in order to parch hickory nuts. Parching, a technology employed by both archaeological and modern societies, prepares nuts for storage by killing mold, fungi, and insects (Talalay et al. 1984). It destroys the embryos, thereby precluding germination during storage. Gardner (1997) notes that nut parching can be easily accomplished by stirring nuts over heated stones in pits. Ethnographic observations have recorded other means. For example, traditional west-Ghana groups process shea nuts (*Vitellaria paradoxa*) for the modern nut butter industry (e.g., Chalfin 2007; Casey 2004) using a variety of methods: stirring them in ceramic pots over a fire, on half of a large ceramic storage vessel laid over a fire, or roasting them in a clay oven; temperatures in the latter two reach between 90 to 150°C. (Boffa et al. 1996; Dei et al. 2007; Newland 1919). I would argue that a convenient alternative would be to parch them on a prepared clay surface. Multiple fires kept burning for long periods of time would keep the surfaces hot enough for parching. In our experimental surfaces, we easily maintained surface temperatures of 50-100°C simply by allowing coals to smolder. Future experimental research should focus on trying to replicate this proposed parching process and noting the material correlates it leaves behind.

A unique expedient hearth that warrants special attention is Feature 117, dating to the Paleoindian occupation, in Zone T (see Homsey 2004: Plates 6.46-6.55). Feature 117 is a large ash-rich feature with a highly burned periphery. At about a meter in length, 80 cm wide and 17 cm deep, it overlaps with the dimensions for surface hearths. Yet, with the exception of size, Feature 117 looks more like an expedient hearth than a surface hearth. It is not lined with rocks, although angular fragments of thermally altered limestone are visible in thin section. Its fill is dominated almost exclusively by ash (surprisingly, given the extensive decalcification at this depth) (Homsey 2004). The periphery is dark red and appears to be burned (Homsey 2004). Microartifacts are heavily dispersed, comprising about five percent of the coarse fraction. The dominant microartifact is burned bone, much of it identified as fish (Homsey 2004: Plates 6.50, 6.51). Burned shell is also present, as well as possible burned quadrate (Walker, personal communication 2004). Partially combusted material (Homsey 2004) and charcoal incompletely combusted to ash indicate low to moderate temperatures. Intact ash aggregates (Homsey 2004: Plate 6.55) demonstrate that this feature has remained amazingly undisturbed through the millennia. These similarities with expedient hearths attest to the antiquity of the expedient hearth technology and highlight the continuity in technology through time at Dust Cave.

Many of the expedient hearths are stratified, such that the charcoal forms a thin, lower lens, while ash makes up the rest. The ash portion is also sometimes bedded, as in the unnamed feature present in DC-99-36. In thin section, I observed several micro-layers (<1 mm) of ashes from separate fuel sources (Figure 3.13e). In some cases, layers consisting solely of lozenge shaped ash crystals, indicative of deciduous species, overlie layers consisting of spherulite crystals, indicative of leaves and/or (possibly) nuts (Courty et al. 1989:107; Wattez and Courty 1987). In other cases, as is shown in lozenge shaped crystals overlie elongated rhomboid shaped crystals, possibly representing pine fuel (Courty et al. 1989; Wattez and Courty 1987). Interestingly, spherulite and lozenge crystals dominate the ashes in samples dating to the Kirk Stemmed and later (circa 8,000 B.C.), while rhomboid and lozenge crystals dominant the ashes pre-dating this (Homsey 2004). This may represent changing vegetation concurrent with middle Holocene warming in the Middle Tennessee Valley, or it may represent changing patterns in fuel exploitation.

Finally, bedded ashes and charcoal are characteristic of fires that smolder for long periods, during which time charcoal slowly converts to ash. These features may have doubled as "sleeping fires." Based on ethnographic analogy, we know that modern hunter-gatherers often place coals near a cave wall to reflect both light and heat

---
[4] As byproducts of food processing, nutshells would have been a nuisance to the site's occupants. Rather than littering the site or the talus slope with nutshells, occupants could simply dispose of them by burning, especially because the nuts are useful as fuel. Hickory and walnut shells have relatively high fat contents, such that they burn hot and with relatively little smoke (Lopinot 1984).

(Galanidou 1997; Gorecki 1988). As they smolder overnight, these pits would form ash rich pits with charcoal bases. Such fires would provide welcome warmth in a chilly cave. Furthermore, the prepared surfaces, with all these low temperature, relatively smokeless fires on them, would have retained heat rather nicely. While the primary purpose of these hearths may have been cooking, they may have doubled as sleeping fires.

Organization. Looking at the spatial distribution of expedient hearths, we can see that there are two main clusters (Figure 3.9c). Those focused around the periphery, along the northwest walls, and those focused around the southwest wall. The Test Trench, which cuts through the center of the entrance chamber (see Figure 3.5), partially accounts for this bimodal clustering since shallow charcoal/ash pits often went overlooked during excavation. Overall, they focus on the front-center of the entrance chamber. They are not as tightly clustered as surface or pit hearths ($R=.588$, $p<.001$), lending some support to their interpretation as being expedient and useful for a variety of purposes, from smoking fish to heating boiling stones, to warming the cave. Expedient hearths could be quickly made anywhere a prepared surface provided the appropriate substrate. As Figure 3.9c illustrates, the space occupied by expedient hearths corresponds very closely to prepared surface space. The hearths tend to focus somewhat along the southwest and northeast walls. The position of some of these expedient hearths may have allowed them to double as sleeping fires.

Pit Hearths (Figure 3.14)
Description. In contrast to the expedient hearths described above are sub-surface hearths, which I refer to here as "pit hearths" since they appear as pits dug into the substrate. Examples for which I had thin sections include features 41, 412, 419, 443, and 449. Typically basin-shaped in cross section, they average about 15 cm in depth, and always intrude a prepared surface (Figure 3.14a). They are always circular in shape, and though they range in size from 50 to 100 cm in diameter and 15 to 30 cm deep, they have a surprisingly consistent width to depth ratio of 3.5. Ash content exceeds charcoal. Feature fill can be characterized as gray to gray-brown silty loams with approximately 30% sand-sized (and larger) charcoal distributed throughout (some pieces up to 1 cm) (Homsey 2004:Plate 6.58). After ash, carbonized nutshell is the most common microartifact, making up approximately 10-15% of the coarse fraction (Figure 3.14b) followed by lightly to moderately dispersed sand-sized fragments of fire-cracked rock (Figure 3.14e), and lightly dispersed burned bone and shell. Their loose, heterogeneous fill contains moderate to heavy amounts (~20%) of dispersed burned prepared surface clasts, and mixed and compound clasts, the latter which Sherwood (2001) attributes to reworking due to scuffling, trampling and re-deposition. Most ash occurs as dispersed individual ash crystals, rather than in articulated aggregates. Unlike expedient hearths, layers of ash are not preserved. Rather, the chaotic fabric and lack of calcitic pseudomorphs suggests disturbance. Their poor sorting is indicative of gravitational deposition (versus water or wind), which may include dumping. Some are slightly stratified with remnant bedding preserved (e.g., Feature 41), suggesting more than one depositional event.

Most interestingly, pit hearths contain a great deal of fine sand- and silt-sized fragments of partially combusted organic material (figure 3.14d). In addition to partially combusted organics, charcoal incompletely combusted to ash crystals occurs frequently in pit hearths (Figure 3.14c), suggestive of low temperature fires. The degree of burning in bone suggests temperatures on the order of 200-300°C (Homsey 2004). Geochemically, these features have exceptionally high Sr and K values (>.005 and >.10, respectively), indicative of combusted materials such as nuts. Calcium oxalate spherulites, associated with the reproductive organs of angiosperms (which includes nuts), are the most abundant ash crystals present, further arguing that nuts played a key role in the formation of these pit deposits.

Another interesting aspect of the Dust Cave pit hearths is the type of fire-cracked rock (FCR) they contain. Although a variety of raw materials existed for use in cooking, such as river cobbles from the Tennessee River and weathered gravels from the upland plateau, the occupants of Dust Cave appear to have made use of the fossiliferous limestone outcropping along the bluff line the cave is formed in. Moreover, only a massive, blocky variety (biomicrite) was utilized in the pit hearths, although thinner bedded varieties are quite common along the bluff and are found in other hearth contexts. Experimental and petrographic studies demonstrated that this biomicrite underwent the least alternation, degradation, and fracturing of all the locally available materials when fired above 300°C (Homsey 2009). Thus, it appears that the occupants of Dust Cave preferentially selected the blockier, more resistant variety of limestone for the processing activities occurring in pit hearths.

Interpretation. The great consistency in shape, size, and content contrasts with the variability described above for expedient and surface hearths. It has been argued that consistency in shape and size indicates low functional variability (Fortier 1983; Stafford 1991). This morphological characteristic, coupled with the relative lack of bone or shell in these pits, suggests to me that these features served a single purpose. Ethnographically pit hearths appear in a number of food contexts: processing fatty meats; preparing fructan-rich plants foods (e.g., camas, agave) for storage and later consumption; and cooking foods such as acorn breads, corn, fish, and starchy tubers for immediate consumption (Dering 1999; Smith and McNees 1999; Wandsnider and Sodha 1997). Hearth size varies, depending on the food processed and the social context (e.g., domestic, ceremonial), though shape is usually cylindrical or bottle-shaped (Wandsnider and Sodha 1997). Rocks often serve as an intermediary heating element, though they are not necessarily essential to the cooking technology (Wandsnider and Sodha 1997).

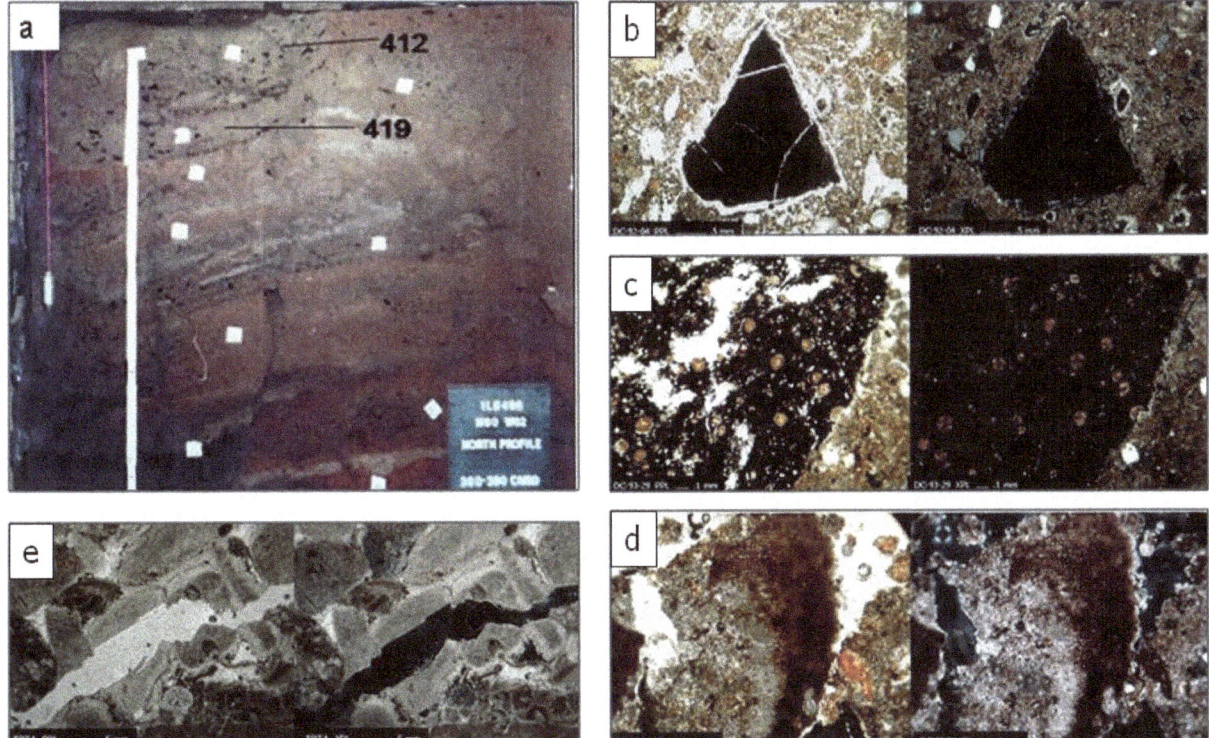

Figure 3.14. Field image of Features 412 and 419 (pit hearths) (a) and photomicrographs (PPL left, XPL right) of nutshell (b), charcoal incompletely combusted to spherulite ash crystals (c), partially combusted organic material (d) and angular fractures in thermally altered limestone (e).

Based on high Sr concentrations, carbonized nutshell, and spherulite ash crystals, I hypothesize that these hearths represent the byproducts of nut processing. We know from ethnohistoric accounts that Southeastern Indians highly valued hickory nut oil, which they used for cooking and seasoning (Hudson 1976:301). The procedure for obtaining oil involved boiling the nutmeats. Nuts were first cracked into small pieces using nutting stones, then thrown into a pot of boiling water, shells and all. With time, the shells and nutmeat would sink to the bottom while oil floated to the top as a milky emulsion which they then skimmed off and preserved. According to Hudson (1976), one hundred pounds of hickory nuts yielded approximately one gallon of oil.

While the pre-ceramic populations working at Dust Cave would not have used ceramic pots, boiling can also be accomplished by digging a pit into the ground, lining it with animal skins and filling the hole with water (Munson 1986; Stafford 1991; Talalay et al. 1984). Using rocks as heating elements, prehistoric cooks could boil the water. This would entail keeping boiling stones handy, so that hot rocks could continually be added to the water as cooled rocks were removed. For convenience's sake, boiling stones were most likely kept hot in fires adjacent to boiling pits. Wandsnider and Sodha (1997) have documented this practice ethnographically, further noting that by first transferring heat to a rock element, a moderate heat environment (>100°C) in the hearth could be maintained. After processing the nuts, these pits probably were filled in, either intentionally, or accidentally, through foot traffic and/or animal activity. The micro-scale remnant bedding seen in Feature 41 lends some support for the argument that they were filled in intentionally, but later reworked through post-depositional activity.

Stafford (1991) describes a pit common at the upland site of Buckshaw Bridge in the lower Illinois River valley, which he believes functioned as oil extraction pits. He describes them as fairly steep sided pits approximately 150 cm in diameter and 45 cm in depth. While these pits are much larger than the Dust Cave hearths, the width to depth ratios are nearly identical at each site: 3.22 at Buckshaw Bridge and 3.46 at Dust Cave (the larger size may simply reflect the fact that Buckshaw Bridge is an open-air site lacking the space constraints of Dust Cave). Pit fill consists of "dark brown sediment with heavy charcoal mottling," fill that would be considered "midden" if found outside the confines of a pit feature, and suggests (as I do) that the pits were filled with redeposited material. Several of the Buckshaw Bridge pits exhibited evidence of in situ oxidation due to heating.

Gardner (1997:174) believes that the pits discussed by Stafford are indeed nut processing pits, but that oil production was not involved. Rather, he suggests that the pits more likely represent nut parching, a process which could be easily accomplished by stirring nuts over heated stones in the pits. The parching process (described above, previous section) would leave features very similar to those characterized as nut *boiling* pits (Gardner

1997:174). Gardner was referring to morphological similarities, but I would argue that parching pits would also look similar geochemically and micro-morphologically: both would appear as low temperature pits high in Sr and K. Perhaps the only way to test this would be to look at the fire cracked rock for evidence of wet or dry heating. Such an endeavor should be part of future research; experimentation is vital to answering this question. Interestingly, Ferris et al. (2007) note that traditional families in Uganda parch shea nuts *prior* to boiling them for oil extraction; heating the nuts precludes germination which can reduce oil quality and result in a bitter taste. This raises the interesting possibility that both parching and boiling was occurring at Dust Cave, with parching preceding boiling to enhance nut oil flavor. Regardless of whether the nuts were boiled or parched, their processing would result in copious amounts of combusted materials requiring refuse disposal (Stafford 1991).

Finally, it should be noted that Sr may derive from nutshell used as a secondary fuel source, rather than through the primary processing of nuts. If the fires used to heat boiling stones were burned using nutshell, and if the pit hearths were filled in with the coals from these fires, than the resulting pit fill would have very high Sr values, without them necessarily having been for the purpose of boiling nuts. As Hudson notes, Indians boiled soups and stews regularly, so it is possible that these pits are the byproducts of other kinds of boiling too. The presence of burned bone and shell, though light (<2%), may indicate other uses of the pits, but these may have become incorporated into the pit during infilling. Interestingly, though, pit hearths do not appear at Dust Cave until the Kirk Stemmed component, around 8,000 B.C., a time corresponding to the spread of hickory trees into the Tennessee Valley (Delcourt and Delcourt 1987). This temporal correlation lends persuasive evidence, albeit circumstantial, that pit hearths represent nut processing pits. I will revisit this temporal correlation in chapter 5.

Organization. Spatially, pit hearths focus in the center of the entrance chamber, but skewed towards the east side (Figure 3.9d). It appears, then, that nut processing occurred within the general "food processing" area (defined by surface and expedient hearths), but somewhat on the edge of that area. This may reflect the natural geometry of the cave: the ceiling here slopes up towards the east, so positioning them on this side may have maximized ventilation. Alternatively, this pattern may be embedded in cultural practices which led to a separation between foods prepared for immediate consumption, and those processed for storage (i.e., nuts, nut oil). It has been argued that the prevalence of nuts at Dust Cave, coupled with the discrete clustering of nut processing pits, may reflect a pattern of gendered labor (Hollenbach 2009; Homsey et al. 2010). We know from ethnohistorical accounts of Southeastern Indians that food preparation and processing was the job of women (Hudson 1976: 264-266). Taking an evolutionary perspective, Hollenbach (2009:214-215) has argued that gathering resources predictable in time and space (such as nuts) is related to the need of women to obtain stable nutrition for themselves and their children. She further argues that women likely processed and prepared plant foods, noting that the allocation of food preparation to women holds across ethnographic foraging groups (Hawkes 1996; Kelly 1995; Panter-Brick 2002). Considering nut processing as a subset of food preparation, it is interesting to note that among the traditional west-Ghana and Ugandan groups that currently process shea nuts for the modern nut butter industry, processing is the exclusive domain of women (Boffa et al 1996; Chalfin 2007; Casey 2004). Thus, assuming that the primary responsibility for gathering, food processing and preparation was in the hands of women—as it was among historic-period Southeastern Indians—then not only are we seeing gender at Dust Cave, but perhaps gendered space as well (McMillian et al. 2008).

Fireplace Rake-out (Figure 3.15)
Fireplace rake-out occurs as combusted materials that have been re-deposited from the original burning location. Rake-out includes stones used in cooking, primary refuse resulting from the cleaning out of coals from hearths, secondary refuse deposited some distance away from the original burning location, and charcoal rings. Each is described below, followed by an interpretation of the technology represented. I do not interpret nor map these individually since they cannot be differentiated without the aid of thin sections. However, I map collectively charcoal and ash pits, the distribution of which yields some valuable information about the organization of refuse disposal at Dust Cave.

Accessory Pits
Description. Associated with surface hearths are small charcoal pits containing numerous rocks, often thermally altered. The pits average 30 cm in diameter and 5-6 cm deep, with saucer-shaped profiles. Charcoal dominates feature fill, while ash is a minimal constituent (<20%), though this probably reflects the fact that most of my samples came from below the seasonal inundation depth (350 cmbd) and are therefore decalcified. These pits always intrude another feature, often a hearth, and show no evidence of being burned in place, though the hearths they are associated with are burned. Geochemically, they have low Sr/Ca and K/P (<0 .003 and <0.10, respectively) which reflects the high charcoal and low ash content of these features (Homsey and Capo 2006). An example of a fireplace accessory pit is Feature 429, which intrudes Feature 117, the Paleoindian expedient hearth described earlier. While fire-cracked rock was not noted in thin section, in the field the feature contained numerous fist-sized limestone rocks exhibiting characteristics of thermal alteration, including angular fissures and a friable texture (Homsey 2009).

Interpretation. The association described above suggests that these features may be the remnants of piles of cooking stones, ready by the side of the hearth. Since they are a secondary addition to hearths, I refer to them as "accessory" pits. Gorecki (1991) has documented cooking stone piles in his ethnographic research among New Guinea horticulturalists.

Primary Refuse: Scrape-out

Description. Leafing through feature forms and excavation field notes, it quickly becomes apparent that many features form part of larger hearth complexes consisting of a main hearth intruded by smaller charcoal-rich pits, often just off to the side of the hearth. Feature 136 was a large hearth exhibiting several burning episodes. Several smaller, roughly circular charcoal pits intruded the hearth, including features 136d, 136e, and 136f. These smaller pits were less than five cm deep with saucer shaped profiles. Often, the periphery of these pits was noted by concentrations of large charcoal fragments and ash.

Unfortunately, most of the hearth complexes this well preserved date to the Eva/Morrow Mountain component, which was excavated before the systematic collection of micromorphology samples from features. Micromorphology samples were taken from only three features matching the above description: 222, 410, and 420. The sample from Feature 222, part of the larger Feature 223 complex, was excavated in 1998 and could not be located. Thus, the following discussion is based on only two features and therefore should not be considered a representative sample.

Like accessory pits, scrape-out pits are roughly circular, generally less than 30 cm in diameter and about five cm deep. Also like accessory pits, scrape-out co-occurs with surface hearths. They consist predominantly of charcoal, though may contain a moderate to heavy amount of dispersed ash as well (~30%). Both features 410 and 420 contained moderate to heavy dispersed burned microartifacts (shell and bone). Both also contained sand-sized fragments of fire-cracked rock. They exhibit no evidence of *in situ* burning and always intrude the burned periphery of a larger hearth feature. Geochemically, these features have low Sr/Ca and K/P values (<.003 and <.10, respectively), which—as with accessory pits and rake-out—reflects the high charcoal and low ash content.

Interpretation. Scrape-out is a kind of rake-out, one which is re-deposited from the original burning location, but moved only a short distance from the original burning location. While scrape-out pits look morphologically similar to accessory pits, they differ in two ways: (1) they lack fire-cracked rock, and (2) they may contain more ash, up to 40%. The lack of articulated ash aggregates and poorly sorted, porphyritic microstructures are consistent with disturbed and re-deposited materials. Ripped up clasts of burned prepared surfaces were observed in Feature 420, further supporting an interpretation of re-deposited materials. Scrape-out pits are coals raked out of larger hearths to clear them of built up combusted materials. They are not pits dug in which to dispose of the coals, but rather accumulate as coals are scraped out and brushed to the side.

Admittedly, these scrape-out pits may not be contemporaneous with the hearths they are located near. Even if we had radiocarbon dates from each of the pits, the error ranges would likely be too large to assume contemporaneity. However, based on their small size, lack of *in situ* burning, and intrusive nature they do not appear to be "stand alone" features, but rather associated with some other activity. This scrape out may accumulate after several burning episodes, or even after multiple occupations. Scrape-out as defined here can be considered primary refuse since it directly reflects hearth cleaning but is not swept away, collected or re-deposited at a distant location (Schiffer 1987).

Secondary Refuse

Description. Secondary refuse comes in two morphologies: charcoal lenses (< 5cm thick) and small charcoal pits not in association with *in situ* fireplaces (< 5 cm deep), both of which occur towards the rear of the cave, usually towards the northwest wall. It is very important to note that these pits are *not* burned in place. While both types consist predominantly of charcoal, ash may make up to 40% of the groundmass. Individual charcoal grains may be quite large, sometimes greater than a centimeter, giving deposits the appearance in the field of having less ash than they actually contain. Geochemically, they have low Sr/Ca and K/P values (<.005 and <.15, respectively), which—as with accessory pits—reflects the high charcoal content relative to ash[5] (Homsey and Capo 2006).

Micromorphological analysis of both lenses and pits revealed unsorted, loose microstructures with approximately 30-40% porosity (Homsey 2004: Plate 9.72, 9.73). They contain a variety of burned and unburned microartifacts, including shell, bone, and lithics. Of the bone artifacts, bones identified as fish accounted for about a quarter of the total. Also identified were soil aggregates, sand-sized fragments of thermally altered limestone, and ash aggregates. Some ash aggregates (Homsey 2004: Plate 9.74) are rounded, typical of transport and redeposition. Most pits exhibit a range of combusted materials, from partially combusted organic materials to fully combusted ash crystals. These characteristics suggest to me that the source of the sediment varies and that no single activity is responsible for their deposition. Their poor sorting and lack of *in situ* structures (e.g., calcitic pseudomorphs or intact bedding) support an interpretation of re-deposited, dumped materials. It is unlikely that they were not transported far or frequently, based on the large size and fragments of intact cellular structure in some of the grains of wood charcoal. The heavy amounts of soil aggregates (20-30%) may represent soil adhering to whatever materials (e.g., vegetative matter) that were burned (Sherwood 2001). Light micritic (i.e., fine grained calcitic) coatings of vesicles and channels associated with rhizomorphic activity abound as do fecal pellets, suggesting that root

---

[5] It should be noted that most of these pits tested came from below the seasonal inundation level where the dissolution of calcite-rich ash has "artificially" enriched them in charcoal.

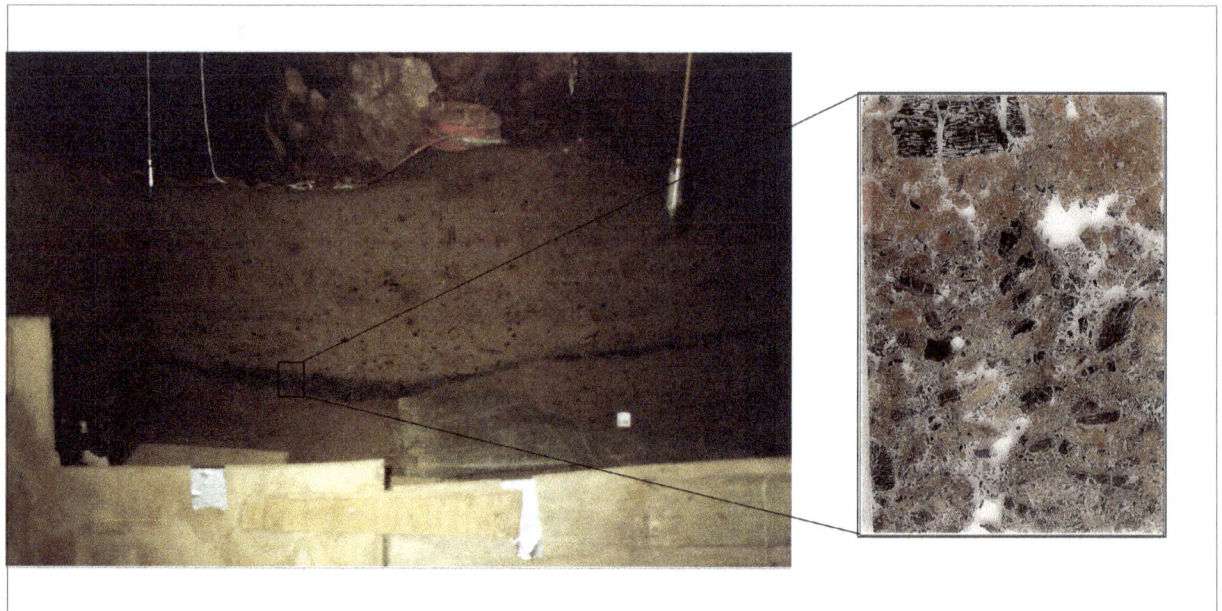

Figure 3.15. Field image of Feature 301, a charcoal lens (a) and scanned thin section of feature fill illustrating the cross-bedded charcoal grains.

and earthworm activity flourished in the soft refuse deposits.

Feature 301, a charcoal lens located in the far rear of the cave at the entrance to the west passageway (Figure 3.15), shows a slight preferred orientation of most charcoal grains, suggesting re-deposition via sweeping (Goldberg, personal communication 2003). The grains are cross-bedded, with the charcoal grains in most of the slide dip slightly to the left, while the grains in the lower right hand corner appear to trend in the opposite direction. This suggests that sweeping did not always occur in the same direction. The high porosity and poor sorting support sweeping as the transport agent (vs. a process that would compact sediments, or sort them such as fluvial activity).

Interpretation. As the above description demonstrates, these charcoal deposits are not burned in situ but rather have been redeposited. The poor sorting and high porosity in these features suggests a gravitational transport agent, such as dumping or sweeping. The bedding seen in Feature 301 supports sweeping as the most likely transport mechanism, at least for that particular feature. Moreover, the wide variety of plant and animal materials in the fill, coupled with the range of combustion apparent in plant remains, strongly indicates that these materials derive from more than one source and/or activity. I therefore interpret these deposits to represent refuse redeposited away from the original burning location. Because they are not in association or proximity to in situ fireplaces, they cannot be classified as scrape out. Rather, I argue that these features represent secondary refuse deposits (*sensu* Schiffer 1987), dumped away from the center of activity. The position of rake-out—essentially refuse—towards the rear of the cave is consistent with the disposal of coals by modern hunter-gatherers (Galanidou 1997, 2001; Gorecki 1991).

Charcoal Rings
Description. Charcoal rings most likely represent post-depositional alteration of charcoal pits, both accessory and rake-out. In the field, rings of charcoal surround a matrix of sediment that looks just like the zone in which the feature formed. Feature 387, a charcoal ring intruding Zone T8, exemplifies the morphology of a charcoal ring in cross section. In thin section, rings exhibit fine fluvial laminations of silt and clay, and oriented, elongated charcoal grains wrapped around silts and clays, as well as charcoal coatings of voids (see Homsey 2004:Plates 6.9, 6.10; 6.77), all of which indicate a fluvial agent of re-deposition.

Interpretation. Two mechanisms may account for the formation of charcoal rings. First, they may result from water dripping through the cave ceiling, which disperses charcoal (and possibly ash) towards the outside. Ash, much lighter than charcoal, may be washed away entirely (or dissolved as part of the decalcification process). The presence of slacking crusts, in Feature 369 for example (Homsey 2004: Plate 6.78), lends some support for this interpretation (Courty et al. 1989). Alternatively, the rings may form when slackwaters saturate sediments, allowing the lighter ash to float away while the heavier charcoal resettles to the bottom and sides. Sediments later infilled the resulting depression, leaving behind a charcoal ring. Rings are especially prevalent in Zones P, Q, and R, suggesting that the cave may have been more wet during this time interval. I will return to this idea in the next chapter when I discuss the effect of fluvial activity on the organization of deposits and the changing use of the cave through time.

Organization of Fireplace Rake-out
Without micromorphology samples, it is nearly impossible to differentiate primary from secondary refuse. It is even difficult to differentiate accessory from

refuse pits since oftentimes rocks were removed prior to feature excavation and tossed out, mistakenly taken for roof spall. Nor did feature forms and photographs offer much help. Photographs often did not have high enough quality to distinguish among types and feature forms often lacked pertinent information such as profiles or fill description. Thus, since micromorphology samples are not available for all of the features at Dust Cave, I mapped together all charcoal and ash pits that did not clearly display physical properties characteristic of *in situ* fireplaces (Homsey 2004, Figures 6.18, 6.19).

A Nearest Neighbor Analysis of ash pits indicated that they do not cluster nearly as tightly as other feature types ($R=.520$, $.005<p<.01$). Charcoal pits show a similarly dispersed pattern ($R=.622$, $p<.001$). Although the distribution of charcoal pits and ash pits reveal little patterning, two trends are worth noting. First, while pits appear to cluster somewhat towards the cave walls, it is important to note that poor lighting and a lack of familiarity with the cave stratigraphy during excavation of the Test Trench meant that many features went unrecognized. Thus, the paucity of pits in the Test Trench initially gives one the impression of greater clustering than actually exists. Second, some of the pits overlap with the same areas covered with prepared surfaces (see Figure 3.9c), while others occur beyond their boundaries. Those that co-occur with the prepared surfaces probably represent a combination of fireplace accessories and "scrape-out," though without detailed field notes and micromorphology samples, it is impossible to differentiate between the two. Other charcoal pits occur well beyond the boundaries of the prepared surfaces. The fact that they occur "off site" so to speak suggests their use predominantly as rake-out and refuse disposal.

Mixed Burning
Mixed burning deposits occur when the burned surface and the combusted materials (ash and charcoal) are mixed through post-depositional processes, though the original constituents are still distinguishable (Sherwood 2001:157). Generally, these large-scale deposits occur as zones and were not excavated separately as features. Bioturbation, trampling, and sheetwash likely account for most of the mixing. Mixed burning deposits include middens and charcoal stringers.

Middens
Description. Tabular, heterogeneous ash-rich zones occur across large portions of the floor of the cave in most components, most notably the Eva/Morrow Mountain and Kirk Stemmed components (e.g., K1, J3b, P3). These are not pits, and they display no internal stratification. Micromorphological analysis reveals that the matrix is composed of combusted materials—primarily dispersed ash (~50%) and burned microartifacts (~5% shell, bone, and lithic debitage)—in a chaotic fabric (Homsey 2004:Plates 6.80-6.82). Poor sorting suggests gravitational deposition, which is consistent with dumping behavior. Evidence for post-depositional biological activity comes in the form of extensive fecal pellets and a porous fabric, often lacking clear sedimentological features. Such extensive biological activity is unsurprising given the soft, porous nature of the combusted materials. Geochemical analysis shows these deposits to have exceptionally high Sr/Ca and K/P values (>.005 and >.20, respectively), indicative of ash, especially from hickory nut and/or fish bones. Partially combusted materials, oxalate spherulite ash crystals and nut charcoal are common, suggesting that the materials dumped are primarily coming from expedient and pit hearths. Thin section DC-96-28 shows slight bedding of zone J3b, dipping (in a convex, "scooped" fashion), about 15 degrees to the left hand side of the slide, giving the impression of multiple dumping episodes (Homsey 2004:182).

Interpretation. Despite being excavated as zones, the depositional history of these deposits clearly has an anthropogenic source, transport agent, and deposition mechanism. Based on detailed thin section observations, Sherwood (2001) has previously described these as the byproducts of multiple dumping episodes derived from intensive burning activity. My own thin section analysis corroborates her interpretation. Since they derive from dumped combusted materials, they can be thought of as exceptionally large rake-out deposits; but because their original sedimentary structures are extensively disturbed by bioturbation, I classify them as mixed burning deposits (*sensu* Sherwood 2001). I refer to them as middens to differentiate them from the less disturbed rake-out deposits occurring as discrete pits.

Organization. These zones can usually be traced throughout the entrance chamber, and tend to thicken towards the northwest wall (Sherwood 2001), an area that appears to be a toss zone. While excavating this portion of the cave during the 2002 field season, excavators noted heavy densities of broken artifacts (both stone and bone), discarded cores, lithic debitage, and large fist-sized fragments of prepared surfaces. The prepared surface fragments suggest that surfaces were periodically torn up or, at the least, broken up during cleaning, and tossed in the rear of the cave, away from the center of daily domestic activities. Examples of middens include Zones E1, K1, J3b, and P3.

Charcoal Stringers
Description. Stringers are thin lenticular zones of charcoal less than two cm thick (but usually less than 1 cm) which occur only below 400 cmbd (zones R through U). In the field, we called these stringers "stains" since they appeared as thin veneers staining the underlying deposits. They may extend for several meters. Zone U2a exemplifies a typical charcoal stringer (Figure 3.16a, b). Lying unconformably between U1 and U2 at 445 cmbd, U2a could be followed for over three meters. It had an undulatory and ephemeral appearance and was difficult to follow spatially as it came and went. Due to their thinness and ephemeral nature, excavators usually could not remove stringers separately as features, but we did take micromorphology and chemical samples from them. In thin section, fluvial laminations of fining upward silt and clay are ubiquitous, indicative of sheetwash over these

deposits (Figure 3.16c). Preferentially oriented, elongated and bedded charcoal grains also occur with great frequency in Zones U6 and T2c. Moreover, micromorphological analysis of thin sections revealed that charcoal coats the inside surface of many vughs and vesicles (i.e., pore spaces) (Figure 3.16d). Feature 381, one of the few stains deep enough for excavators to remove as a feature, contained a distinct micro-lens (<1 cm) of sand-sized quartz forming an unconformable boundary with the overlying feature fill, as well as the underlying Zone T (Figure 3.16e). This unconformable coarse lens reflects a small-scale fluvial event with enough velocity to erode some of the original T2, though just how much erosion occurred is impossible to say. Geochemically speaking, stringers have very low Sr/Ca (<.003) and K/P (<.05), which reflects the loss of Sr and K below 350 cmbd. Charcoal dominates stringers since decalcification has leached and dissolved fragile ash crystals.

Interpretation and Organization. I suggest that stringers represent former charcoal and/or ash deposits, perhaps rake-out, that have experienced extensive post-depositional fluvial activity—enough so as to destroy the original shape and sedimentary structures of the deposit and spread charcoal and ash across a large portion of the cave floor. Charcoal stringers almost exclusively occur below 400 cmbd, with most of them occurring between 420 and 450 cmbd. In addition, the majority of stringers occur east of the Test Trench, including zone U2a, and Features 486 and 381. Zone T2c, a charcoal stringer consisting of about 20% ash (relatively high compared to other stringers) occurs just west of the Test Trench, adjacent to Feature 423, the rock basin previously discussed which represents the washed out fill of that former hearth. In general, though, most stringers occur in the eastern portion of the entrance chamber, an area that Sherwood's (2001) geoarchaeological study of Dust Cave demonstrated to be frequently subjected to flooding and small-scale erosion. While such heavily disturbed deposits can yield little cultural information, they do provide a wealth of information about natural processes and the geological constraints that people inhabiting the cave at a certain time period would have faced. In this respect then, they still serve as valuable sources of cultural information.

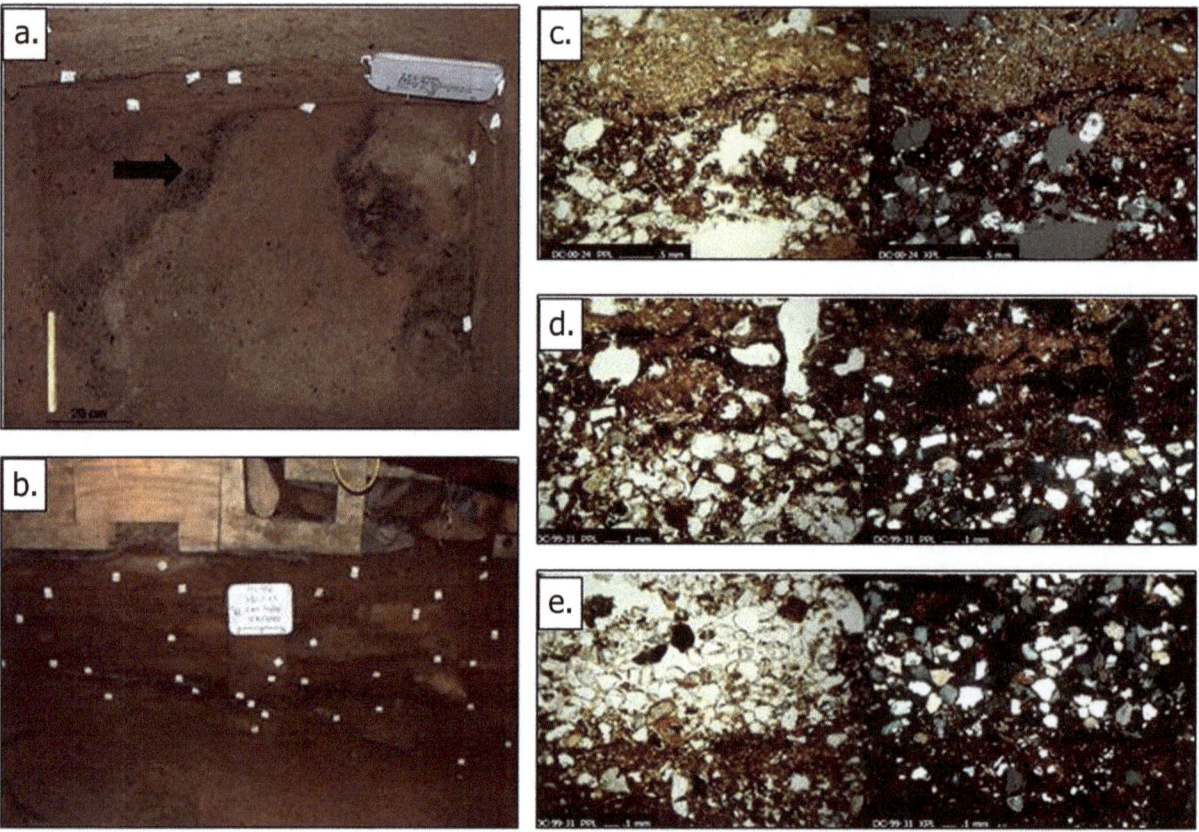

Figure 3.16. Field image of Feature 381 (stringer) in plan view (a) and cross-section (b); photomicrographs (PPL left, XPL right) of undulatory charcoal grains and fining upward bedding (c), charcoal lined voids (d), and unconformable boundary with underlying zone T2.

UNBURNED FEATURES

Burials

Description and Interpretation. Burials include both human and domestic dog (*Canis familiaris*) interments. Human interments range from adults (n=12), to sub-adults (n=17), to infants (n=4) (Hogue 1994). None of the burials contained cultural material in unequivocal association with the remains. Mortality data indicate that 44% of the individuals died before age five, a figure consistent with prehistoric populations elsewhere in the region (Hogue 2003). Average age at death for adult females was determined at 38.62 +/- 14.38 (n=8) and 24.87 +/- 9.40 for adult males (n=4) (Hogue 2003). This older age for women contrasts to other prehistoric populations in which women have a shorter life span than men, a statistic generally attributed to childbirth (Hogue 2003). Hogue (1994) characterizes the overall health of the Dust Cave population as good and similar to that of other hunter-gatherer populations in the region.

Between 1990 and 1994, poor lighting led us to believe that burial pits did not exist. Since we had so much difficulty discerning pit outline in the cave, we often assigned arbitrary pit boundaries. Over the years, as lighting improved and we became more familiar with the burial fill, we did identify pit outlines (Homsey 2004), solving the enigma of the "missing burial pits." Burials excavated between 1996 and 2000 average approximately 12 cm in depth, compared to 20 cm for those excavated between 1990 and 1994, confirming that we dug much too deep in the early years of excavation. No micromorphology samples exist from burial context.

Four domestic dog burials have been uncovered (Morey 1994; Walker et al. 2005). One dog was recovered buried with a Benton projectile point adjacent to the cranium (Walker et al. 2005:86). One *Canis* burial of particular interest was excavated from the lower levels of the Early Side-Notched component in Test Unit F. Morey (1994: 169) considers this individual to be too small to be a gray wolf, but the femur is also too long and slender to be a dog. Morphologically, this individual may be a coyote (*canis lactrans*), although Morey (1994:169) notes that the geographic range of coyotes during the Early Holocene may have been considerably west of Alabama. Based on recent identification of damage to the lower vertebrae of three of the canines, Walker et al. (2005: 88) suggest that the dogs of Dust Cave may have served as pack animals.

Organization. Burials are located along the periphery of the cave, focusing primarily along the northwest and southwest walls (Figure 3.17a). One burial is located along the northeast wall. A Nearest Neighbor analysis indicates only slight clustering (R=.648, $.02<p<.05$). However, if the one burial along the northeast wall is omitted as anomalous, the clustering is greater (R=.581, $p<.001$). Canine burials (not pictured) follow this same pattern; two of the four canine burials are located adjacent to human interments. Such a pattern of rear burial comes as no surprise, since this is away from the focus of domestic activities. Also, as previously discussed, back areas of the cave correspond to areas of refuse, and so it may be that the cave's inhabitants chose to dig burial pits into the softer fill comprising the midden deposits. Ethnographic patterns of burial also follow this pattern (Galanidou 2000:29).

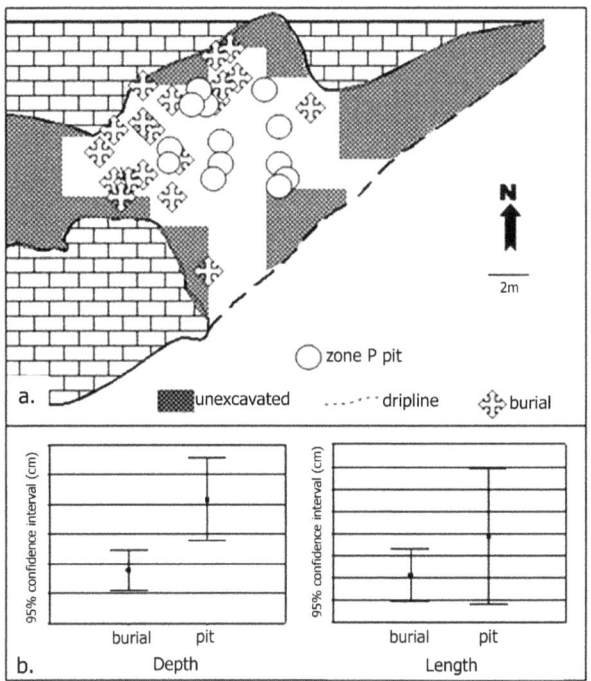

Figure 3.17. Location of human burials and Zone P pits (a) and error graphs showing that length does not differ significantly between burials and pits, but depth does (b).

Storage and/or Secondary Refuse

Description. Perhaps the most enigmatic deposit at Dust Cave is a series of deep, intrusive pits originating at the top of zone P/base of zone N, approximately 300 cmbd (Figure 3.18). Many of these pits were difficult to discern during excavation, especially if a profile was not available. Indeed, many of the pits were identified not in the field, but rather based on later examination of profile exposures and drawings. As a result, many were excavated not as features, but as zones. The 18 pits evaluated here consist of Features 19 and 34 and zones P2, P8/P8a, P9, P11, P15, P16, P17, P19, P20, P21, P22, P23, P24, P25, P27, and P29. Sherwood (2001) has suggested that these are burials, based on two in which excavators found several disarticulated juvenile metatarsals and vertebrae. Based on this assumption, she further argues that the use of the cave shifted from a habitation to an ossuary site during this time period. Based on a radiocarbon date from Feature 34 (6050 +/- 100 uncal. B.P.), she proposes a tentative Eva/Morrow Mountain association. Closer inspection of Feature 34 reveals that it was excavated in 1991 as a definite burial, containing a cranium, ribs, and long bones. Stratigraphically, it begins at 280 cmbd, about 10-20 cm higher than the majority of the pits in question. It differs significantly in morphology: it is about 20 cm deep, 40 cm long, and has a concave, basin shaped profile. In contrast, most of the other zone P pits average about 40 cm deep, 80 cm long, and exhibit roughly bell-shaped profiles with a flattened bottom (Figure 3.18). Moreover, these pits lack human remains, with the exception of disarticulated juvenile bones found in two of the pits. Based on these attributes, Feature 34 does not appear to be one of the Zone P pits, and so the Eva/Morrow Mountain association attributed to it may not reflect the true temporal affiliation for the other Zone P pits. Based on intact Zone N surfaces overlying these pits, I argue that they date to the Kirk Stemmed component—probably representing the latest Kirk occupation. Future radiocarbon sampling should attempt to refine the cultural affiliation of these pits.

Based on their irregular morphology and lack of cultural material, nine of the Zone P pits (P2, P16, P17, P19, P20, P21, P22, P23, and P29) are probably animal burrows (Homsey 2004). The remaining nine pits (P8/P8a, P9, P11, P13, P15, P24, P25, and Features 19 and 34) have rectangular profiles with relatively flat bottoms. This morphology is characteristic of the Dust Cave burial pits; however, at 80 cm long and 40 cm deep, they are much larger than burials. The error graphs shown in Figure 3.17b illustrate that while the mean length for burials and the Zone P pits overlap at the 95% confidence interval, mean depth does not. A students t-test statistically confirms that the difference is significant ($t=2.18$, $p=.002$), indicating that the Zone P pits do not derive from the same population as burial pits.

Unfortunately, since most of these pits were not identified in the field and therefore not excavated as features, they were not sampled for micromorphology analysis; only two samples accidentally cross-cut these pits (P8/P8a and P11). Field observations describe feature fill as heterogeneous, loose, silty loams with a friable texture. Flecks of charcoal, smeared ash, and sand and gravel-sized clasts of burned red clay are dispersed throughout the fill. Six of the nine bell-shaped pits have large, flat limestone rocks in them. Based on thin section observations of the two samples available, the fill is loosely packed, porous, and has a vughy to complex microstructure (Homsey 2004: Plate 6.105). Within the chaotic fabric, aggregates <1mm are common as are sand-sized fragments of burned red clay and mixed and compound clasts. Microartifacts are dispersed throughout and consist of shell, bone, and microdebitage. Interestingly, microartifacts are often incorporated into aggregates (Homsey 2004: Plate 6.106), indicating just how disturbed and reworked the fill is. In one case (Zone P11), a large aggregate containing preserved root features was observed oriented perpendicular to the bedding of the fill, suggesting that it became incorporated into the feature fill during a separate depositional event and/or disturbance. Poor sorting, a lack of graded bedding, and a complex microstructure indicate deposition via gravitational infilling (Homsey 2004). Some of the pits are internally stratified (e.g., P8/346, see Figure 3.18), suggesting more than one depositional episode. Finally, pits "bottom out" in all kinds of deposits. Initially, I thought that the flat bottoms may have been created because the pit abruptly ended at a hard surface (i.e., prepared clay surface), but closer inspection of each of the nine pits in question showed that only one pit has a base resting on such a surface. The other eight ended in soft, bioturbated deposits (typically Zone P7, P3, or Q).

Organization. Because the spatial distribution of the Zone P pits is important to their interpretation, I first consider their organization before making an interpretation. When mapped, the pits form a distribution subtly different from that of burial pits (see Figure 3.17a). A few of them occur towards the rear; one of these (P11) did contain disarticulated juvenile remains (metatarsals, vertebrae). The other pits occur slightly south and east of known burials, in space that hearths and processing pits usually occupy. This different distribution compared to burial pits helps to support an argument that they form a distinct feature class from burials. As already noted, the four pits east of the Test Trench are most likely animal and/or bioturbation disturbances, though the pit in the far northeast is clearly not (based on size and shape). The western pits form a fairly distinct "line" immediately west of the Test Trench along W64. As will be further discussed in chapter 5, this line is sandwiched by Kirk Stemmed component hearths to the east, and primary and secondary refuse to the west.

Interpretation. The Zone P pits differ from burial pits in several significant ways. First, they lack articulated human remains. Second, they are statistically deeper than burial pits. Third, some exhibit internal stratification. Finally, they occur further south of known burials, farther away from walls. At four times deeper than burial pits, the Zone P pit size is consistent with that of later Woodland period storage pits. Moreover, their nearly straight sides and flat bottoms are also consistent with that of storage pits (Wilson 1985). Historically, southeastern Indians stored nuts below ground in pits with similar shapes and sizes as the zone P pits (Wilson 1985:41). The loose, heterogeneous feature fill is consistent with what we would expect of pits filled in with refuse, suggesting that if these pits were used for storage at one time, they were converted into refuse pits later in their "life cycle" (*sensu* Moeller 1992; Schroedl 1986). Such fill is also consistent with that of burial fill, but again, these pits are much deeper than known burial pits. The fact that several of them are stratified (e.g., P8/P8a) indicates more than one depositional episode, more likely to happen during discard than burial. The few disarticulated human remains could come from discarded cremation remains, or they may have become incorporated into the pit during construction or infilling.

Interestingly, Ahler (2004) has noted similarly shaped and sized pits in the late Early through Middle Archaic layers at Modoc in southern Illinois. Ahler (1993) and Styles et al. (1983) key the pits as "pit features" (Figure 3.19). These pits bear a striking resemblance to the Dust Cave pits, so much so that some even have thin "fired lenses" of sediment overlying them, similar to the intact surfaces overlying the pits at Dust Cave. Based on their large size, distinct shape and spatial positioning towards the rear of the shelter, Ahler interprets them to be storage pits (Ahler, personal communication 2004). Working from published profiles, I estimate that the Modoc pits average 68 cm in length and 28 cm in depth, yielding a depth to diameter ratio of approximately 0.42. This value compares favorably to the 0.5 depth to diameter ratio for the Dust Cave pits. Additionally, the mean depth and length of the Modoc pits overlap that of the Dust Cave pits at the 95% confidence level. If the two largest pits at Modoc are eliminated, the standard deviation around mean length decreases and the Modoc pits and Dust pits overlap even more. The Modoc pits are discussed further in chapter 5.

The description given above does not rule out a burial context for the Zone P pits; indeed, the shape and fill are as consistent with a burial context as they are with a storage context. In other words, these characteristics are not function-specific. Assuming a burial context may lead to assumptions about site use, but the same can certainly be said of assuming a storage context. Lacking other evidence, I lean towards storage, based on the large size, organization inside the cave and lack of articulated human remains. Hopefully, future botanical studies of pit fill will elucidate their contents, and, by extension, their function.

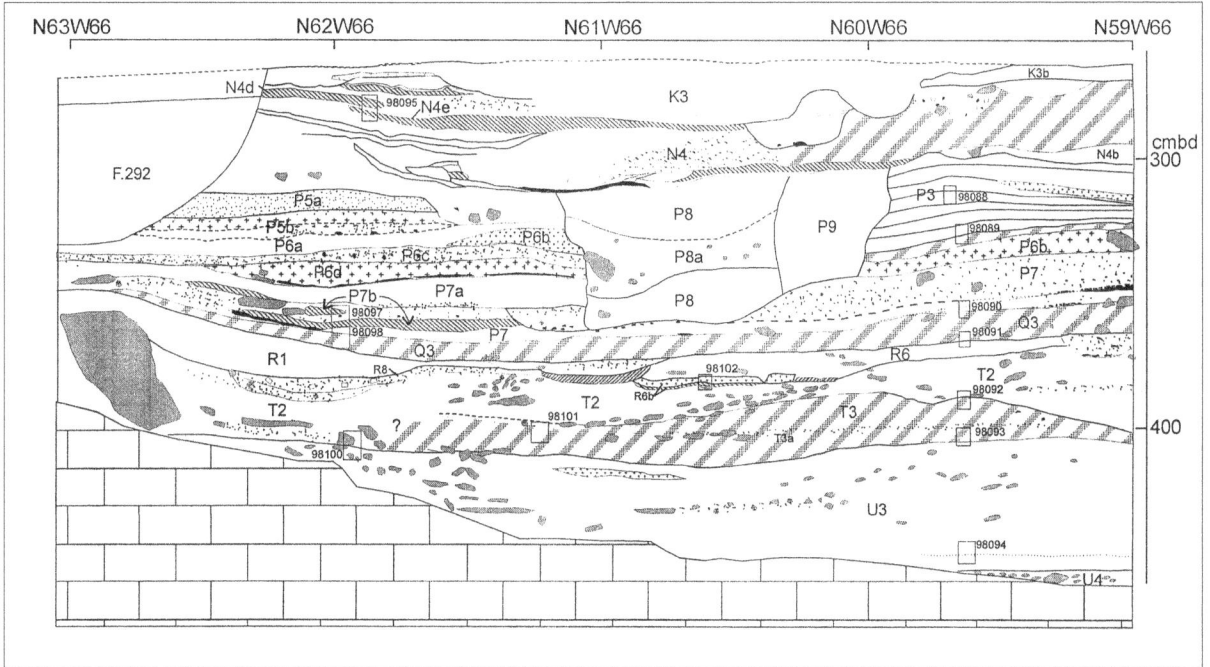

Figure 3.18. Examples of pit intrusive into Zone P (P8/P8a) at Dust Cave (modified from Sherwood 2001:Figure 8.8)

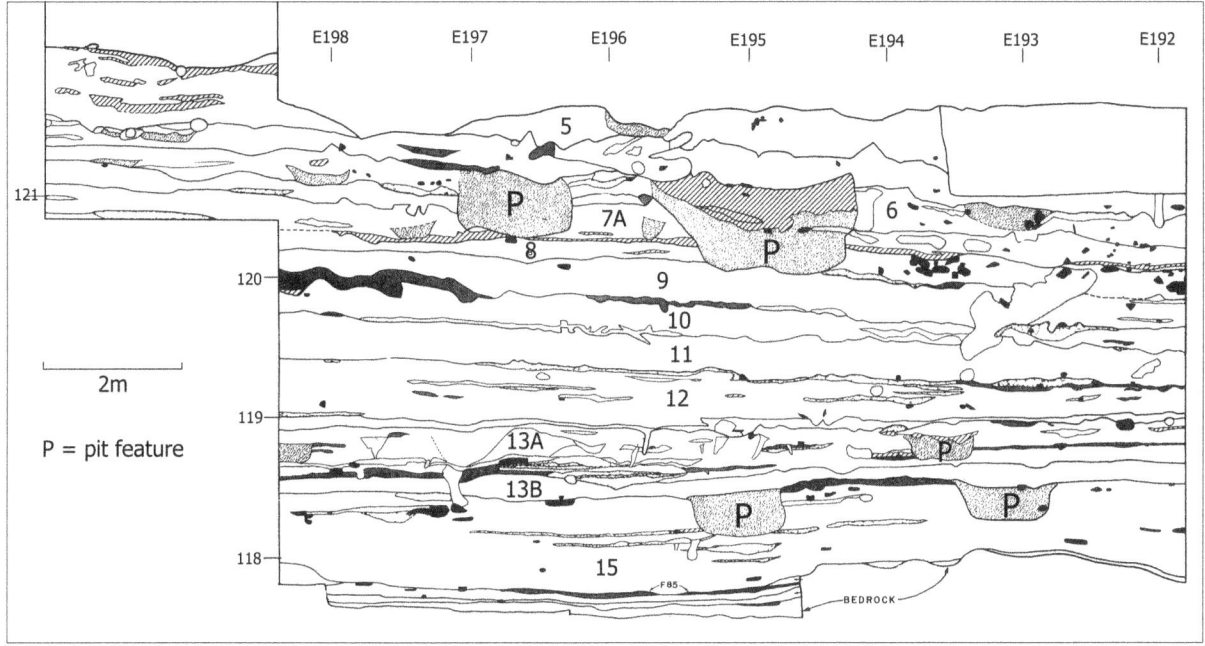

Figure 3.19. Representative stratigraphy showing the pit features (P) at Modoc Rockshelter (modified from Styles et al. 1983:Figure 13.4).

SUMMARY

The integration of macromorphology, micromorphology, and geochemistry has elucidated several salient points crucial for interpretation of human behavior at Dust Cave. These points include (1) the recognition of great diversity in the activities represented by features; (2) the realization that not all charcoal features are hearths; and (3) the recognition of important post-depositional processes affecting cave deposits.

(1) A great diversity of features characterizes the Dust Cave deposits. Burned deposits include in situ fireplaces, fireplace rakeout, and mixed burning. In situ fireplaces consist of prepared surfaces, surface hearths, expedient hearths, and pit hearths. The recognition of several types of hearths highlights the variation the term "hearth" may mask. At Dust Cave, hearths range from formal, rock-lined surface hearths for broiling food to informal fires built on top of clay surfaces for rapid grilling and/or roasting of foods in coals. Perhaps most important is the identification of pit hearths, which represent not food preparation for immediate consumption, but nut processing to extend the storage life of hickory nuts and/or extract nut oil. Recognizing that nut processing occurred at Dust Cave is vital to accurately assessing site function through time, a theme which is explored further in the next chapter. Fireplace rake-out includes primary refuse scraped out from hearths, secondary refuse redeposited in the rear of the cave, and accessory cooking stone piles placed near cooking fires. Mixed burning includes middens derived from massive amounts of combusted material, multiple burned layers formed from the repeated construction of surfaces over time, and charcoal stringers resulting from post-depositional water activity. Finally, unburned deposits include human and canine burials, and possibly storage pits.

(2) Nearly a decade ago, researchers realized that we should not interpret the use of formal lithic tools based on their morphology alone (Keeley 1980; Semenov 1964). Microscopic use wear studies conducted in the 1990s demonstrated that their actual use often did not conform to expectations based on appearance. The same holds true for archaeological features. Just as we needed to add microscopic and chemical analyses to better interpret lithics, so we should also add them to feature studies on a regular basis. To illustrate this point, recall Feature 301, the large charcoal pit located in the rear of the cave. Based on the abundance of charcoal, its large size, and a basin-shaped profile, excavators identified it as a hearth on the feature form. This designation struck later researchers as odd given its position in the cave. Located in the rear of the cave at the entrance to the west passageway, with only about one meter of headroom, it did not seem like a conducive place to locate a large fire. Additionally, the brisk draft that frequently blows through the west passageway would have made it difficult to maintain a fire. Micromorphological analysis revealed two important aspects of this feature that proved vital to a correct interpretation of function. First, this "hearth" showed no signs of in situ burning. Second, its loose fill, reworked clasts and ash aggregates, and cross-bedded charcoal grains indicated re-deposition, most likely from sweeping. Feature 301 is now categorized as fireplace rake-out, re-deposited in the back of the cave, away from the center of activity. Given the intensity of burning at Dust Cave, occasional cleaning would have been a must, and the presence of rake-out should come as no surprise.

I emphasize this inaccuracy not to criticize early excavation at the site, but to point out a problem that pervades archaeological excavation in general. The terminology we use has a large effect on how we perceive the archaeological record. By thinking of everything as a hearth, we risk glossing over immense diversity in human activity. This research has demonstrated that many of the charcoal pits we see at Dust Cave are not hearths: they are not burned in place, but rather are re-deposited. In some cases, we can even reconstruct the transport agent involved, such as sweeping or dumping. Thus, the multidisciplinary approach taken in this study has achieved a much more holistic and accurate interpretation of feature function, and therefore of human behavior.

(3) Several post-depositional processes have so altered some of the Dust Cave deposits that they have completely obscured their original morphology, thereby severely hindering our attempts to reconstruct human behavior at the site. Perhaps the most destructive process at the cave has been decalcification. Decalcification leads to the dissolution of calcitic sediments (i.e., ash), and their subsequent compaction. The result is shallow features dominated by charcoal. For years, researchers at Dust Cave have interpreted these small, shallow charcoal pits to represent ephemeral occupation of the site. This research demonstrates that decalcification, rather than ephemeral occupation, more likely accounts for the small size of these features. A second important post-depositional process that has greatly altered deposits at Dust Cave is water activity, in the form of sheetwash, slackwater, and/or water drips through the cave ceiling. Dripping water is probably responsible, at least in some part, for the numerous charcoal rings found at the site, especially in the lower reaches of the cave stratigraphy. Slackwater may also account for some of these rings. Sheetwash is the most probable process responsible for the charcoal stringers and the destruction of characteristic hearth signatures, especially in the lowermost deposits.

In conclusion, an integrated, multidisciplinary study has elucidated the nature of activities occurring at Dust Cave. Despite the cave's rather small size, a great variety of activities are represented, including cooking, nut processing, refuse disposal, sleeping, burial, and potentially storage during the Kirk Stemmed component. Cooking technologies range from broiling to boiling to roasting. Most cooking and processing-related features occur over prepared surfaces in the center of the entrance chamber. The presence of large numbers of pit hearths and massive midden deposits suggest that nut processing received high priority and accounts for much of the debris dumped at the rear of the cave. The high Sr and K values of both pit hearths and middens strengthen this interpretation. Thick rake-out and midden deposits, especially towards the rear of the cave, suggest that burning occurred on a large-scale. Burning resulted from nut processing, heating of cooking stones, and cooking. This diversity suggests the cave's use as more than a simple overnight camp. That nut processing figures so prominently suggests that people may have come to Dust Cave with the goal of gathering hickory nuts for oil extraction. Finally, most feature types represented at Dust Cave are multipurpose. Cooking hearths may have doubled as sleeping hearths and prepared surfaces may have helped to retain heat. Hearths likely doubled as foci of tool maintenance and socializing. Only pit hearths appear to have had a single purpose, though these, too, may have been used for other types of boiling. Features of all types occur repeatedly in the same locations over time, suggesting that the occupants of Dust Cave utilized a space conserving strategy. The only clear segmentation of space exists between domestic space and refuse disposal. Finally, the close spacing among features reflects the natural constraints of the cave interior, as well as the relatively short anticipated length of stay at the site.

Chapter 4

RECONSTRUCTING THE SPATIAL ORGANIZATION AT DUST CAVE

EVALUATING THE UNITS OF ANALYSIS

Before examining spatial variation, it is first necessary to critically evaluate stratigraphic integrity and decide on the unit of analysis. To make sure that the contextual unit chosen is the smallest one that can be confidently defined, several factors must be carefully evaluated, including microstratigraphy and radiocarbon dates. Over 40 radiocarbon dates exist for Dust Cave, most of which are pictured in Figure 4.1. Overall, there is a strong positive correlation between depth below datum and radiocarbon age. Using this data, coupled with detailed microstratigraphic control, I examine spatial variation among cultural components for two reasons. First, thanks to the large number of radiocarbon dates, we can constrain components with acceptable confidence; we do not have this kind of control for smaller ethno-stratigraphic units (*sensu* Stein 1990). Second, studying variation at the cultural component level is intuitively satisfying since previous analyses (*e.g.*, Hollenbach 2007, 2003; Meeks 1998; Randall 2003, 2001; Walker 1998, 2007; Walker et al. 2001) have used this same level as the comparative unit.

COMPONENT COMPARISONS

Component Compositions (Figure 4.2)

Paleoindian (10,650-9,200 cal. B.C.). The Paleoindian component consists of 33 features. By far, the predominant type is the charcoal stinger, accounting for 33% of the total (N=11). These are followed by charcoal pits (N=9, 27%) and charcoal/ash concentrations (N=5, 15%). There is one expedient hearth (Feature 117), and two rock clusters that appear to be surface hearths post-depositionally altered by water flow (Features 384 and 423). Three features (six percent) could not be identified.

Early Side Notched (10,000-9,000 cal. B.C.). The Early Side Notched component consists of 32 features. Charcoal pits account for 44% of the assemblage (N=14) while charcoal concentrations account for another 25% (N=8). Stringers account for less than seven percent of the total, compared to over a third of the total for the Paleoindian. No surface hearths are evident; however, I interpret one of the two rock pits (Feature 403) to be a hearth post-depositionally altered by water flow.

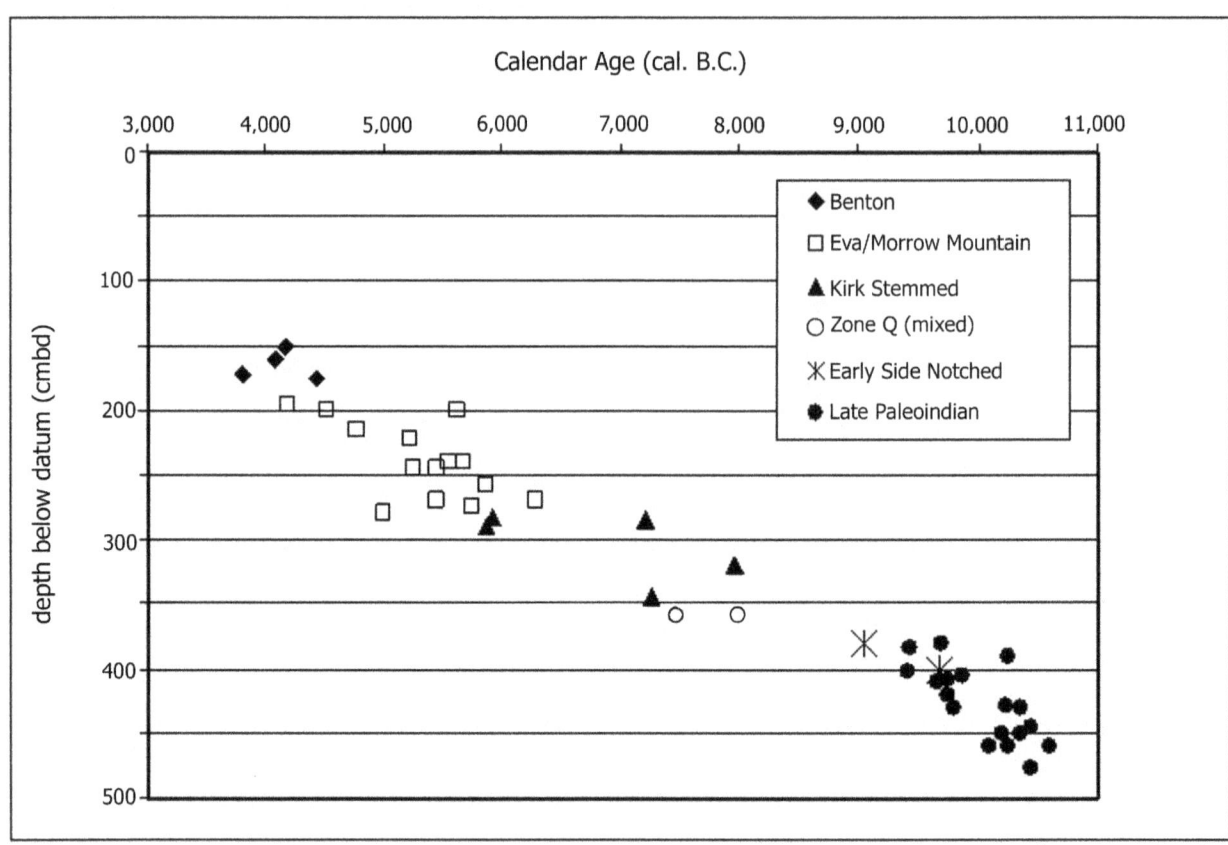

Figure 4.1. Dust Cave calibrated radiocarbon dates by component and depth.

There is one possible pit hearth. If it is indeed a pit hearth, it is the earliest in the Dust Cave sequence. Charcoal pits could not be further identified due to substantial post-depositional alteration (decalcification and fluvial activity). Many of the charcoal pits were full of burned fish bones, suggesting their possible use as expedient hearths for smoking fish; the absence of ash due to decalcification makes it difficult to assign these features as expedients hearths. Three features, or 9%, could not be identified.

Kirk Stemmed (8,200-5,800 cal. B.C.). The Kirk Stemmed component consists of 53 features, 23% of which are charcoal pits, and another 12% of which are ash pits. Three hearths account for 6% of the assemblage. Pit hearths substantially increase over the Early Side Notched component, at 10% of the total assemblage (N=5). Expedient hearths appear with certainty for the first time, accounting for 14% of the total assemblage. One large rock pit accounts for just under 2% of the total assemblage; this feature is the largest feature at the site (Feature 111) and may be an earth oven. Burials also appear for the first time during the Kirk Stemmed component. Three burials account for 6% of the total. Eight features, or 15%, could not be identified with certainty.

Eva/Morrow Mountain (6,400-4,000 cal. B.C.). A noticeable increase in feature frequency and diversity occurs during the Eva/Morrow Mountain component. The number of features, 193, is nearly a fourfold increase over that of the Kirk Stemmed component, despite the fact that they both represent occupations of approximately 2,400 years. Of the 193 features, over 40% consist of charcoal pits (N=71) and ash pits (N=10). Seven percent are surface hearths (N=13), eight percent are pit hearths (N=15), and five percent are expedient hearths (N=9). There are also six rock clusters (3%). Human burials account for seven percent of the total (N=13). Canine burials appear for the first time, accounting for just under 2% of the total (N=3). Twenty-four features, or about 12% of the assemblage, could not be identified.

Benton (4,500-3,600 cal. B.C.). During the Benton component, feature frequency (N=27) and diversity decrease markedly. As with most components, charcoal pits make up the majority of features, in this case 41% (N=14). Surface hearths account for 11% of the assemblage (N=3); expedient hearths increase notably, accounting for 22% of the assemblage (N=3). There is only one pit hearth, less than 4% of the total. There are three human burials (11%) and one canine burial (4%). Three features, or 11%, could not be identified.

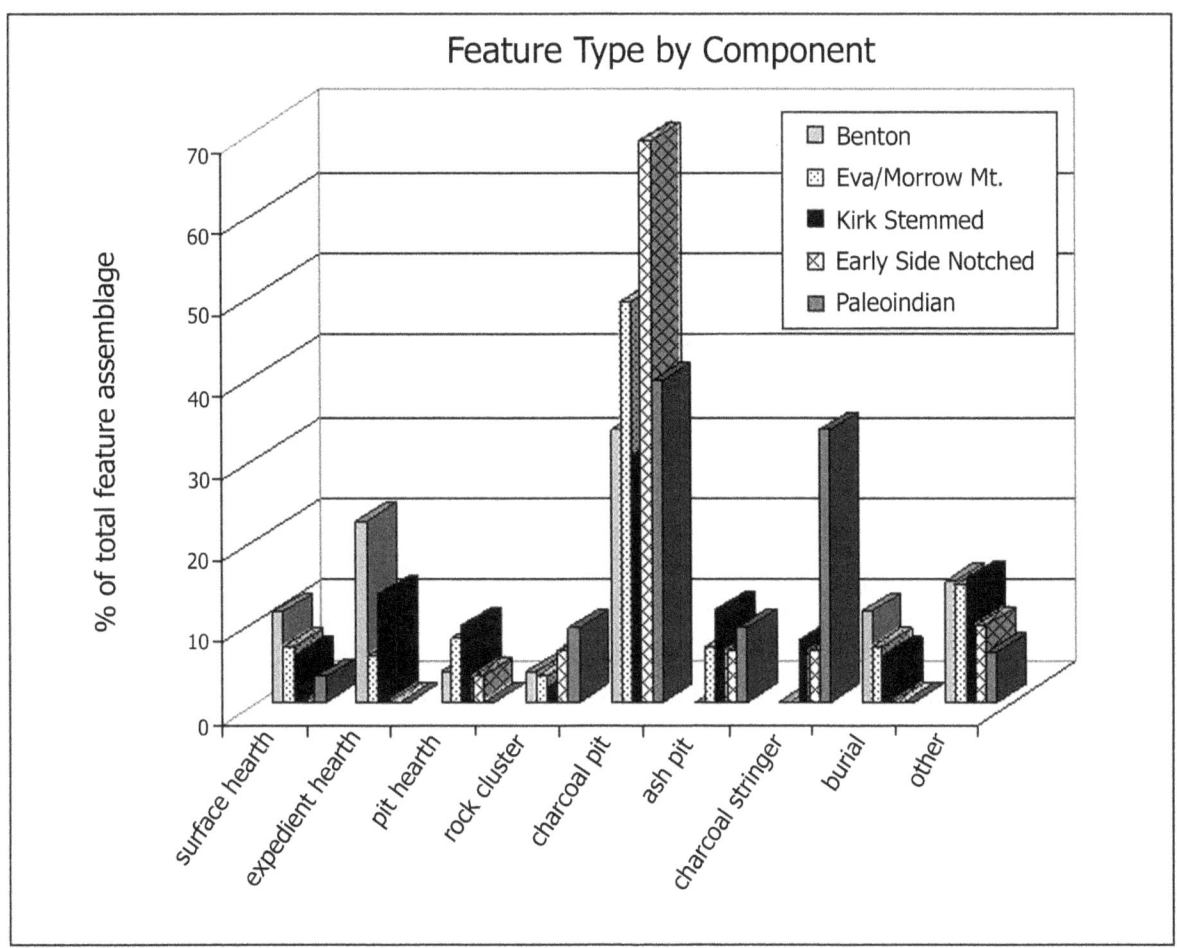

Figure 4.2. Feature distribution by type from the Paleoindian through Benton occupations.

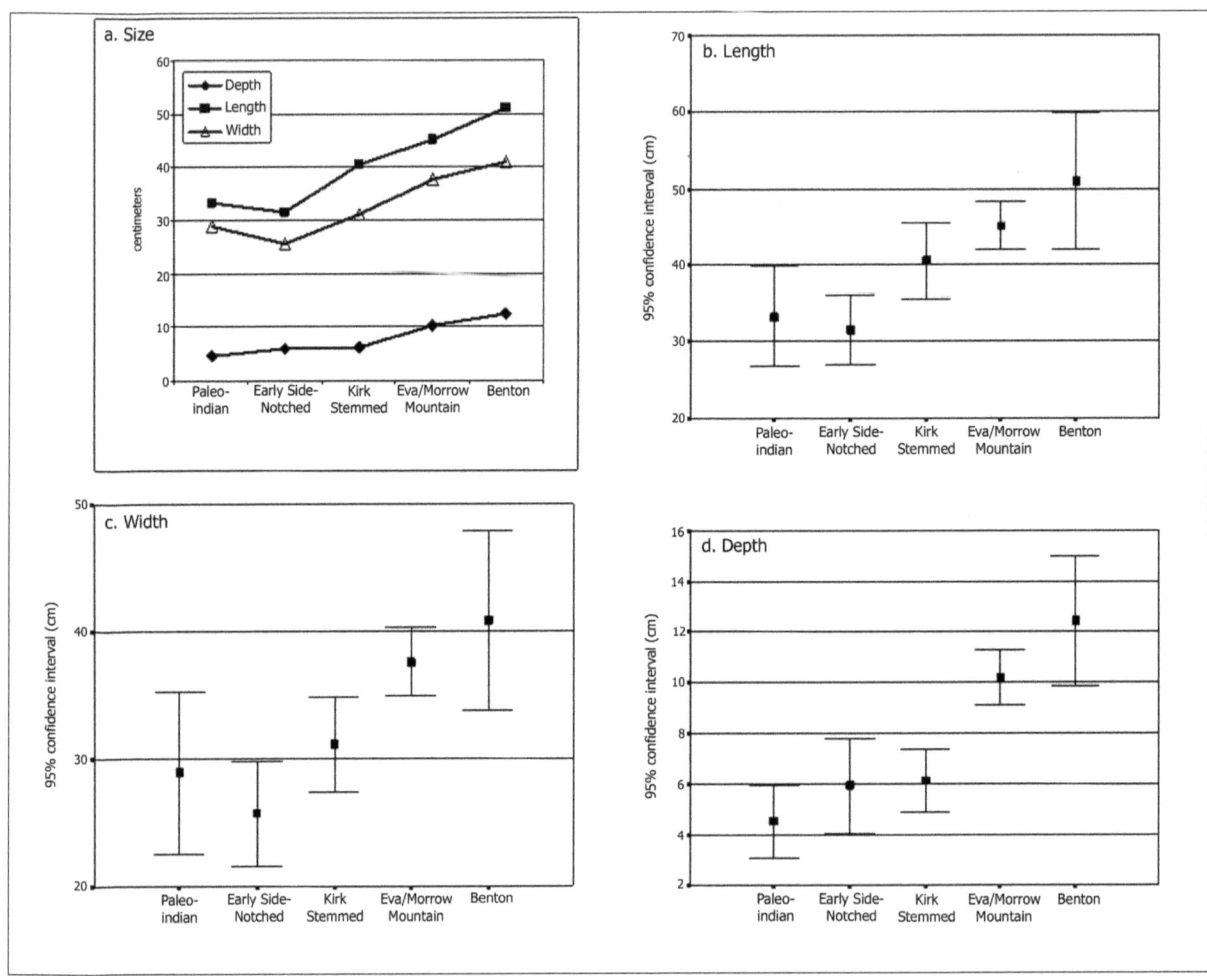

Figure 4.3. Average feature size through time (a), comparison of feature length by component (b), comparison of feature width by component (c), and comparison of feature depth by component.

Overall, feature size increases noticeably through time (Figure 4.3). The Benton and Eva/Morrow Mountain features are substantially larger than features dating to the earlier period, especially the Early Side Notched and Paleoindian components. Error graphs constructed for the average length, width, and depth indicate that the Benton and Eva/Morrow Mountain features are significantly larger than Early Side Notched and Paleoindian features at the 95% confidence level. Benton and Eva/Morrow Mountain features are also significantly deeper than Kirk Stemmed, Early Side Notched and Paleoindian features at the 95% confidence level. Looking at these data, it would be easy to simply conclude that the intensity of occupation increases through time. Yet we know from the geochemical data that decalcification is a prominent postdepositional process at Dust Cave that results in the dissolution of ash and compaction of sediments. This would account for the marked decrease in feature depth during the earliest occupations. The decrease in average depth is probably also related to the large numbers of thin charcoal stringers in the earliest component. The explanation for why Benton features are the largest, despite the restricted headroom, is less obvious. I suggest that the smaller Eva/Morrow Mountain and Kirk Stemmed features relative to the larger Benton features is a function of limited horizontal space resulting *from* intense occupation. As the cave was used more intensively with more features per unit area, it may have been necessary to keep the size of hearths and other habitation features down so as not to impede nearby activity. During the Benton component, horizontal space was at less of a premium, so larger feature sizes would have been less obtrusive.

There is surprisingly little change from component to component, suggesting similar use of the cave through time using similar technology (see Figure 4.2). In all components, charcoal pits comprise the majority of the assemblage, followed by hearths of all types. However, there are a couple of significant changes through time that are worthy to note. First, "charcoal stringers" dominate the Paleoindian assemblage, but drop off significantly after that, disappearing entirely by the Eva/Morrow Mountain component. Second, pit hearths first appear in the Early Side Notched (3%), peak during the Kirk Stemmed component (10%), decrease slightly in the Eva/Morrow Mountain component (8%), then decrease markedly during the Benton component (4%). Third, expedient hearths become common during the Kirk Stemmed component, during which time they are twice as common as surface hearths (14% vs. 6%). Expedient hearths decrease during the subsequent period, so that they occur with the same frequency as surface hearths (6 and 7%, respectively). Finally, during the Benton component, expedient hearths increase again, dominating hearth types at 22%. Finally, burials appear for the first time during the late Kirk Stemmed component and increase in frequency and proportion through time.

Component Diversity
A Simpson diversity index (L) was calculated in order to determine how diverse the feature assemblage is for each component (Figure 4.4) This measure of diversity considers both richness (the number of classes represented) and heterogeneity (frequency distribution of items per class). The index is expressed as a ratio of the number of items in each class to the total number of individuals in all classes. The resulting value (L) ranges from 0 to 1, with 0 representing the highest diversity and 1 representing no diversity. In other words, the smaller L is, the greater the diversity. Hall (1985) argues the case that low diversity characterizes limited activity sites, while higher diversity indicates more generalized, multipurpose activities. The Benton, Eva/Morrow Mountain, and Paleoindian occupations are similarly diverse, having diversity indices of 0.171, 0.184, and 0.193, respectively. The Kirk Stemmed component has much greater diversity (L=0.115), while the Early Side Notched exhibits much less diversity (L=0.25).

The low diversity of the Early Side Notched stems from its lack of richness and heterogeneity; only eight of the 12 feature classes identified were represented. Moreover, nearly all the features belong to one feature class (charcoal pits, N=14). Erosion, (and subsequent deflation), post-depositional decalcification, and fluvial activity are likely the culprit for this low diversity. These are discussed more fully in the following section. While the Paleoindian component had only seven classes represented, features were more evenly distributed among these, thereby yielding a high diversity index. In contrast, 11 feature classes are represented by the Kirk Stemmed component. While the Eva/Morrow Mountain component also had 11 classes represented, features in the Kirk Stemmed component were more evenly distributed (greatest heterogeneity) than during the Eva/Morrow Mountain component.

Overall, the high diversity indices indicate that a wide array of activities occurred at the site during all five components, and that it functioned as more than a simple overnight camp. The lower diversity of the Paleoindian and Early Side Notched occupations could reflect more specialized use of the site; however, taphonomic processes have more likely obscured originally greater diversity. During the Kirk Stemmed component, diversity increases considerably, suggesting that the site did not function in any specialized way, but rather as a residential base camp at which residents undertook a full range of domestic and maintenance activities, including burial, nut processing, and storage. Finally, during the Middle Archaic, diversity decreases, suggesting that Dust Cave became increasingly specialized. Most notably, storage pits disappear. The high proportion of pit hearths for nut processing suggests that nut processing may be the specialized activity occurring at the site.

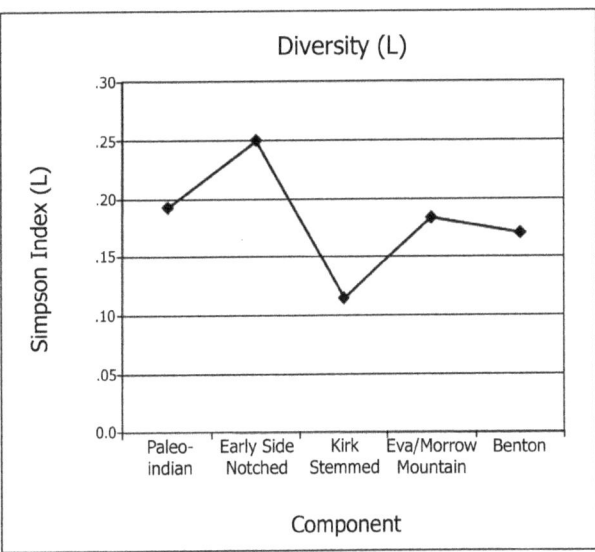

Figure 4.4. Simpson L diversity indices through time.

THE ORGANIZATION OF SPACE THROUGH TIME

An analysis of the spatial organization of features at Dust Cave was undertaken in order to look for patterns in the distribution of different features for each component. I examine the role natural constraints play in feature location, such as the morphology of the cave ceiling and floor, position of the dripline, and microtopography. I also explore cultural patterning, and look for evidence of a space consuming/space conserving strategy by occupants of the cave. Finally, I compare and contrast the Dust Cave pattern to the ethnographic record of cave/rockshelter use by modern hunter-gatherers. It should be noted that in the figures that follow, features are mapped to maximize individual feature visibility; they do not necessarily represent true cross-cutting relationships and/or contemporaneity within the cultural component.

Late Paleoindian Occupation, 10,650-9,200 cal. B.C.
During the Late Paleoindian component (Zones U, T), features cluster in the front central portion of the shelter, suggesting that the majority of activity occurred here (Figure 4.5). This clustering is statistically significant ($R=.577$, $.1<p<.05$). Most of the features are charcoal pits (n=20), probably a combination of fireplace accessories and rake-out. Unfortunately, I was not able to confidently differentiate between the two unless I had thin sections; feature forms were not always complete (e.g., no profile was drawn) and photographs often lacked the requisite resolution. If any of these pits were expedient hearths, poor ash preservation precludes positive identification. The other features consist of ash pits (n=2), hearths (n=1), and rock pits (n=2). Small patches of prepared surfaces (~20cm) have been noted in the general area mapped in Figure 4.5.

Overall, the impression one gets of the Paleoindian is of a rather ephemeral occupation. However, post-depositional processes can account for this seemingly sparse occupation. As discussed earlier, the deposits at this

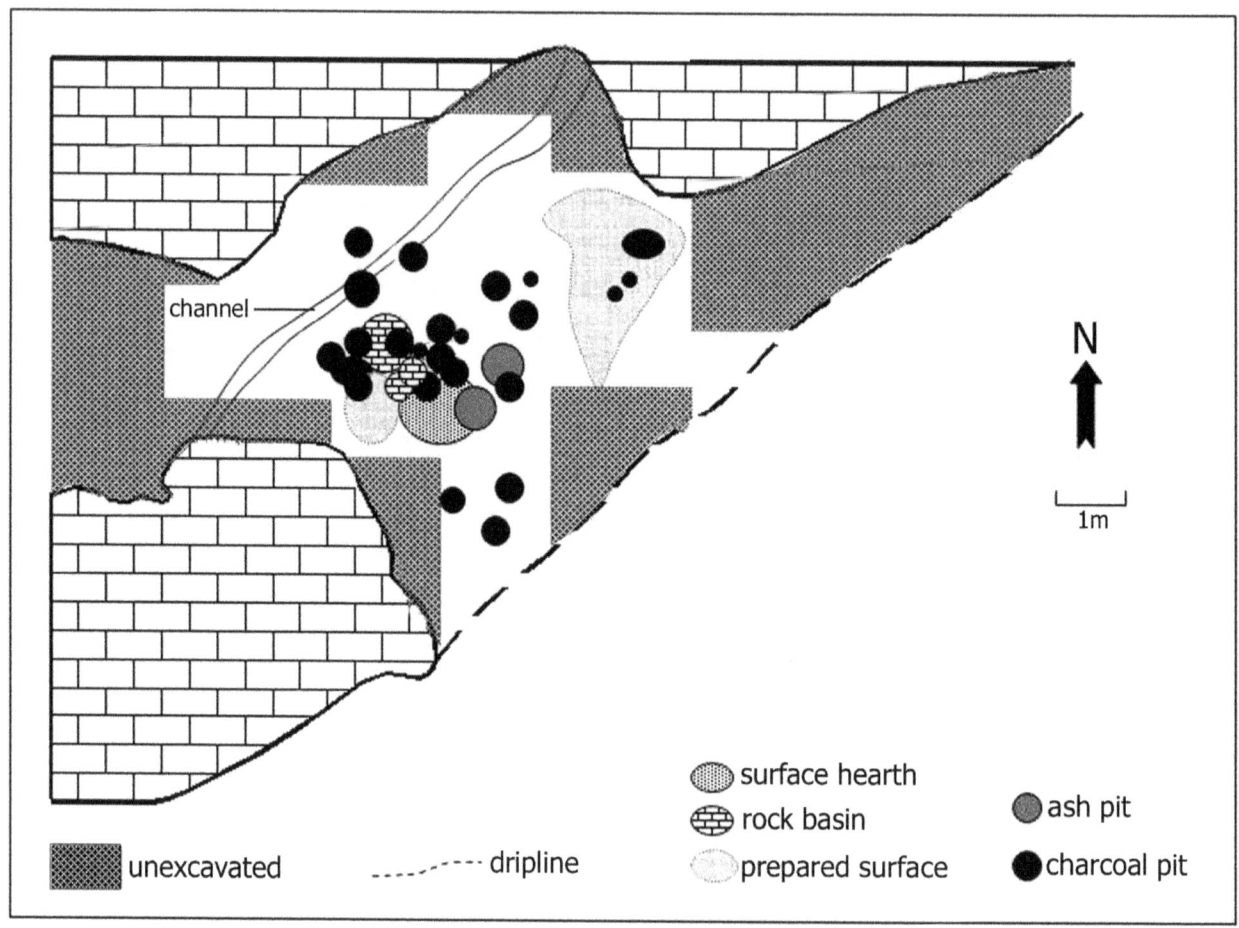

Figure 4.5. Distribution of features in Late Paleoindian component.

depth are severely decalcified, causing features to be significantly shallower than features below the zone of seasonal inundation (i.e., below 350 cmbd). Moreover, the dissolution of ash resulting from decalcification leads to pits dominated by charcoal.

Periodic flooding of the cave also gives one the impression of a more ephemeral occupation than probably existed at this time. Note that features do not occur northwest of the channel. Two geologic controls probably account for this pattern. First, the bedrock floor of the cave slopes upward in the rear, greatly reducing floor space. Second a phreatic channel allows water to flow in a northeast-southwest direction. This channel would have carried water during wet periods. Sherwood's (2001) research suggests that the driest part of the cave would have been southeast of the channel, while the northwest side would have typically been a wet and damp microenvironment. Based on her geoarchaeological reconstruction, it comes as no surprise that habitation features concentrated south of the channel.

Lithics, bone and shell all concentrate in the rear, in units N63W66-67 (along the northwest wall), suggesting that this area served as a convenient dump area for stone and food debris (Figure 4.6). The lithic distribution has a bimodal pattern that encloses the hearth area in a pattern reminiscent of a drop zone (*sensu* Binford 1978). Shell also exhibits this bimodal pattern. Bone concentrates in the far northwest corner. The lack of artifactual data east of the Test Trench is misleading; artifacts have not yet been sorted and tabulated for Zones T and U. Given the extent of fluvial reworking of sediments back here, it is unlikely that artifact distributions would reflect the original organization.

The area devoid of features south of the northeast wall also experienced periodic flooding, as evidenced by myriad charcoal stringers so thin that excavators could not remove them separately. The thin charcoal stain at the U1/U2 interface (Zone U2a, 460 cmbd) is a good example of this phenomenon. It covers nearly the entire floor of the entrance chamber east of the Test Trench, and area greater than 6 m^2 (see Homsey 2004: Plate 6.92). In thin section, the boundary exhibits fine fluvial laminations and the charcoal is bedded (see Homsey 2004: Plate 6.94). Within Zone U2a was a slightly thicker concentration of charcoal which we excavated as Feature 486. This feature also displays bedded charcoal. Feature 381, another charcoal stringer that was excavated as a feature, revealed a disconformity between Zone T2 below and the feature above (see Homsey 2004:Plates 6.96 and 6.97). Clearly, erosion had taken place, albeit at a small scale. A second incidence of widespread charcoal staining occurs between Zones T2 and T3, approximately 415 cmbd. This Zone, T2c is a stringer of charcoal and ash spreading out for several meters on the west side of the Test Trench in the vicinity of Feature 423.

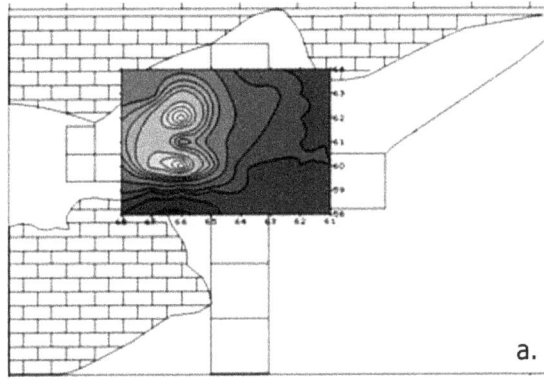

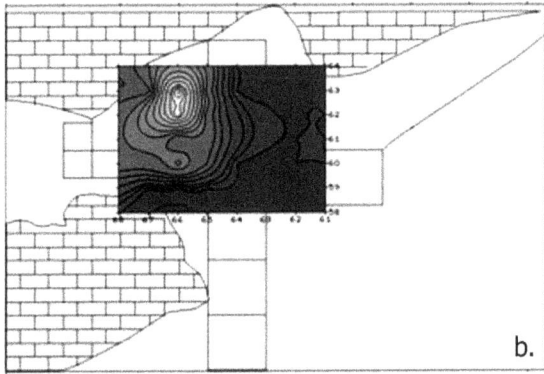

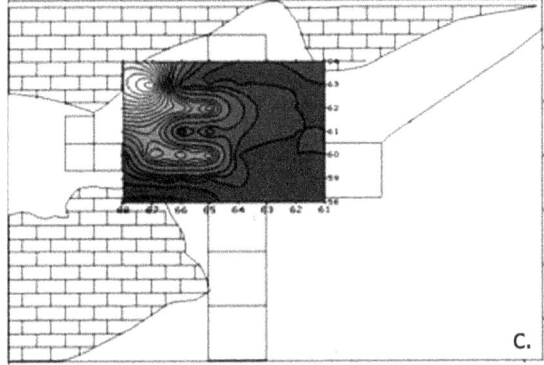

Figure 4.6. Distribution of lithics (a), bone (b) and shell (c), Late Paleoindian component.

Interestingly, these stringers often overlie patches of undisturbed prepared surfaces (e.g., U1a and T2g). Both of these surface remnants appear on the east side of the Test Trench, towards the northeast wall where there are no features. The presence of prepared surfaces implies that activity did occur here and that other features must have existed at one time. Thus, it would appear that periodic flooding washed away evidence for much of the habitation and domestic activities that occurred here during the Late Paleoindian period. Based on the diversity of lithic tool types, Detwiler-Hollenbach (1999) suggests that Dust Cave served as a base camp; the data presented here neither confirm nor refute this claim, though they do suggest that the apparent ephemeral occupation masks the greater feature diversity that may once have existed. If Dust Cave did serve as a base camp, it would have been seasonal since faunal and botanical data indicate a late summer to early fall occupation (as well as a possible spring occupation) (Walker 1998; Detwiler-Hollenbach 2001). The dominance of scrapers suggests that hide processing was also an important activity (Meeks 1994). Use-wear studies support this interpretation, with butchering, hide working and hunting being the most common activities identified by the polishes present (Meeks 1998; Walker et al. 2001). Finally, the association of formal unifaces almost exclusively with the Late Paleoindian deposits reflects a different use of the site compared to later occupations (Randall 2001).

Early Side Notched Component, 10,000-9,000 cal. B.C.
The Early Side Notched feature distribution (Zone R) looks very similar to the Paleoindian (Figure 4.7). Only features from Zone R are mapped, since Zone Q contains a mixture of Early Side Notched and Kirk Stemmed features. The most noticeable difference is that charcoal pits, presumably rake-out, now occupy the north side of the channel. The majority of charcoal pits in the west central portion of the cave are mostly charcoal rings, possibly formed by water dropping from the ceiling or slackwaters. This activity has obscured the original morphology and fill to such a great extent that I could not accurately determine function for this time period. However, the fact that lithics, bone and shell cluster tightly in the far northwest corner suggests that this area served as a secondary dumping zone (Figure 4.8) (though note bone has a more dispersed distribution). Given this refuse pattern, the charcoal pits located in the rear probably represent rake-out as well. It is important to remember that the Early Side Notched component is truncated by erosion, such that the overlying Kirk Corner Notched (Early Archaic) component is no longer an intact occupation (Sherwood et al. 2004). The heavy concentrations of artifacts in the far northwest corner may therefore be "enriched" so to speak from erosion of overlying sediments and subsequent deflation of relatively heavier artifacts.

As they did during the Late Paleoindian period, features cluster in the front-center portion of the shelter, though more tightly ($R=.39$, $p < .001$). They are also located slightly further to the west than in the earlier Paleoindian period. During the Early Side Notched, the front of the cave would have been damp and frequently wet (Sherwood 2001). The rear would have been much drier, thereby explaining the focus of habitation in this area. In fact, Zone R probably represents the first intensive use of the rear of the cave due to the finally dry substrate (Sherwood 2001).

There are no surface hearths representing the Early Side Notched, but this probably reflects taphonomic processes more than human behavior. Although there initially appears to be no hearths, the one large rock basin (Feature 403) is probably a hearth altered post depositionally by water activity. In situ cooking is also indicated by Zone R1, an accumulation of large rake-out deposits. Thin sections from charcoal pits dating to Zone R contain exceptionally heavy amounts of burned fish

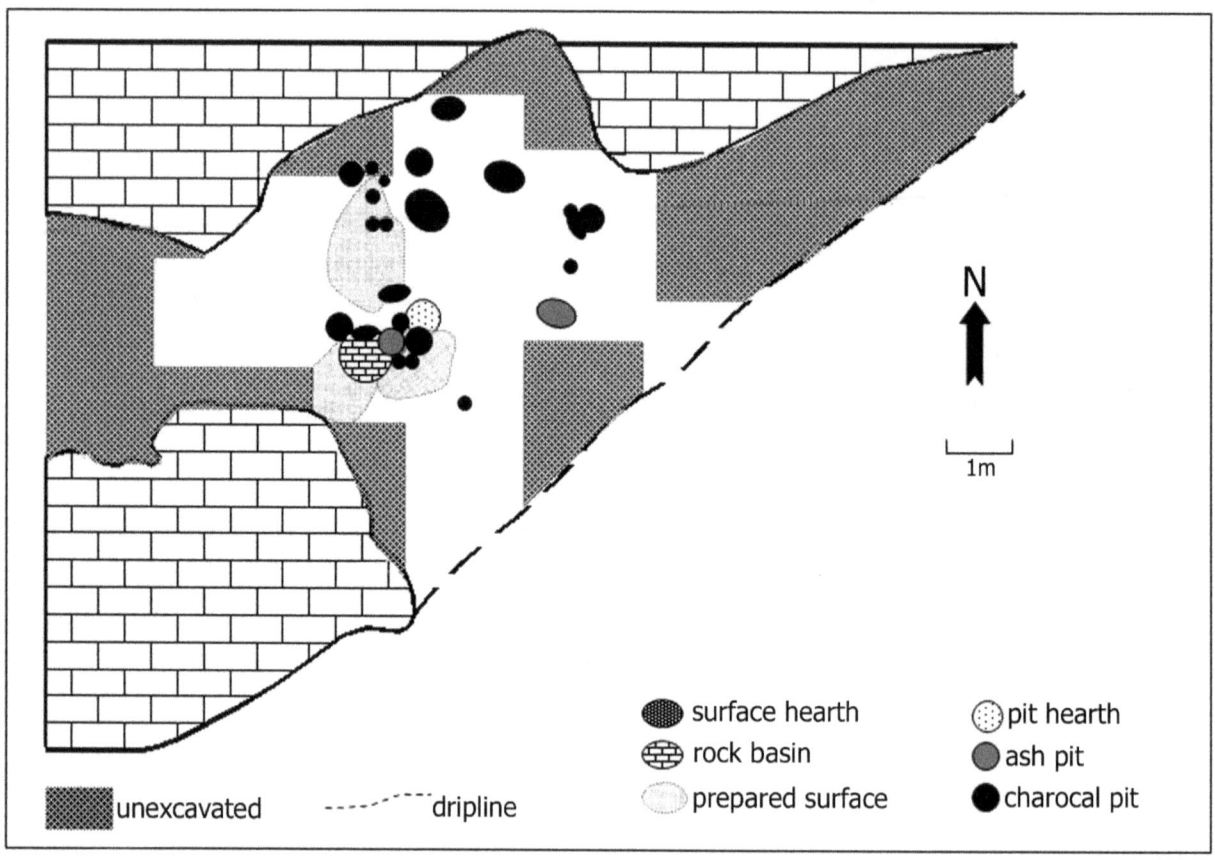

Figure 4.7. Feature distribution for the Early Side Notched Component.

and bone. Gastropod is also common, but not nearly as common as fish. Feature 405, a dense charcoal pit, was so full of fish bones that excavators noticed them even in the field. I suspect that this feature results from the grilling or smoking of fish, as would have been done in an expedient hearth. I did not map this and similar pits as expedient hearths due to the lack of ash and the absence of an obvious prepared surface substrate. However, both these conditions may well be a function of the taphonomic processes already discussed. The prevalence of fish suggests that fish processing and/or cooking played a significant role in the function of these pits. This is perhaps not surprising given the prevalence of fish in the Early Archaic and Paleoindian faunal assemblage, which is second only to waterfowl (Walker 1998, 2007; Walker et al. 2001).

In sum, occupants of Dust Cave during the Early Side Notched component focused their activities in the west-central portion of the entrance chamber. This shift reflects the wet environment of the front portion and the relative dry environment of the rear. The extremely low diversity of features is most likely a function of various taphonomic processes. Despite this, many activities are represented, including cooking (broiling and grilling/smoking), possible nut processing, and refuse disposal. This use of the cave appears to be a general continuation of previous use of the site during the Paleoindian period, with the possible addition of nut processing.

Kirk Stemmed Component, 8,200-5,800 cal. B.C.

Not until the Kirk Stemmed Component (Zone P) do we see more significant changes in use of Dust Cave (Figure 4.9). First, the number of features nearly doubles from 33 to 53. At first glance, this would seem to represent a significant increase in occupational intensity. However, this increase is not surprising given that the Kirk Stemmed component represents nearly twice the amount of time as the preceding Early Side Notched component. Second, and more significantly, new feature types emerge, including pit hearths, possible storage pits, and burials. The Kirk Stemmed component has the highest diversity indices of all the occupations represented at the site. This diversity of feature types, coupled with the great diversity in lithic tools and uses (Meeks 1994), suggest that a wide array of domestic and maintenance activities occurred, a pattern consistent with that of a residential base camp (*sensu* Bense 1994). Interestingly, the frequency of scrapers decreases markedly, indicating a substantial reduction in hide working and butchering activities.

Prepared surfaces cover a much wider area of the cave than they did previously. In contrast to the earlier periods, most features occur in the *east*-central portion of the shelter. Perhaps this is because the ceiling slopes up toward the east side, offering the most headroom. Overall, features are clustered (N=.466, $p < .001$), but less so than the Early Side Notched. Pit hearths and expedient hearths dominate the pits on the east side, while charcoal and ash pits dominate the features on the west side.

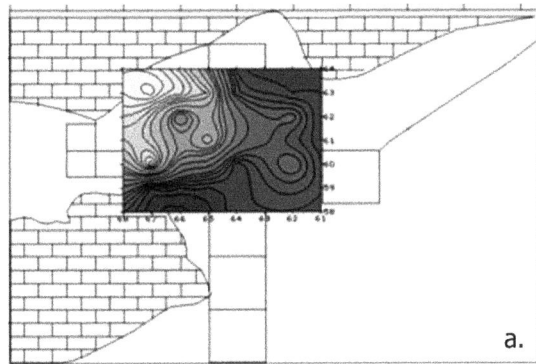

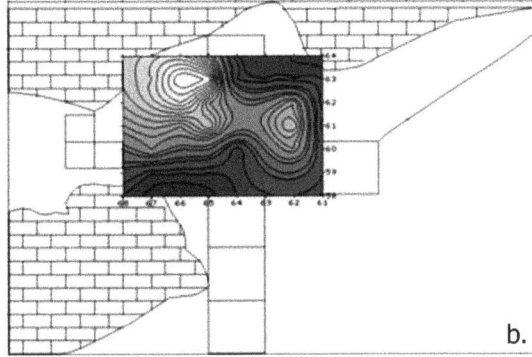

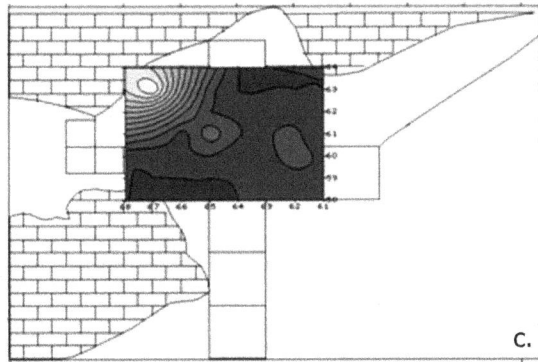

Figure 4.8. Distribution of lithics (a), bone (b) and shell (c), Early Side Notched component.

Examination of Figure 4.9 reveals a suspicious empty "hole" in the center of the entrance chamber, between the surface hearths and prepared surfaces. This space corresponds to Test Unit F, the first test pit excavated at Dust Cave in 1994. Due to poor lighting and cramped conditions, feature identification and excavation was minimal. While excavators usually identified and excavated large features such as surface hearths, ephemeral charcoal and ash pits were often simply noted as "concentrations" on individual level forms and removed along with the general zone matrix. Despite going back through all the level forms for Test Unit F (as well as the entire Test Trench), I identified no definitive features.

Hearths of all types tend to occur in a cluster in the central to east-central portion of the entrance chamber, with pit hearths and expedient hearths located somewhat more to the east than surface hearths. The overlap in cooking and nut processing within the same general area of the cave suggests that the activities associated with each were not separated, a pattern consistent with a space conserving strategy.

The only clear distinction in the use of space is between domestic activities and refuse disposal. Secondary refuse disposal apparently occurred in the western portion of the cave, towards the west passageway where the ceiling was lower. The western charcoal and ash features occur as shallow pits and rings intrusive into a series of superimposed zones representing a sequence of massive ashy deposits (Zones P5, P6a, P6b, and P6c). Sherwood (2001) has interpreted these to have depositional histories very different from the intact prepared surfaces to the east. Based on the chaotic structure of these deposits, dispersed ash and charcoal, burned microartifacts and clasts of burned red clay, they appear to represent multiple and extensive rake-out deposits—a "toss zone" in essence (Sherwood 2001:270).

The disposal of refuse in the far northwest corner is corroborated by the distribution of lithic, bone and shell remains. Figure 4.10 illustrates the clear pattern of disposal of all artifact classes in the rear of the cave, concentrating in units the northwest corner. While this pattern constitutes a continuation of the refuse disposal pattern seen in the earlier Archaic and Paleoindian occupations, it is even more significant now given the concentration of domestic activity on the other side of the cave. Conscious removal of waste from around the domestic area may signify that the occupants anticipated stays of longer duration than in earlier occupations and that they made a greater effort to keep the living/sleeping areas clean.

In sum, activity during the Kirk Stemmed component focused on the center to eastern portion of the cave. Myriad activities, typical of a residential base camp, are represented, including cooking, grilling/smoking, nut processing and, possibly, some storage. Prepared surfaces underlie nearly all these deposits, but are extensively disturbed by Middle Archaic pit digging. A space conserving strategy is implied by the limited activity segmentation and the multipurpose nature of these pits. The only segmentation of activity is between domestic behavior and waste disposal, which occurs exclusively in the far west to northwestern portion of the cave. The fact that Dust Cave occupants took the time to dispose of waste away from the center of domestic life further suggests a fairly long anticipated stay at the base camp. This cleaning out may also reflect the removal of the previous occupants' refuse when setting up a new camp, an activity which in and of itself suggests a fairly extensive stay (relative to an overnight camp).

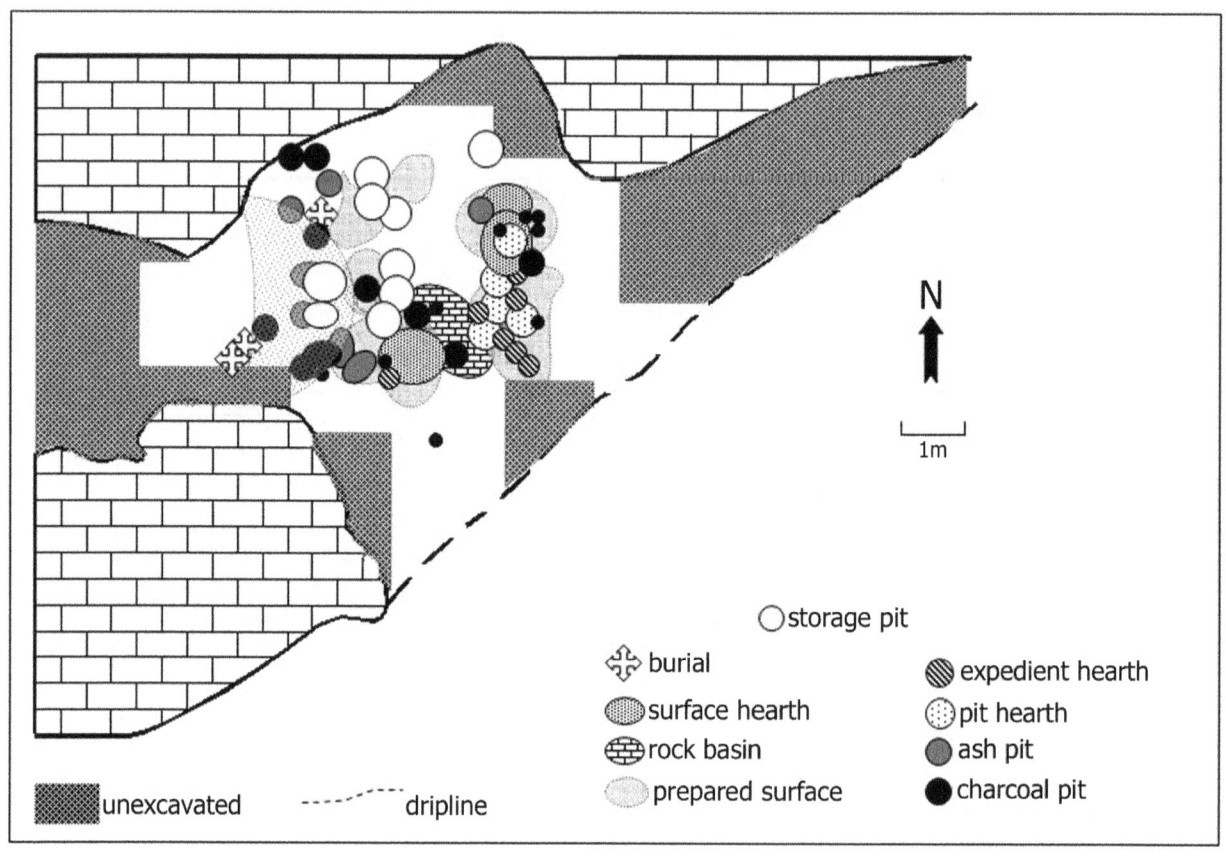

Figure 4.9. Feature distribution for the Kirk Stemmed Component.

Eva/Morrow Mt. Component, 6,400-4,000 cal. B.C.
The Eva/Morrow Mountain component (Zones N, K, J, and E) shows even more change (Figure 4.11). Despite being occupied for the same length of time as the earlier Kirk Stemmed component, there is a four-fold increase in the number of features (n=193). Rake-out and hearths dominate this assemblage. Spatially, Eva/Morrow Mountain features shift towards the dripline, presumably because the cave ceiling slopes down about half a meter towards the rear, limiting head room. Visually, features appear to be far less clustered than in previous periods; a nearest neighbor analysis quantifies this observation ($R=.780$, $p < .001$). Indeed, an R value of .78 indicates that the distribution of features is more evenly distributed than clustered. As in the Kirk Stemmed component, though to an even greater degree, features are superimposed and space appears to have been reused repeatedly. This redundancy has resulted in the vertical "stacking" of prepared surfaces and hearths. Space does not appear to be segmented, except between refuse/burial and domestic activities. The only other exception may be the separation of pit hearths, which focus in the east-central portion of the entrance chamber.

A review of features by individual zone (i.e., N, K, J and E) demonstrated that features occurred widely dispersed across the cave floor during all four zones, rather than resulting from several superimposed patterns created during each time sub-period (Homsey 2004). Likewise, prepared surfaces also occur widely dispersed across the cave floor during the entire 2,400 years. Burials also occur in the rear of the cave for all sub-periods, with the exception of one burial in Zone K, located towards the dripline. Thus, from looking at these maps one gets the impression of a continuation of the same kinds of activity through time.

Zone N is a caveat to the above. With only 12 features, occupation intensity appears to be less than in later zones. Features spread out over the expanse of the cave floor, rather than cluster in a small area, as might be expected of a temporary camp occupied only briefly. Prepared surfaces occur as small patches, rather than the coalescing surfaces characteristic of Zones J, K, and E. There are fewer hearths as well: two versus five in Zone J and six in Zone E. A trough in the geochemical and magnetic susceptibility curves (see Figure 3.7) reflects this limited habitation intensity. The beginning of Zone N may represent a hiatus in occupation at Dust Cave. Zone N is a tabular, red clay deposit formed primarily of slope wash (Sherwood 2001). The red color appears to be due to the limited anthropogenic input. Extensive root activity may indicate a period of non-occupation during which time vegetation took hold. A hiatus between zones N and P is further strengthened by numerous animal burrows on the eastern side of the cave, just inside the dripline. Numerous burials intrude Zone P from Zone N, prompting Sherwood et al. (2004) to argue that the cave functioned primarily as a burial place rather than a habitation or specialized activity site during this time.

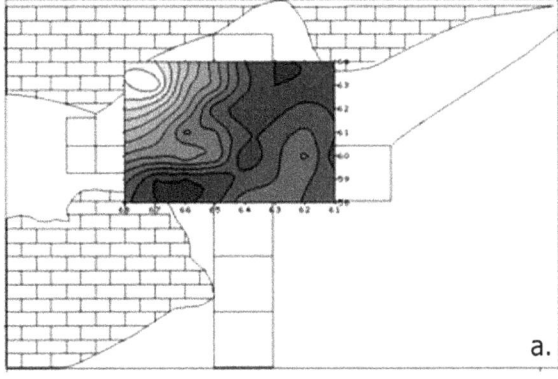

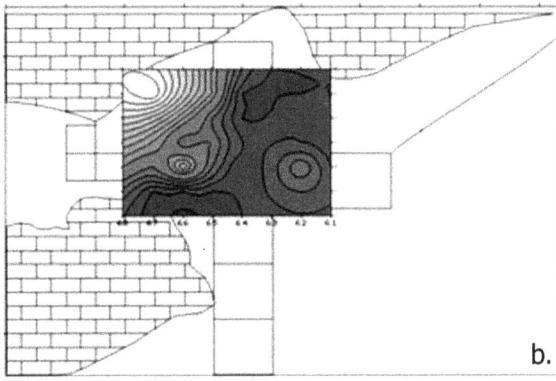

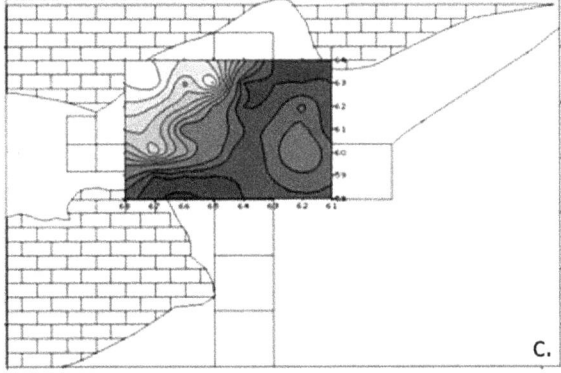

Figure 4.10. Distribution of lithics (a), bone (b) and shell (c), Kirk Stemmed component.

Fireplace rake-out occurs to the west as it did in the earlier Kirk-Stemmed component. Feature 301, over a meter long and a meter wide, dominates the deposits back here. A second area of refuse disposal existed toward the back northwest wall in what appears to be a general toss zone. Burials also occur here, a pattern consistent with the ethnographic record (Gorecki 1988, 1991). This is unsurprising, for it makes practical sense to dig burial pits into the soft, ashy sediments comprising the midden deposits (e.g., Zones J3, J1, K3, E1). In addition to rake-out, all kinds of discarded and broken artifacts and lithic cores have been found along the north wall during excavation. Large ash pits and large fragments of prepared surfaces are frequent as well. Distribution maps of lithics, bone and shell remains illustrate this general pattern of refuse disposal (Figure 4.12). Note that lithics appear to cluster in the extreme corners of the cave, peripheral to the habitation features. To some extent, these maps represent the poorer artifact recovery from the Test Trench. Despite this artificial gap in the distribution, general trends such as that described above are still discernable.

Zones J3, K3, and E1 represent thick midden deposits extending across much of the cave floor, but thickening towards the rear wall. It is in these zones that many charcoal and ash pits occur. Interestingly, these zones are extremely ash-rich, compared to the charcoal-rich rake-out deposits that dominate the west passageway. The nearly total lack of charcoal in Zones J3, K3 and E1 suggest intensive burning and complete combustion of material (Sherwood 2001). These sediments are not trampled, likely because the low headroom limited foot traffic. By the time Zone J was deposited, ceiling height in the rear would have been less than two meters; by Zone K, less than 1.5 meters (Homsey 200). Thus, the rear of the entrance chamber no longer had the necessary "standing room" for precluding its use for domestic activities.

Unlike the Kirk Stemmed component, storage pits do not occur in the Eva/Morrow Mountain component. If storage did occur, which presumably it did given the continued importance of nut processing, then the question becomes, where did it occur? One possibility is that storage took place in subterranean pits outside the dripline. However, such pits would have been vulnerable to water, animals, and more rapid decay. Moreover, no pits indicative of storage were identified during the excavation of the talus slope. A more satisfying answer is that the inhabitants of Dust Cave used baskets (Hollenbach 2009). Possible basketry impressions in prepared surface fragments lend some support for this hypothesis, though these impressions may represent the impressions of textile sleeping mats or other material culture.

In sum, the Eva/Morrow Mountain component was a time of significant change compared to earlier occupations at Dust Cave. The overall high feature diversity, phosphorus concentration, and lithic density all point to extremely intense occupation, but the decreased diversity compared to the Kirk Stemmed, lack of storage facilities, and less segmentation of space indicates a subtle change in the use of the site—at the very least, a shorter anticipated stay. Finally, the large numbers of pit hearths, prepared surfaces, and copious volume of combusted materials, coupled with the significant increase in hickory nut charcoal and nutting stones, suggest a strong emphasis on nut processing. The Eva/Morrow Mountain occupation, then, appears to represent use of the site as a special purpose plant extraction camp. As I will argue in the following chapter, the shift toward use of extraction camps may represent a shift from a more residential mobility strategy to a more logistical mobility strategy.

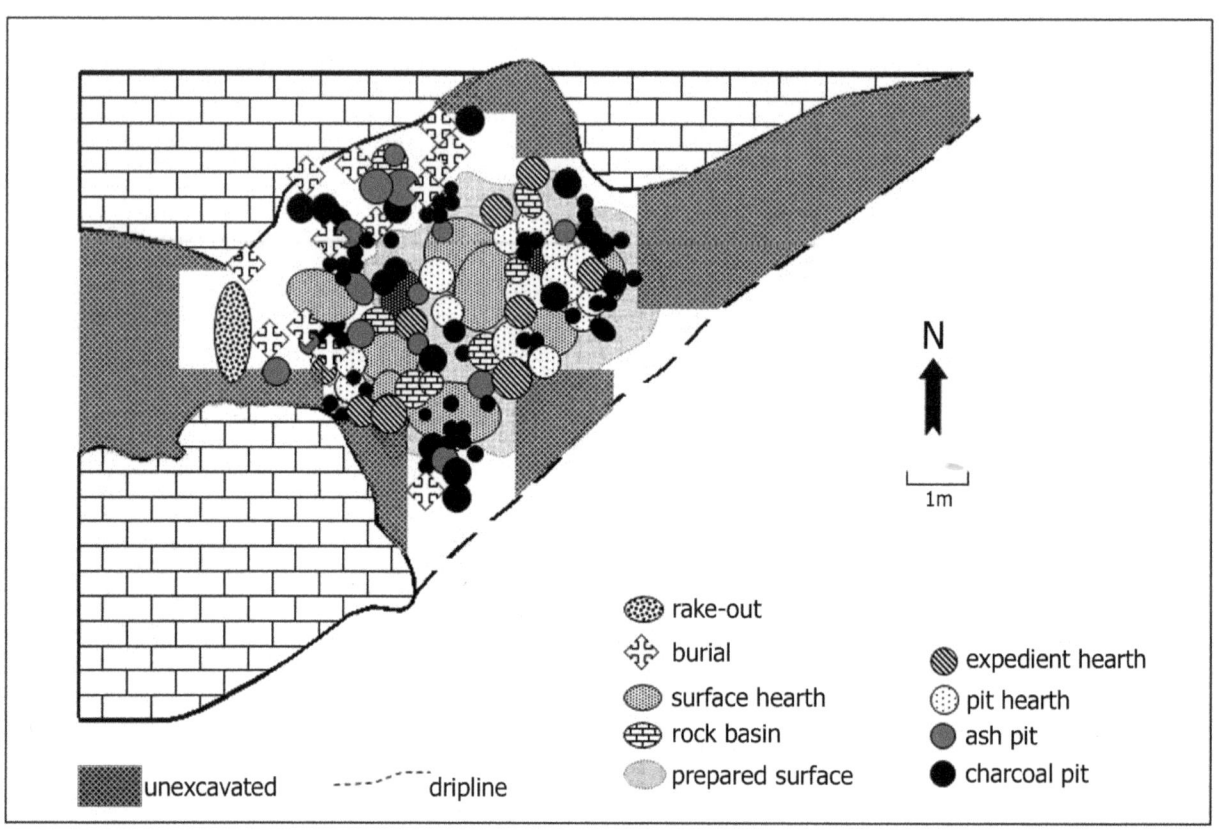

Figure 4.11. Distribution of features in Eva/Morrow Mountain Component.

Benton Component, 4,500-3,600 cal. B.C.

Following the Eva/Morrow Mountain component, occupation of the cave significantly decreases (Zone D) (Figure 4.13). This is most likely a function of decreasing headroom; by about 3,600 cal. B.C., headroom would have been less than 1.5 meters (less than the height of an average male). Overall, the feature distribution is clustered ($R=.5$, $p<.001$), but spatially they form two distinct clusters. In the west-central portion of the cave, about a meter from the southwestern wall, are three hearths and associated charcoal pits (a combination of scrape-out and accessory pits—these could not be differentiated based on feature forms and photographs), three expedient hearths, and one possible nut processing pit (Feature 41). On the east side of the cave are three more expedient hearths and several charcoal pits. Since rocks are not mentioned on the feature form descriptions, these most likely represent scrape-out as the expedient hearths are re-used. Prepared surfaces occur in a band across the front of the cave floor, towards the dripline. Each cluster of features overlies the surfaces. This bimodal clustering most likely reflects the paucity of cooking, processing and refuse features excavated during the initial Test Trench excavations, rather than any significant cultural behavior. Finally, four burials occur in the rear of the cave, three in the northwest and one along the northeast wall.

Given the restricted headroom, one might expect hearths to be located further forward, closer to the dripline. Features on the east side do indeed shift forward relative to earlier occupations. However, features to the west actually shift *back* relative to earlier occupations. Such a pattern seems counterintuitive at first but it is important to note that these hearths lie opposite the west passageway. While excavating at Dust Cave, one quickly experiences the cool draft that blows from the back of the cave along this passageway (resulting from summer temperature variation). Dust Cave occupants may have built surface hearths in this area to maximize the natural ventilation afforded by the passage. Interestingly, expedient hearths account for 22% of the feature assemblage (compared to 11% for surface hearths), or 60% of the hearth assemblage. Expedient hearths may reflect the need for lower temperature, less smoky cooking hearths in a low-headroom environment; large hearths may simply have produced too much smoke.

A question arises from looking at the spatial distribution of features in the Benton occupation: where is the refuse? None of the charcoal pits can be characterized as secondary refuse (rake-out) and both feature clusters appear to relate solely to cooking and/or nut processing activities. Two possibilities exist. First, ashes may have been dumped in the rear of the cave. Sherwood (2001) has noted that the sediments furthest north in zone D are decalcified, so it is possible that they have been obliterated beyond recognition. However, even charcoal deposits are conspicuously absent. A more likely scenario is that refuse was tossed outside the cave into the talus. Support for this hypothesis comes from level forms for the Test Trench. Excavators consistently referred to deposits from Zone D lying beyond the dripline as "midden" deposits. These midden deposits are described as consisting of 20% scattered charcoal; shell, bone, broken tools, and lithic debitage, and burned red clay fragments. This description is very similar to what I noted occurring along the north wall during the Eva/Morrow Mountain. This, then, may be the Benton "toss zone." Given the reduced size of the entrance chamber, it is perhaps not surprising that refuse would be discarded outside the cave.

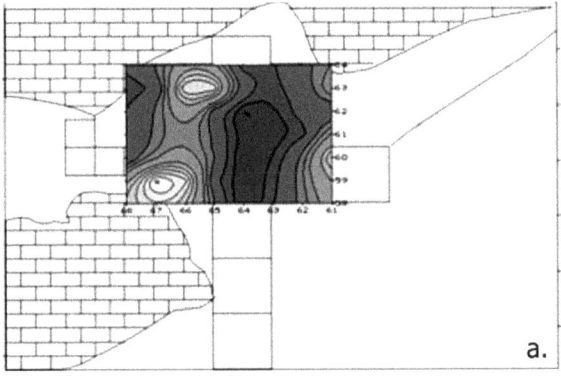

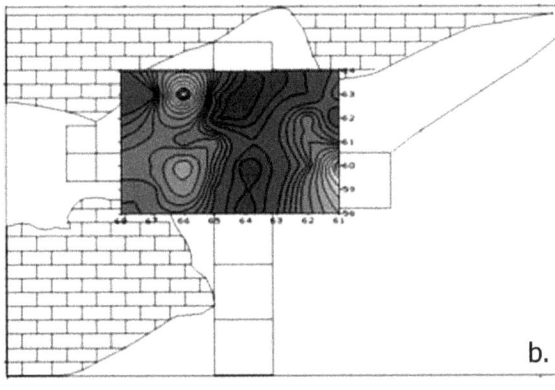

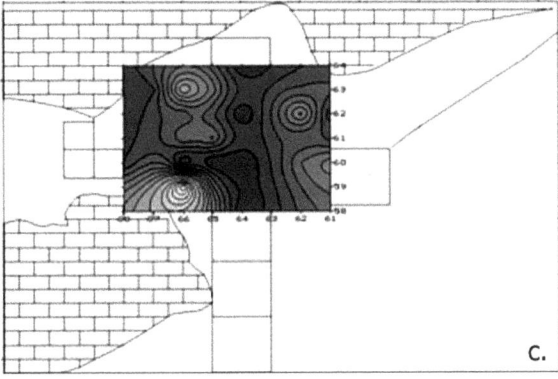

Figure 4.12. Distribution of lithics (a), bone (b), and shell (c), Eva/Morrow Mt. Component.

The distribution of lithics, bone and shell support the interpretation that a discrete refuse zone does not occur inside the cave (Figures 4.14). Unlike the other components, all three artifact categories show little, if any, patterning during the Benton component. Lithics appear to have been swept to the sides of the cave, away from the hearth area, but not in the kind of discrete pattern observed during the earlier occupations. The bone and shell distributions overlap with the western hearth cluster, as if they were not removed from the area. Perhaps this reflects a short anticipated stay at the site. Interestingly, shell only occurs on the west side, suggesting that shell processing was restricted to surface hearth cooking. Bone appears on both sides, with a peak overlapping each hearth concentration.

The Benton occupation signifies a drastic reduction in the use of Dust Cave. The Benton component represents the accumulation of more than 7,000 years worth of deposition, most of it through anthropogenic processes. By 3,600 cal B.C., lowered headroom precluded further occupation of the site. Sterile colluvial sediments accumulated over the next 5,000 years, yielding a sedimentation rate of less than one centimeter per century, far less than the average six centimeters per century during peak occupation of the site. Ultimately, the intense use of the site, which gives us such a rich database from which to interpret hunter-gatherer behavior in the Midsouth, precluded future occupation.

SUMMARY

Through time, the microenvironment of Dust Cave changed, influencing both where human activity concentrated and the preservation of that activity. During the Paleoindian and Early Archaic, the dominant control on human activity was a wet substrate due to periodic flooding, either as water flowing through the phreatic channel, or sheetwash originating from the front of the cave. During the Middle Archaic, flooding no longer determined the foci of occupation. Rather, ceiling height and the location of the dripline appear to have had the most significant impact on the location of activities. Galanidou (1997:26) has suggested that microtopography "is no insurmountable obstacle; it is cultural perceptions and degrees of mobility that constrain the uses made of caves and rockshelters." I do not argue against the influence cultural factors have on hunter-gather use of caves and rockshelters, but I do believe that the microtopography of their living space constrains them more than Galanidou suggests.

While physical constraints on the use of space at Dust Cave are the most obvious, I was able to isolate some cultural patterns of interest. First (1), the lack of segmented space indicates a space conserving strategy typical of groups who anticipate staying for a substantial period of time, perhaps a few weeks. It should be kept in mind, however, that the physically small size of Dust Cave may have forced its occupants to adapt more of a space conserving strategy than they would have in a larger space. The diversity of features representing activities ranging from cooking to nut processing to sleeping to large-scale refuse give us some additional confidence in a stay of more than just a few days.

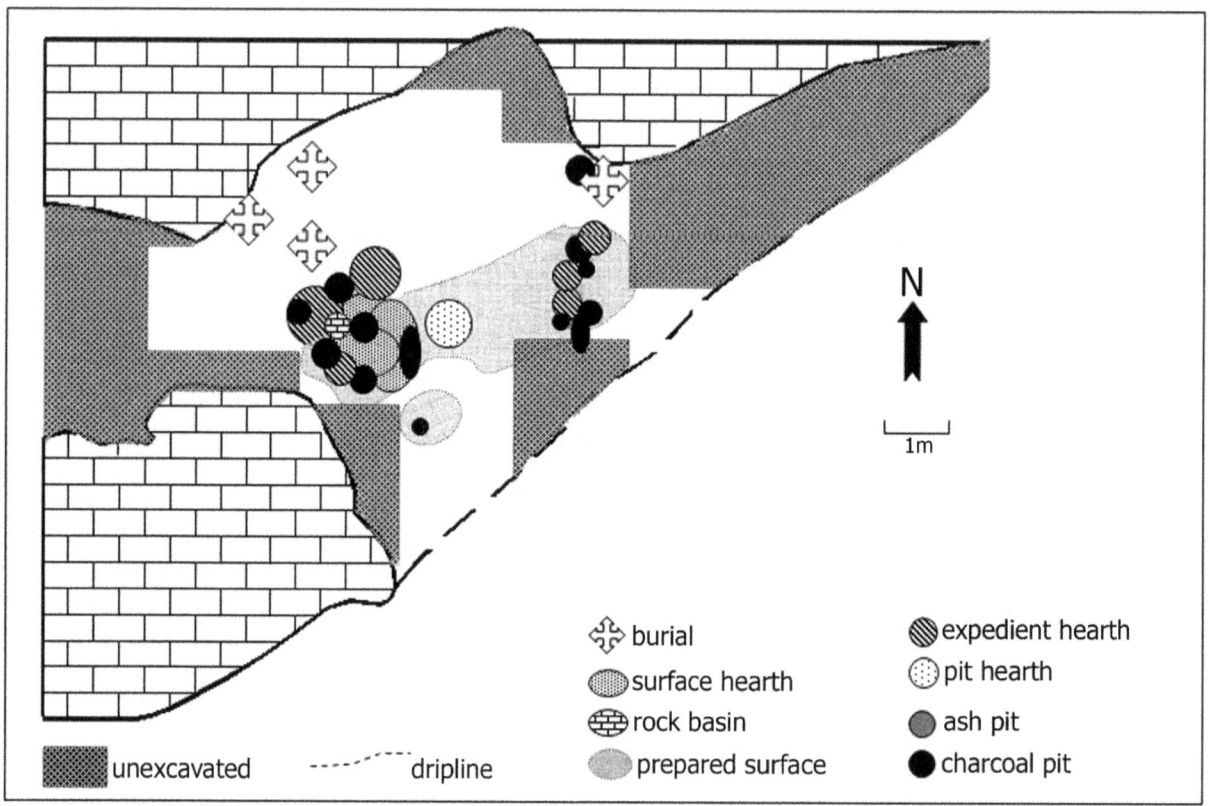

Figure 4.13. Distribution of features in Benton Component.

Second (2), this analysis has allowed interpretations of site use to be made. The overall high diversity of features suggests use of the cave as more than just an overnight camp or lay station (*sensu* Thomas 1985). During the Late Paleoindian and Early Side-Notched occupations, the cave appears to have served as a seasonal residential camp, visited during the later summer to early fall, and perhaps again in the spring (Walker 1998). The high percentage of scrapers during the Late Paleoindian component (Meeks 1994), coupled with the majority of tools exhibiting butchering and hide working use wear patterns (Walker et al. 2001), suggest that the site functioned as a hunting camp. It may therefore have served as a habitual-use site, a place to which hunter-gatherers came to repeatedly (*sensu* Anderson 1996).

During the Kirk Stemmed component, use of the site appears to have shifted to that of a base camp, based on the high feature and artifact diversity, segregation of domestic and refuse space, and possible storage pits. It is important to consider the length of time spanned by the Kirk Component when interpreting occupation. The Kirk Stemmed component spans nearly 2,400 years, almost two times that of the earlier Paleoindian and Early Side Notched components. If occupation intensity remained constant over time, we would expect about two times as many features. In fact, this is exactly what we observe: 56 features in the Kirk component versus 33 and 32 in the Paleoindian and Early Side Notched, respectively. The flat curve in P concentration, lithic density, and magnetic susceptibility (see Figure 3.7) also reflects fairly constant occupation intensity. Diversity increases sharply, however, and new feature types emerge, including storage pits and processing pits. This increased diversity is consistent with a more generalized set of activities, including domestic and maintenance activities. The presence of storage may reflect shifting use of the site towards that of a base camp, albeit seasonal. Faunal and botanical data suggest a fall/early winter occupation (Walker et al. 2001). The marked decrease in scrapers further suggests a decline in the importance of hunting and hide processing activities.

The Eva/Morrow Mountain component, on the other hand, has far more observed features than we would expect if occupation remained constant over time. The Eva/Morrow Mountain spans about two times as long as the Paleoindian, but has *four* times as many features, suggesting that the intensity in use increased significantly over the earlier period. Despite this increased intensity, feature *diversity* decreases and storage pits (which date to the Kirk/Eva interface) disappear, suggesting a subtle change in use of the site. Hall (1985) has argued that low diversity indices result from limited activity sites; i.e., specialized sites focused on a particular activity. During the Eva/Morrow Mountain occupation, processing pits account for almost eight percent of features, nutting stones are common, the relative proportion of hickory nut charcoal increases significantly, and thick midden deposits accumulate, all of which support an interpretation of nut processing as the primary activity at the site. Thus, the use of Dust Cave during this time period is best characterized as an intensively utilized plant extraction and/or processing site.

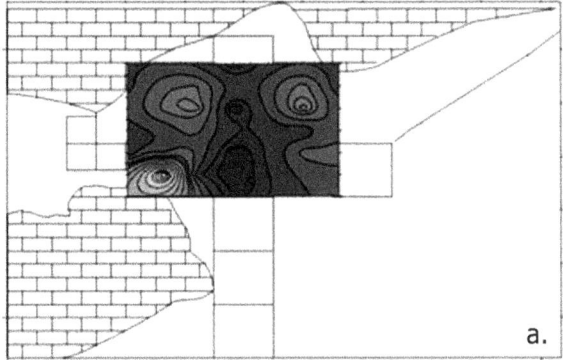

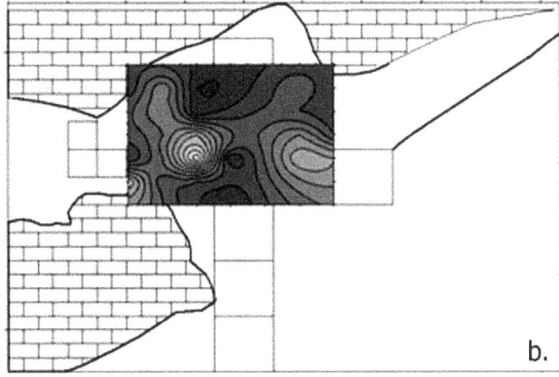

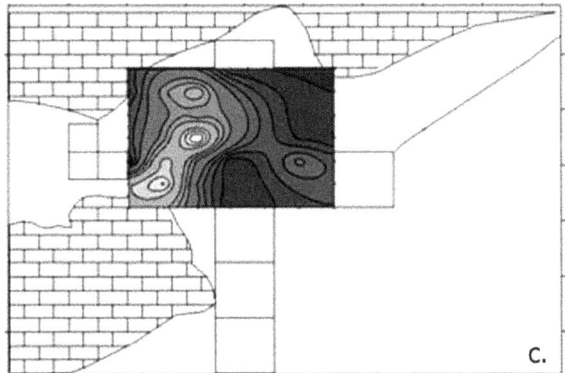

Figure 4.14. Distribution of lithics (a), bone (b) and shell (c), Benton component.

The Benton occupation appears to be a fairly ephemeral camp. Lasting just over 1,000 years, we would expect about the same number of features as occurred during the Paleoindian component (33), assuming constant use of the site. What we observe is 27 features, or 20% fewer than expected. This observation comes as no surprise given the limited headroom available. Diversity decreases again, also reflecting the geologic constraints on activity. Interestingly, while diversity decreases, it still remains greater than during the Paleoindian or Early Side Notched. However, as previously discussed, taphonomic processes likely mask greater original diversity. The early feature assemblage is dominated by charcoal pits and stringers, artificially decreasing feature richness. While we cannot determine site use with much certainty during these two early periods, the identification of post-depositional processes which have greatly obscured feature morphology is crucial to preventing misinterpretation of site use. Occupation intensity was definitely greater than the small, shallow features suggest, but just how intensively the site was used is open to some debate.

In sum, the use of Dust Cave differs in *intensity* of use over time, more so than *types* of activities occurring. The exception to this trend is the addition of nut processing and storage during the Kirk Stemmed component, which continues into the Middle Archaic. Thus, it appears that something happened around 8,000 B.C. which prompted hunter-gatherers to use Dust Cave in a new way, as well as more intensively. The question is, what? I hypothesize that hunter-gather use of caves in the Midsouth intensified due to an ameliorating middle Holocene climate. Computer-generated climate reconstructions for the Middle Tennessee River Valley suggest that by 8,000 B.C. annual temperatures increased more than two degrees and annual precipitation decreased by about 200 mm/year (Bryson 1999a, b; see Homsey 2004:Appendix C). These warmer and drier conditions are just right for hickory trees (Thompson et al. 1999), the remains of which dominate the botanical record at Dust Cave. Indeed, pollen reconstructions demonstrate that hickory trees (among others) began to migrate into the Middle Tennessee River Valley between 8,000 and 6,000 B.C. (Delcourt and Delcourt 1987). At Dust Cave, these changes coincide with the appearance of nut processing pits, the increase in feature diversity, and intensified cave use beginning with the Kirk Stemmed component. In the following chapter, I compare the feature assemblage and organization at Dust Cave to other regional caves, including Stanfield-Worley Rockshelter, Russell Cave, and Modoc Rockshelter. As will be shown, many of the changes seen at Dust Cave are also reflected in the feature assemblage at these caves.

Chapter 5

DUST CAVE IN REGIONAL CONTEXT

It is important not to consider sites in isolation, but rather to compare them to other archaeological sites of similar antiquity in order to establish how the use and spatial organization of a site is linked to the site's role within a broader, regional settlement system (Binford 1982, 1980; Galanidou 2000; Nicholas and Kramer 2001). I therefore compare the Dust Cave feature assemblage to three other cave and rockshelter sites, two in the Middle Tennessee Valley, and one outside the Tennessee Valley. Three criteria influenced site selection. First, the site must date to the same time period as Dust Cave, between 10,650 and 3,600 cal B.C. (10,500 to 5,200 uncal. B.P.), or at least overlap with this range. Second, the site must contain preserved feature remains with comparable data. On this point, I had to be flexible; micromorphology and chemical samples were rarely, if ever, collected from cave and rockshelter sites (Dust Cave and Stanfield-Worley Rockshelter excepted). For this reason, I limit my inter-site comparison to occupation intensity, presence/absence of prepared surfaces, and feature morphology, content, and (where possible) distribution. Third, I wanted sites within the Middle Tennessee Valley to compare and contrast cave use through time in the valley. I also wanted some sites outside of the valley in order to get a sense of whether caves served the same function as a place in the Midsouth as they do in the more restricted landscape of the Middle Tennessee Valley. This chapter concludes by comparing these cave and rockshelter sites to nearby open-air sites. Drawing upon the influential models of settlement and subsistence strategies summarized in chapter 1, I draw conclusions about the changing use of caves and rockshelters in the hunter-gatherer landscape of the American Midsouth.

CAVE AND ROCKELTER SITES IN THE PROJECT AREA

In addition to Dust Cave, the three additional sites chosen for this comparative study include Stanfield-Worley Bluff Shelter, located in Colbert County, northwestern Alabama; Russell Cave, located in Jackson County, northeastern Alabama; and Modoc Rockshelter, located in Randolph County in southern Illinois (Figure 5.1). It should be noted that because these sites were excavated during the 1950s and 60s, calibrated radiocarbon dates do not exist. Thus, I compare the sites to Dust Cave using uncalibrated dates. Table 5.1 summarizes the components/zones and radiocarbon which correspond to the uncalibrated dates and components from Dust Cave. These correlations are not exact, but are as precise as possible given the available data. These three sites are compared to Dust Cave in terms of feature diversity, occupational intensity, spatial organization of deposits, and site function.

Figure 5.1. Location of cave and rockshelter sites discussed in chapter 5.

Stanfield-Worley Bluff Shelter

The Stanfield-Worley Bluff Shelter (1Ct125) is a sandstone rockshelter formed in the Hartselle Formation and located in the upland forests of Colbert County, northwest Alabama, approximately 12 miles south of Dust Cave. The shelter extends some 15 meters out from the rear wall, creating a protected living space of nearly 2,500 m^2 (Walthall 1980). Excavations conducted within the living area and on the talus slope outside the shelter indicate that the site was occupied intermittently for over 8,000 years, from the Early Archaic through the Late Woodland. Unlike Dust Cave, Stanfield-Worley contains a true Dalton component, indicating that potentially different cultural groups made use of these two shelters, at least during the Late Paleoindian-Archaic transition. In addition to being a rockshelter, rather than a cave, Stanfield-Worley is much larger and shaped differently than Dust Cave. For these reasons, Stanfield-Worley serves as a useful comparison to Dust Cave in examining the use of space in caves and rockshelters. Dug in 1960-1961 by David DeJarnette, excavations at Stanfield-Worley represent one of the first attempts to systematically investigate a rockshelter site in eastern North America. Deposits were screened through ¼ inch mesh, though flotation samples were not taken. Additional test excavations were conducted during the summer of 2001 by Kandace Detwiler-Hollenbach and Asa Randall. During this season, flotation samples were taken, as well as 13 micromorphology samples, six of which represent feature sediments. DeJarnette and his crew uncovered 95 features, including 11 burials, during the 1960-61 excavations. The remaining 84 features were originally classified as rock-filled storage pits (n=10), refuse and/or "midden-filled depressions" (n=58), hearths (n=18), and "fire-hardened masses" (n=5). Six features could not be identified. During the 2001 field season, Detwiler-Hollenbach and Randall recorded and floated six additional features including one possible prepared surface.

Russell Cave

Russell Cave is located in northeast Alabama, approximately seven miles from the Tennessee River. Like Dust Cave, it is a true cavern, formed from the dissolution of the Monteagle Limestone (Griffen 1974). The Smithsonian Institute and the National Geographic society together excavated Russell Cave in 1953; the National Park Service further excavated it in 1962 (Griffen 1974). The deposits date from 8,500 to 1,000 years B.P., spanning the Early, Middle, and Late Archaic, and Woodland periods (Table 5.1). The levels dating from 8,500 to 5,500 years B.P. correspond to the Kirk Stemmed (Layer G), Eva/Morrow Mountain (Layer F), and Benton (Layer F) components at Dust Cave. Occupants restricted their activity to the entrance chamber, approximately 33 m long and 50 m deep, for a total area of 1,650 m^2. The sinkhole in front of the cavern contains a spring-fed pool which flows into the chamber beside the rock shelter. At times in prehistory, this pool likely flooded the cave, especially during the Early Archaic (Griffen 1974). Excavations uncovered features of myriad types, including what excavators called storage pits, unknown ash pits, cooking pits, and post-holes. They also found six burials and four textile impressions in hard red clay. The latter material may represent prepared surfaces, and are discussed further later.

Modoc Rockshelter

Modoc Rockshelter is located in Randolph County in southern Illinois, along the eastern edge of the Mississippi River floodplain and approximately two miles east of the present town of Prairie du Rocher (Ahler 1993; Fowler 1959; Styles et al. 1983). The Illinois state museum excavated the site several times, first during the 1950s, and twice again in 1984 and 1987 (Ahler 1993). The shelter is formed by an overhang of the Aux Vase Sandstone (Fowler 1959). The overhang essentially contains two sites: the Main shelter (the larger one, 100 m long and 10 m deep) and the West Shelter which is significantly smaller (Ahler 1993). Since the West and Main shelters were not necessarily used in the same way through time (Ahler 1993), I focus primarily on the Main shelter unless otherwise noted. Nearly five meters of cultural deposits represent more than 6,000 years of occupation, from approximately 9,000 to 3,000 uncal. B.P. (Ahler 1993). These dates overlap the Paleoindian through Middle Archaic components at Dust Cave. The microstratigraphy of Modoc Rockshelter is complex; Fowler (1959) describes the habitation features as being so "numerous and superimposed that it was not possible to separate them and get an accurate count." Nevertheless, the many features that researchers excavated appear to be a good representative sample of the variety of feature types at the site. Feature types include what Fowler refers to as fire-pits, ash beds, and clay-lined pits of unknown use (N=4). Unlike Dust Cave, post-molds were recovered, suggesting that the Modoc occupants built temporary structures such as windbreaks; given the long, open overhang, the use of windbreaks is unsurprising. They also found 22 burials, all of which dated between 8,500 and 4,600 uncal. B.P. Thin superimposed beds of intact surfaces are locally preserved, suggesting the possible presence of a prepared clay surface technology.

Table 5.1. Radiocarbon dates (uncalibrated) at Dust Cave and corresponding components and/or zones for other sites.

Dates (uncal. B.P)	Dust Cave	Stanfield-Worley Bluff Shelter	Russell Cave	Modoc Rockshelter[6]
6,000-5,200	Benton	Zone B	Zone F	4-3
7,000-6,000	Eva/Morrow Mountain	Zone B	Zone F	7-5
8,500-7,000	Kirk Stemmed	Zone D (Dalton)	Zone G	15-8/9
10,000-9,000	Early Side Notched			16
10,500-10,000	Paleoindian			

---

[6] Based on West Shelter stratigraphy.

INTER-SITE COMPARISON

Feature Diversity

Stanfield-Worley Bluff Shelter. At first glance, feature diversity at Stanfield-Worley is less than at Dust Cave. For the Dalton component (Zone D), only five feature types are described by DeJarnette et al. (1962): fire pits, midden-filled depressions, fire-hardened clay, and pits (some of which are referred to as refuse pits). Fire pits are described as approximately a meter in diameter, and having ash, charcoal, and fire-reddened earth surrounding them, a description consistent with surface hearths; they are therefore referred to as surface hearths from here on. Fire-hardened clay masses are described (DeJarnette et al. 1962, 1963) as circular to oval patches of compact, reddish yellow deposits about 12 inches in thickness, often flecked with charcoal and ash, underlying charcoal and ash deposits. A patch of such a mass was uncovered during the 2001 excavations and micromorphology samples taken for analysis. The samples come from a compact layer of yellowish red silty clay loam with charcoal and ash flecking throughout. Micromorphological analyses (Homsey 2010) revealed a very silty matrix—much siltier than the Dust Cave surfaces. The matrix contained lightly dispersed nut and wood charcoal incompletely combusted to ash. The unconformable boundary between the silty clay loam and overlying charcoal and ash is sharp. The rubification appears to be due to the oxidation of iron oxides during burning. In this respect the Stanfield-Worley clay masses are similar to the Dust Cave prepared surfaces. Unlike the Dust Cave surfaces, however, the lack of heavy residual clays, weathered limestone and ceiling rain suggest that the source of the material is not from a cave interior. Translocated clays, root casts, papules of *terra rosa*, and rounded silt aggregates all indicate a pedogenic origin. This is perhaps not surprising given that Stanfield-Worley is formed within the Hartselle Sandstone and residual cave clay (formed from the chemical dissolution of limestone) would not have been readily available like it would have been at karst sites like Dust Cave. Interestingly, one large angular fragment of burned biomicritic Tuscumbia Limestone was identified, suggesting that the occupants of Stanfield-Worley traveled down in elevation to select the same material for fire stones as did the occupants of Dust Cave (Homsey 2009). Based on the field descriptions, coupled with the micromorphological analyses, I suggest that the Stanfield-Worley clay masses served as prepared surfaces, and so refer to them as such from here on out.

DeJarnette (1962, 1963) describes midden-filled depressions, which occur only during the Dalton component, as shallow, irregular depressions (10-15 cm deep). He interprets them to represent "midden accumulation in natural depressions." The original feature forms record these depressions as dark brown loams with moderate to heavy charcoal content. I coded them as charcoal pits for the sake of analysis. Their restricted spatial distribution on the far right hand side of the shelter (see below) is compelling evidence that these "middens" reflect refuse deposits, as DeJarnette's descriptive term suggests.

Diversity increases in both richness and heterogeneity during the Middle and Late Archaic (Zones A, B). Hearths (N=14) and prepared surfaces (N=4) increase in number, though there is only one midden-filled depression. Pits come in four varieties: circular refuse pits, rock-filled storage pits, miscellaneous refuse pits, and unknown pits (DeJarnette et al. 1962, 1963). Rock-filled storage pits are large, approximately 80 cm in diameter and 20 cm deep, though the standard deviation around the means is large (25 and 30 cm, respectively). These pits contain large rocks, many of which had been used as anvils or mortars. These pits may have functioned as nutting stone "caches" for future occupation; however, the fact that many also contain large concentrations of large mammal bone (likely deer) and aquatic snail shell suggest storage of various materials. Circular refuse pits are similar to the rock-filled storage pits, except that they lack the large rocks and nutting stones. DeJarnette describes the miscellaneous refuse pits excavated during 1961 as small, circular and irregular holes. However, those excavated during the 1963 season which adjoin the back wall are extremely large, nearly a meter in length and almost 25 cm in depth. I could not tell from the feature forms what the contents of these pits are; it is doubtful the contents from this season were ever analyzed. Finally, several of the "unknown pits" matched descriptions very close to the charcoal and ash pits found at Dust Cave. The fact that they intruded prepared surfaces in nearly every case strengthened this interpretation.

The lack of obvious charcoal and ash pits at Stanfield-Worley most likely reflects taphonomic processes rather than differences in use of the site. Due to the openness of the bluff, the site acted more as an open-air preservation environment than a true cave such as Dust Cave. Perhaps more importantly, the siliceous sandstone shelter does not offer the same buffering capacity that the calcareous walls of Dust Cave offer to otherwise acidic sediments. The lack of discrete microstratigraphy attests to the influence of post-depositional processes (such as pedogenesis and bioturbation) in homogenizing the deposits. To confound matters more, excavators rarely mentioned the presence of charcoal pits until the 1963 field season. DeJarnette does mention "charcoal/debris in small pits" associated with hearths—these may represent scrape-out, but without photographs and detailed descriptions, it is difficult to say this with any certainty.

In considering how the Stanfield-Worley features compare to the Dust Cave features, I added the Stanfield-Worley features to the scatterplot of feature volume to width/depth of the Dust Cave features (Figure 5.2). In general, the two populations overlap quite nicely at the lower end of the continuum (log volume >3, width/depth <10). What is missing from the Stanfield-Worley feature assemblage are charcoal and ash stringers (width/depth >20) and charcoal and ash concentrations and pits (width/depth between 5 and 25, log volume between 2 and 3.5). Stringers at Dust Cave result from intense post-depositional fluvial activity; their lack at Stanfield-Worley indicates minimal flooding. The lack of charcoal and ash pits most likely results from inadequate feature description and taphonomic processes. Additionally, since excavators dug in four inch (10 cm) levels with shovels, it is likely that they missed small pits and concentrations.

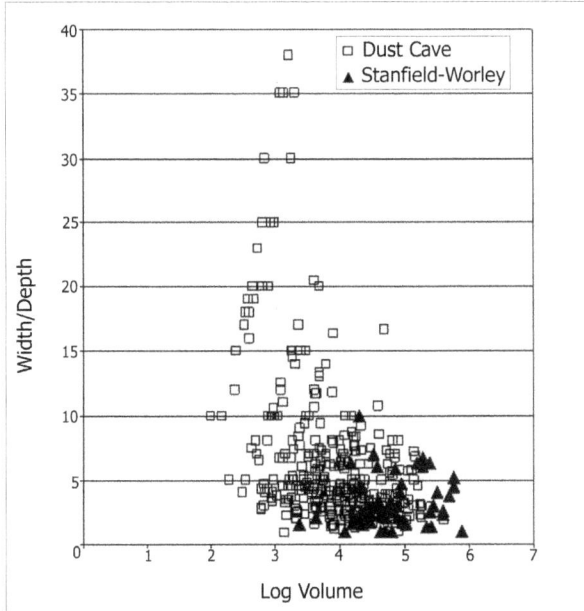

Figure 5.2. Scatterplot of Dust Cave and Stanfield-Worley Bluff Shelter features.

Russell Cave. Original feature forms were not available for Russell Cave. However, Griffen's site report (1974) and his original field notes (1961-1962) were available and yielded some pertinent information. The 1974 site report summarizes the features encountered during excavation. Griffen notes that pit digging accounts for the most serious disruption of stratigraphy at the site. Pits that Griffen notes include burials, possible storage pits, charcoal concentrations, U-shaped ash pits, and "fire-baked areas."

Based on the presence of several textile impressions found in clay masses pulled from the water screens (see Homsey 2004, Plate 8.8), there is good reason to believe that the aforementioned "fire-baked pits" represent prepared surfaces. These remnants originated in layer G, dating to the Early Archaic. Griffen (1974) describes the clay as very compact, but unfired. However, in his field notes (August 2, 1962), he describes these roughly oval areas as "solidly fire-baked." This apparent contradiction may be resolved by remembering that experimental studies conducted during the 2002 Dust Cave field season demonstrated that prepared surfaces range from highly burned directly under a fire to unburned 40 cm away from the fire (Homsey and Sherwood 2010). Indeed, Griffen notes that the periphery of these areas is only

"semi-baked" (August 2, 1962). The masses cover an area of roughly 2.5 by 2 feet (75 by 60 cm). In one instance, excavators drew a circular concentration of ash and charcoal overlying a burned red area (August 17, 1962). Several references are made throughout the notes of "banded white ash and red ash" (e.g., September 6, 1962). This may possibly represent the vertical stacking of surfaces as described by Sherwood (2001).

The report says little about the charcoal concentrations, except that they may have been cooking pits. Not enough information is provided to determine whether such features were burned in place or not; indeed, Griffen himself notes several times throughout his 1961 field book that they were unable to determine whether pits were hearths burned in place or "tossed aside from a fire" (e.g., July 26, 1962). He also notes that they could not determine in the field whether these pits resulted from one or many fires (July 26, 1962). Elsewhere, however, Griffen describes the charcoal lenses in some of the pits as being "separated by lenses of soil" (July 23, 1962), a description consistent with many of the Dust Cave hearths. Finally, sketches of pits in Griffen's field notes indicate clusters of limestone rocks with no ash or charcoal, lying adjacent to charcoal pits. Little detail was provided for ash pits, including dimensions. Using the trowel in a photograph of one such pit, I estimate that they were approximately 35 cm deep and 30-40 cm in diameter. While this depth is nearly twice that of Dust Cave pit hearths, the diameter, shape, and intrusive nature are similar.

The possible storage pits at Russell Cave are large, roughly circular to oval pits approximately a meter in diameter and 30 to 40 cm deep. The latter depth overlaps with the 95% confidence interval for the depth of the Zone P pits at Dust Cave. They are generally rectangular in profile. Like the Zone P pits at Dust Cave, the Russell Cave pits contained a number of rocks, many of which are flat. Griffen notes that none of these pits were rock-lined. Numerous pits were excavated, most of which occurred in the Middle Archaic layers (F, E). Indeed, the pits do not occur prior to the Middle Archaic, though they do continue into the Late Archaic and Woodland periods (Griffen 1974:112). Griffen argued that these pits most likely represent storage, which subsequently became filled in with refuse: "The pits had probably been dug initially for storage purposes…After the stored contents (acorns, nuts?) had been consumed, the pits were filled. Some refuse was included, but…not sufficient to lead us to believe that they had been dug for the primary purpose of refuse disposal (Griffen 1974:10)."

Modoc Rockshelter. In his report of investigations at Modoc Rockshelter, Fowler (1959:38) notes that fire pits and ash lenses were found in all levels, but that they "were so inter-bedded that it was not possible to separate them and get an accurate count." Fire pits, presumably hearths, occur in two varieties: prepared fireplaces and rock-lined fireplaces. Post-molds were also uncovered, and are thought to represent wind breaks (Fowler 1959). Twenty-nine (29) burials were also found, 11 of which date to the late Early through Middle Archaic. Four pits of unknown use were found, two dating to the Woodland period and two dating to the late Early Archaic period. These appeared in the field as shallow saucer- or basin-shaped pits lined with sandy clay, but sterile. Their limited numbers and lack of content gives little indication of use or purpose.

Based on the 1984 excavations in the Main Shelter, Ahler (2004, 1984) developed a preliminary typology of feature types, consisting of (1) inclusive, (2) intrusive, and (3) complex features. *Inclusive* features consist of isolated ash lenses, isolated charcoal lenses, and isolated fired sediment lenses with no associated ash or charcoal. Combinations of one or more of the above also occur, including ash/charcoal, ash/fired sediment, and charcoal/fired sediment. *Intrusive* features, those that cross-cut stratigraphic layers, consist of two types: those with high depth to diameter ratios, and those with low depth to diameter ratios. Pits having high depth:diameter ratios are cylindrical with sharply defined walls and bottom. They come in three sizes: small (<38 cm diameter), medium (diameter 40-65 cm), and large (>65 cm diameter). The medium cylindrical pits morphologically match the description for pit hearths at Dust Cave. Pits having low depth:diameter ratios are basin shaped with indistinct boundaries. Shallow basins are less than 15 cm deep and described as "often filled with ash or other evidence of use in cooking or heating" (Ahler 2004). These basins sound morphologically similar to surface hearths at Dust Cave. Other intrusive features include small basins (<65 diameter), large/deep basins (~70 cm diameter), and very large basins (>150 cm diameter).

Complex features are defined as a combination of one or more inclusive features in spatial proximity to, and presumed functional association with, one or more intrusive features. Most complex features consist of small cylindrical pits or shallow basins and an ash/charcoal lens adjacent to the pit and occurring at the surface where the pit or basin originates. In some cases, fired sediments extend along the side walls of the adjacent pit features. This latter description is again consistent with the pit hearths at Dust Cave, which always intrude a prepared surface and which often have small, shallow ash and/or charcoal pits spatially associated with them. Type 3C pits ("large deep basins") are those that are morphologically similar to the Zone P pits at Dust Cave, and which Ahler interprets to be storage pits (see Figures 3.18, 3.19). The pits at Modoc Cave originate in layers 12 and 13A, which date between approximately 7,700 +/- 190 and 8,680 +/- 150 years B.P. (uncal.), corresponding to the Kirk Stemmed component, approximately the same period during which similar pits occur at Dust Cave. Pits re-appear at Modoc in levels 5A and 6, also spanning approximately 7,130 +/-180 to 7,580 +/-190, also overlapping the Kirk Stemmed Component.

Nothing explicitly resembling prepared surfaces was noted in the Modoc Rockshelter report of investigations (Fowler 1959). However, Fowler does note a difference between "prepared fireplaces" and "rock-lined fireplaces." Since many of the prepared surfaces at Dust Cave were described on feature forms as "fireplaces," it is possible that the Modoc fireplaces may also represent prepared surfaces, but this is conjecture only. Thin beds of "fired surfaces" are also discussed in Styles et al. (1983). A glance at the nature of these intact deposits quickly reminds one of those seen in Dust Cave profiles. In his feature typology, Ahler (2004) describes feature type 1B as "fired sediment lenses" which often occur in combination with ash and/or charcoal lenses and which cylindrical pits and/or shallow basins may intrude. Based on this description, it seems very probable that a prepared clay surface technology is represented at Modoc Rockshelter.

Occupational Intensity
Stanfield-Worley Bluff Shelter. There is no quantitative data for traditional occupation proxies, such as lithic density, at Stanfield-Worley Bluff Shelter. Nor can accumulation rates be calculated since there are too few accurate radiocarbon dates. However, based on the increase in projectile point frequency and features of all types, as well as the increased diversity in feature types, occupation intensity clearly increases substantially between the Dalton and later Archaic components.

Russell Cave. The use of Russell Cave was not likely very intensive; fairly low accumulation rates imply that the site was not occupied every year, that the time spent there annually was short, or that the groups were quite small, or some combination of all three (Griffen 1974). Moderate occupation is indicated for the Early Archaic with a slight increase by the Middle Archaic. A decline in intensity during the Late Archaic follows, but then increases again, peaking during the Middle Woodland. Seasonal flooding (especially during the spring) likely precluded more intense occupation during the Early Archaic; the presence of alluvial sediments inter-bedded among cultural sediments corroborates this interpretation.

Modoc Rockshelter. Occupation intensity is based on a comparison of artifact, debitage, faunal and mollusk densities relative to depth, data which can be found in Fowler (1959). Ahler (1993) also discusses occupation intensity. Like Dust Cave, Modoc (West Shelter) was first occupied on bed rock, as soon as it became available for occupation, around 9,000 B.P. Occupation intensity increased slightly through ca. 7,000 B.P., but remained sparse. Several sterile layers interfinger occupational surfaces (Ahler 1993). After 7,000 B.P. activity in both the West and Main shelters increased dramatically. Fowler (1959) notes in the layers dating to this occupation, pits are frequent, the sediment rich in organics, and fire-pits closely bedded. After 4,500 B.P. occupation intensity slackened; by 3,000 B.P., only sporadic use of the West Shelter characterizes the use at the site.

Spatial Organization of Deposits
Stanfield-Worley Bluff Shelter. The organization of deposits at Stanfield-Worley Bluff Shelter contrasts

sharply with that of Dust Cave. Whereas the Dust Cave assemblage exhibited a tightly clustered feature distribution, the Stanfield-Worley assemblage exhibits a much less clustered distribution (Figure 5.3). The Nearest Neighbor ratio for the Dalton component is .80, although this value is statistically insignificant (.5 > p >.2), probably due to the small sample size. All features lie to the northwest of the zone of roof fall, suggesting that the roof fall existed as far back as 8,000 B.C. In general, the two hearths locate centrally, while circular refuse pits focus on the left and "midden-filled depressions" (probably charcoal pits) focus to the far right side of the shelter. If these features do indeed represent refuse deposits, then their positioning far away from domestic activity comes as no surprise. Excavators uncovered two fire hardened clay masses stratigraphically associated with the Dalton component. Interestingly, these patches are associated with numerous, small round depressions in the bedrock floor and adjacent boulders broken off from the brow of the shelter, which Hollenbach (2009:104) interprets to be bedrock mortars. In fact, similar depressions punctuate several large sandstone blocks of roof fall (far left, Figure 5.3). These bedrock mortars not only attest to early nut processing in the middle Tennessee River Valley, but they also represent such an efficient and creative modification to the rockshelter that they may be considered site furniture (*sensu* Binford 1983).

During the Middle and Late Archaic, features are again more evenly distributed than clustered (R=.872, p < .001) (Figure 5.4). There is little apparent patterning, with the exception that features do not extend past the zone of roof fall. There is no central clustering of hearths like that observed at Dust Cave; rather they are scattered throughout the shelter in no apparent pattern. Prepared surfaces cluster somewhat in the right-central portion of the shelter, though this pattern more likely reflects excavation methodology than cultural behavior. Randall (personal communication 2001) suspects that excavators would have encountered these floors more often than they would have recorded them. As during the early years at Dust Cave, the cultural origin of these surfaces is not immediately evident. It was not until water screeners discovered textile impressions on the underside of some of the larger fragments at Dust Cave that researchers began to realize the cultural significance of these unique deposits.

Unlike Dust Cave, burials are not relegated to the rear of the cave, but scattered throughout the shelter. If the different hearth loci reflect different occupations (which they do not necessarily—without detailed stratigraphic context and more radiocarbon dates it is impossible to determine the contemporaneity of features), then burials may have been interred on the opposite side. The only pattern discernable in the Middle through Late Archaic distribution is the miscellaneous refuse pits and rock-lined storage pits placed towards the back wall. Both of these pits types contained several large nutting stones.

The prevalence of nutting stones is staggering; they appear in pits of all kinds, though most commonly in rock-filled storage pits (DeJarnette et al. 1962). Based on this pattern, I suggest that the occupants of Stanfield-Worley cached their nut processing tools for anticipated re-occupation of the site.

Russell Cave. Unfortunately, no information is available to study the spatial organization of deposits at Russell Cave. Even if this data were available, it would mean little since only a small portion of the entrance chamber was excavated.

Modoc Rockshelter. Fowler notes that ash lenses and fire pits consistently occurred about 10 feet from the rock bluff. This undoubtedly afforded additional heat due to the reflection of heat off the back wall. The general living area probably occurred between the fires and the bluff wall, while the refuse (dump) zone is thought to have been outside the fireplace area. In one layer, the distribution of post-molds "made a definite pattern in conjunction with a fire bed and probably represent wind breaks" (Fowler 1959:38). The frequency of habitation features drops sharply above five feet (Late Archaic/Woodland transition), suggesting that after this time, Modoc was occupied more sporadically. Burials are distributed throughout the site. The only noticeable trend in burials is a shift in burial position from tightly flexed to semi-flexed in the later Archaic occupations.

Site Function

Stanfield-Worley Bluff Shelter. The Stanfield-Worley Bluff Shelter was probably occupied intermittently. During the Mississippian and Woodland periods, the site seems to have served as a temporary hunting camp (DeJarnette et al. 1962). This hypothesis is based on the high percentage of projectile points and the relative infrequency of domestic implements (such as pottery). Hunting tools, particularly scrapers, offer some evidence that the site functioned primarily as a hunting camp, though hunting was apparently not practiced to the exclusion of plant gathering and processing. During the Archaic period, the site shows more evidence of having served as a habitation, rather than hunting, camp. A wider array of tools, representing hunting, processing, and manufacturing activities occurs, as well as a very diverse range of feature types. Of particular interest is the large number of nutting stones, caches of mortars and pestles, and prepared surfaces, all of which suggest intense nut processing. Indeed, excavators at Stanfield-Worley often noted parched acorns in pits; Hollenbach (2009:106) came across "several large bags of carbonized acorn meats" in the site collections housed at the DeJarnette Laboratory at the University of Alabama Museums in Moundville, Alabama. Hollenbach's botanical analysis (2009:151) also identified acorn, but in lower quantity than black walnut and hickory. While nut processing seems to have had its roots in the Dalton occupation, there is a clear trend towards intensification over time through the Archaic period.

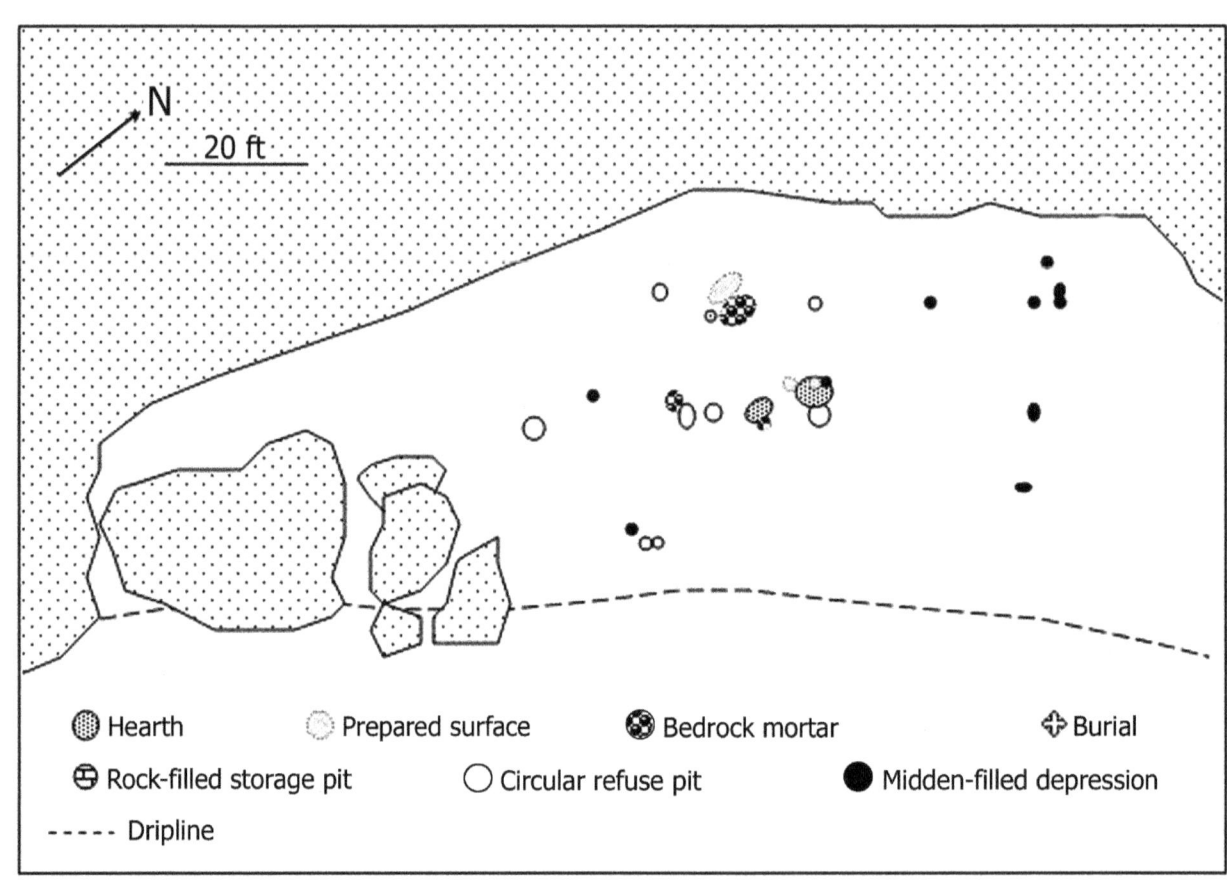

Figure 5.3. Organization of Dalton features at Stanfield-Worley Bluff Shelter.

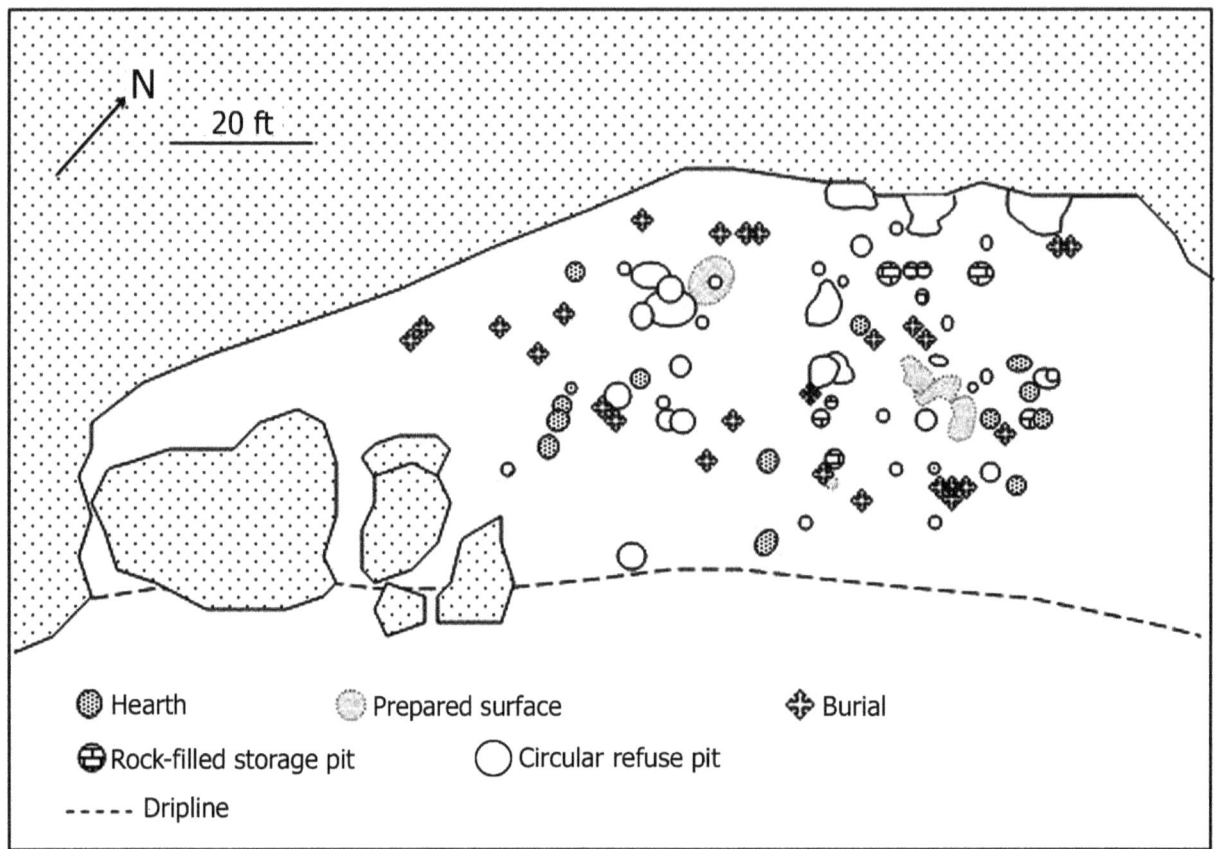

Figure 5.4. Organization of Middle through Late Archaic features at Stanfield-Worley Bluff Shelter.

Russell Cave. As at Dust Cave, there appears to be more change in intensity of activity through time rather than a change in use of the site. During the Early Archaic, occupation was light to moderate, with family groups using the cave as a late fall or winter camp (Griffen 1974: 111). During the Middle Archaic, storage pits appear, but this is the only significant change in the assemblage (Griffen 1974). Other than storage pits, the diversity of tool types and feature types remains fairly constant through time. The only exception in technology is the "re-appearance" of nutting stones in Late Archaic. Sandstone mortars were recovered from the Early Archaic occupation as well, but they are curiously lacking from the Middle Archaic layers. This may indicate that plant processing ceased to occur, though this seems unlikely, especially given the increase in storage facilities. Based on the presence of storage (what Griffen hypothesizes is for acorns and other nuts, the presence of which excavators often noted), prepared surfaces, and possible pit hearths at Russell Cave, I argue that the site functioned primarily as a plant processing site, albeit on a rather small scale, with slightly increasing intensity through time.

Modoc Rockshelter. The intensity of occupation and use of Modoc changed significantly over time. At first, Modoc functioned primarily as a short-term camp (Fowler 1959; Styles et al. 1983), though there is some conflicting evidence for longer-term use (Ahler 1993). Until about 7,000 B.P. occupation was intermittent, especially between 9,000 and 8,500, when the shelter periodically filled in with loess deposits as the valley flooded during early Holocene climatic warming (Fowler 1959). Shortly after 7,000 B.P., Archaic groups reoccupied the site. By the Middle Archaic, selective use of food sources like hickory nuts increased markedly, and people used Modoc for longer periods of time (Ahler 1993; Styles et al. 1983). Increasing artifact, debitage, and feature density all support this hypothesis, as does the increase in grinding implements recovered at the site. Archaic occupation peaked between 6,000 and 5,500 B.C., and the percentage of hickory as a proportion of the total plant assemblage increases to nearly 80%. Ahler (1993) interprets these trends as evidence for use of the site as a base camp. Long term use characterizes the site until about the early Late Archaic. After 3,000 B.P., deer remains and projectile points increase dramatically while domestic and manufacturing tools nearly disappear, leading Fowler (1959) to conclude that Modoc shifted from a domestic habitation to a specialized hunting camp occupied seasonally. This trend compares favorably to those identified at other sites in Illinois, Kentucky and Missouri, in which sites show increasing site specialization. Site surveys in the area indicate that base camp habitation shifted to floodplain locales around 3,500 B.P. (Ahler 1984; Emerson et al. 1986).

Summary
The above comparison of Stanfield-Worley Bluff Shelter, Russell Cave, and Modoc Rockshelter reveal several salient trends occurring from the Early to the Middle Archaic. First, occupation intensity increases at all three sites during the Middle Archaic, just as it does at Dust Cave. This intensity peaks between 7,000 and 4,000 B.P. Secondly, the botanical assemblage at Stanfield-Worley and Modoc indicate a substantial increase in plant use and processing, especially nuts. At Stanfield-Worley, hickory, black walnut, and acorn dominate the plant assemblage by the Middle Archaic; at Modoc—like Dust Cave—hickory dominates, although black walnut and acorn are present in significant quantities. There is no botanical data for Russell Cave, though the site report indicates a probable reliance on acorns and other nuts (Griffen 1974). Finally, at all three sites we see increasing evidence for intensive plant exploitation. At Stanfield-Worley, nutting stones are extremely common and are even stored in pits, some of which seem to be exclusively for nutting tools. At Dust Cave and Modoc Rockshelter (and possibly Russell Cave), evidence for storage pits at the Early Archaic/Middle Archaic transition appears. Thus, the data reviewed here, coupled with the analyses from Dust Cave, indicate that the occupants of caves and rockshelters began to focus on plant exploitation sometime during the late Early Archaic, an activity which intensified with time and peaked during the Middle Archaic. The question that arises, then, is whether sites occupied with the primary purpose of nut processing is unique to caves and rockshelters, or whether this phenomenon occurs at open air sites as well.

OPEN AIR SITES IN THE MIDSOUTH
Evidence for open-air sites specializing in the extraction of nutmeat and nut oil abounds in the Midsouth. At the Buckshaw Bridge site in west-central Illinois, hickory nutshell comprises over 90% of the Middle Archaic botanical assemblage (Asch and Asch 1987; Stafford 1991). Pit features interpreted to be nut boiling pits designed to extract nutmeat and oil are ubiquitous (Stafford 1991:217). These pits, like the pit hearths at Dust Cave, show evidence of *in situ* burning and often contain lenses of nutshell lining their base. Though somewhat larger than those at Dust Cave (166-180 cm in diameter, 45 cm deep), they are round and fairly steep-sided and have similar width to depth ratios as the pits at Dust Cave (3.22 and 3.46, respectively) (Stafford 1991:231). Fuel for fires at Buckshaw Bridge consists primarily of nutshell rather than wood, suggesting that sufficient nutshell was produced to make its use as a fuel a more practical alternative to deadwood. Stafford (1991:227) interprets the Buckshaw Bridge site to be an upland plant processing camp where hickory nuts were processed and the dry nuts and/or oil transported back to a central base camp located at lower elevations. Interestingly, Stafford (1991:218) notes large midden deposits suggesting that a great abundance of waste was being produced. In other words, bulk processing at a short-term camp produces the copious amounts of ashy waste usually considered to be characteristic of a longer-term base camp.

A similar scenario characterizes the Ferry site in southern Illinois. The Ferry site began as a small hunting camp prior to 3,000 B.C. (uncal.). After this point, prepared fireplaces are common, as are large quantities of nutting stones (Fowler 1959). Nutshell dominates the botanical assemblage. Fowler (1959:52) argues that the Ferry site represents a "nut utilizing or collecting" camp. Stafford (1991:219) suggests that the upland sites of Cypress Land and Slim Lake sites also fit the pattern described for the Buckshaw Bridge and Ferry sites.

In contrast to these upland sites, large floodplain sites such as Koster in the Illinois River Valley, Icehouse Bottom in the Little Tennessee River Valley, the Black Earth Site at Carrier Mills, and Indian Knoll in the Green River Valley appear to have been large base camps (Bense 1994; Chapman 1985; Jefferies 1987, 1982; Jefferies and Lynch; Stuever and Holton 1979; Webb 1974). They are characterized by extensive secondary midden deposits, high feature and artifact diversity, and evidence for permanent structures (Chapman 1985; Jefferies 1987; Stafford 1991; Stuever and Holton 1979; Webb 1974). Koster, in particular, comprises a cultural sequence from seasonal hunter-gatherer camps during the Paleoindian to sedentary camps during the Middle Archaic (Brown and Vierra 1985; Struever and Holton 1979). In the Tennessee River Valley, sites such as Eva, Anderson and Mulberry Creek, became the loci for large shell middens, which many have suggested reflect an increasingly sedentary strategy by 6,000-5,000 cal. B.C. (Anderson 2001; Bense 1994; Walthall 1980). Stafford (1991) notes that these river valley sites also have evidence for subterranean storage.

During the first part of the Middle Archaic, settlement and subsistence patterns in the Midsouth paralleled the band-macroband settlement pattern of the Early Archaic (Anderson and Hanson 1988; Bense 1994). Then, around 5,000 B.C., settlement strategies appear to have shifted in several river valleys, including the Lower Ohio and Lower Tennessee River Valleys (Bense 1994; Jefferies 2008) and across the Midwest (Cook 1976; Jefferies and Butler 1982; Lewis 1983; Munson 1980; Stafford 1991). In these valleys, large multi-season base camps emerged consisting of thick midden deposits and "hundreds of domestic-related features," the most common of which are pits and hearths. (Bense 1994:82). Shell middens develop and shell processing pits appear, indicative of a developing riverine adaptation. Baden (1985) has shown that site densities along the Tennessee River in the Tellico Reservoir in East Tennessee increased throughout the Middle Archaic period, with the greatest density of residential bases occurring in the lowlands, along the river and its primary tributaries. In the Midwest and Lower Ohio Valley, it has been argued that these trends reflect an emerging strategy of logistically organized settlement among Middle Archaic populations (Brown and Vierra 1983; Jefferies 2008:274-275).

This is not to suggest that there were no upland sites, only that the relative proportion of upland camps to lowland base camps shifts during the latter half of the Middle Archaic period. Indeed, Jefferies (2008:275) notes that hunter-gatherers established multi-seasonal base camps in lowland areas, which were used in conjunction with upland sites where task-specific activities occurred. This trend appears to occur in the Middle Tennessee Valley as well. For example, in a study of the five-county region around Dust Cave, Goldman-Finn (1994) found that the number of floodplain sites increases from 13 to 20% from the Early to the Middle Archaic. Hollenbach (2009) noted a similar trend in her recent review of settlement patterning in the Middle Tennessee Valley. She showed that during the Kirk Stemmed and Eva/Morrow Mountain phases, sites tend to be located at lower elevation near rivers and major tributaries relative to earlier periods. She also notes a significant decrease in the reoccupation of sites in the Kirk Stemmed and Eva/Morrow Mountain phases suggesting that Middle Archaic populations were re-establishing more new sites rather than reoccupying old ones. These different patterns during the Middle Archaic period suggest a shift in the way hunter-gatherers used the landscape over time, and one that occurs simultaneously with the intensification of hickory nut use, as well as a shift in the exploitation of animals associated with closed habitats (Walker 1998). Such a shift may relate to the drying of sinkholes during the middle Holocene warming and drying trend associated with the Hypsithermal, indicating that Early and Middle Archaic people coped with large scale environmental changes of the Holocene by shifting site locales and subsistence strategies

This is the same pattern that Stafford (1994, 1991) observes in the Lower Illinois River Valley. During the Early Archaic, he argues that numerous residential camps existed throughout a drainage basin, to which foraging groups traveled both within and between seasons (Figure 5.5). He further argues that due to warming and drying during the Middle and Late Archaic, hunter-gatherer settlement strategies shifted in order to take advantage of new resources such as shellfish and upland mast (i.e., nuts including acorn, walnut, and hickory). In this scenario, the majority of upland sites are temporary camps functioning as mast processing sites (i.e., extraction camps), while lowland sites are generally base camps, from which logistical forays were launched to the upland sites.

DISCUSSION AND SUMMARY

There is a clear shift in site use at most of the caves and rockshelters discussed in this chapter. By the Middle Archaic, occupation intensity increases markedly, the use of nutshell (particularly hickory) proliferates, and new feature types emerge, most notably pit hearths and storage pits. Such changes have been documented at numerous upland sites throughout the American Bottom and Southeast, sites which Stafford (1991) convincingly argues functioned as special plant processing loci. I propose that during the Middle Archaic some cave and rockshelter sites functioned similarly to upland, open-air plant extractive sites. Such sites contrast sharply with river valley sites which, by the Middle Archaic, functioned as base camps used to stage resource procurement of upland resources for storage at the base camps (Stafford 1991, 1994).

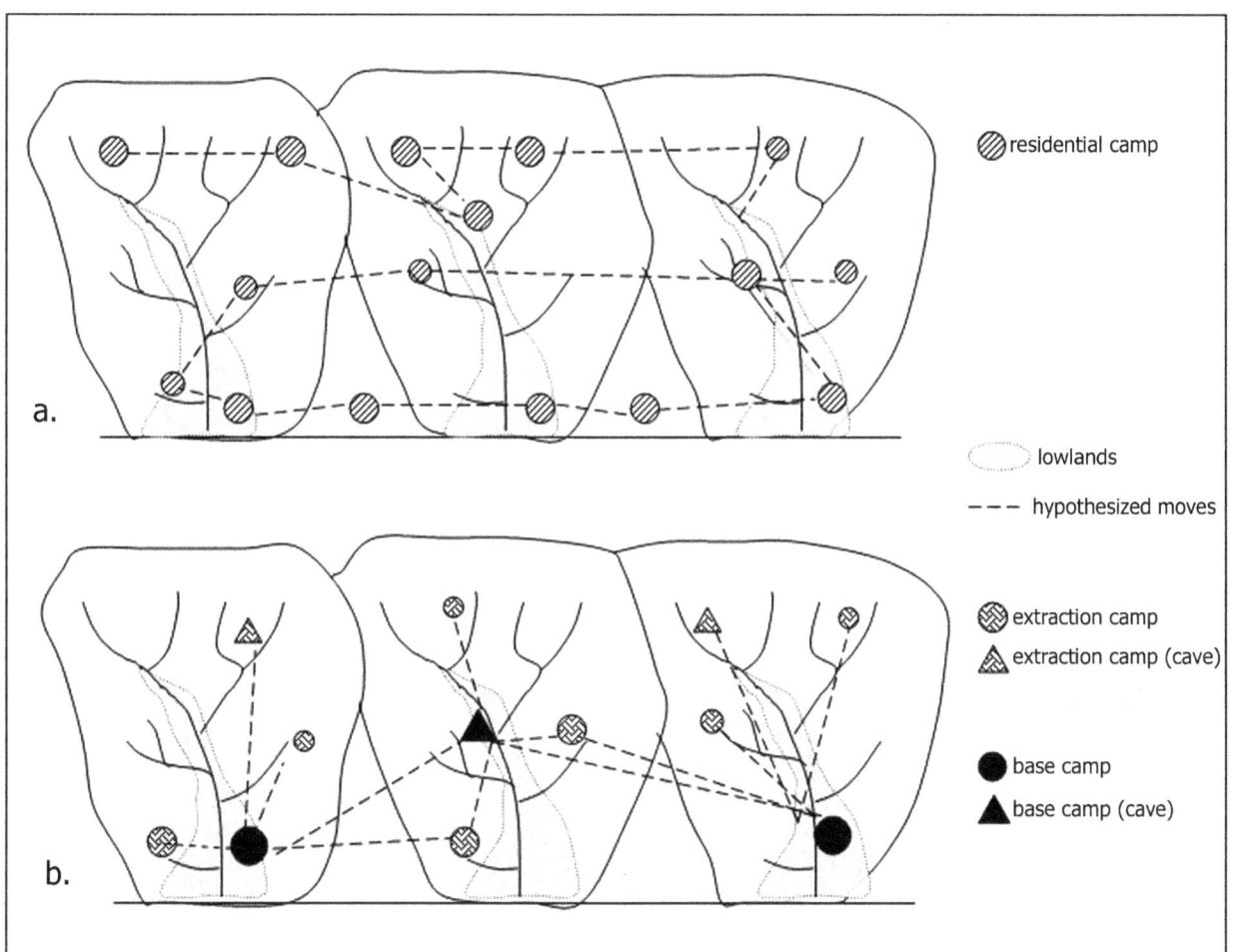

Figure 5.5. Model of Early (a) and Middle (b) Archaic settlement strategies. Site size indicates residence duration and/or frequency of use (modified from Stafford 1994:Figure 5).

Such a scenario fits best with a logistical mobility strategy in which collectors live at a base camp, but target specific resources (such as nuts) which can be moved to consumers (*sensu* Binford 1980). Such a logistical strategy should occur in regions of patchy, heterogeneous resources. There are several characteristics of nut availability which would make a logistical collecting strategy (i.e., low residential mobility) more adaptive. First, nut trees produce at irregular intervals (Gardner 1997; Munson 1986; Talalay et al. 1984). Individual trees rarely yield abundant harvests in consecutive years, thereby adding an element of unpredictability to nut collecting. Second, most nuts are only available for a limited amount of time, usually a few weeks in the late summer to early fall (Talalay et al. 1984:345). This short harvest time is further limited by competition for nuts by animals, especially squirrels. These two factors—irregular production intervals and limited harvest time—add significant spatio-temporal variance to nut collection by creating incongruities in their distribution. Under such circumstances, a logistical mobility strategy used by collectors would be more adaptive in dealing with these incongruities than the residential mobility strategy used by foragers (Binford 1980). A logistical strategy would allow groups to target patchy mast resources by sending logistical collecting parties out with the primary purpose of harvesting and processing nuts which could then be brought back to the base camp—in other words, moving resources to consumers (Binford 1980). Stafford (1991) has already shown that upland sites most likely functioned as logistical camps at which short-term nut processing took place. I propose that many upland caves and rockshelters also functioned as temporary camps occupied with the primary purpose of exploiting mast. Occupation of these sites would be limited by the duration of nuts on the ground, up to a few weeks during the autumn. The intense bulk processing of nuts, through boiling and parching, would easily produce so much waste that the sites would appear to have been occupied for much longer periods of time.

Using a logistical strategy to deal with the spatio-temporal variance associated with mast resources is consistent with the predictions of models developed in optimal foraging theory (e.g., Anderson and Hanson 1988; Bettinger 1991; Dwyer and Minnegal 1985; Kelly 1995; Wilmsen 1973). Several researchers have modeled forager dispersion as a function of the patchiness of food resources (Horn 1968; Dwyer and Minnegal 1985). Heterogeneous resources distributed in a patchy fashion (in space and/or time), are most efficiently exploited by aggregated collectors. Nuts, particularly hickory, fit this model of patchy distribution. Under Horn's (1968) model, they are more effectively exploited from a central base by aggregated groups of collectors (i.e., a logistical foray) than by mobile, dispersed groups.

Using ethnographic data, Kelly (1983, 1995) has also examined the relationship between biomes with low primary biomass and the number of residential moves made by hunter-gatherers per year. Primary biomass is inversely related to the effective abundance of vegetable food. In other words, plants that produce much edible food are said to have low primary biomass while plants that produce little edible food are said to have high primary biomass. For example, in the tropics many tree species have much of their biomass taken up in inedible structural components (i.e., high primary biomass). In contrast, nut-bearing deciduous species such as oak, hickory and walnut invest less energy in structural components and more energy in edible reproductive tissue such as seeds and nuts (i.e., low primary biomass). Thus, in areas of low primary biomass, edible plant matter *increases*. Kelly's (1983) ethnographic data showed a strong negative correlation between overall food density and the number of residential moves per year. In other words, as primary biomass decreases and food density *increases*, mobility *decreases*. Thus we would expect hunter-gatherer groups living in zones of lower primary biomass to make fewer residential moves per year than hunter-gatherer groups living in zones of higher primary biomass.

As the middle Holocene progressed, warmer, drier conditions developed which facilitated the spread of oak-hickory forests over much of the Southeast and American Midsouth. Oak-hickory forests, which produce abundant edible material in the form of acorns and hickory nuts, are considered to be low in primary biomass (Kelly 1983, 1995). Therefore, based on Kelly's research, we would predict decreased hunter-gatherer mobility during the warmer and drier middle Holocene relative to the cooler and wetter early Holocene.

Binford (1980) and Harpending and Davis (1977) further argue that low resource predictability leads to decreased mobility and increased food storage. Food storage is a means by which the temporal availability of resources is extended, thereby making the resource more predictable. Bulk processing of nuts through boiling and parching would turn raw nuts into a resource suitable for storage. Oil could last a long time (Gardner 1997; Talalay et al. 1984). Parching nuts killed the molds, fungi, or insects that led to rapid decomposition (Gardner 1997). Moreover, parching would also kill the nut embryos so that germination could not occur during storage (Gardner 1997; Talalay et al. 1984).

In the American Midsouth, the highest densities of mast trees, especially hickory, would have occurred in the uplands. It appears that during the Middle Archaic in regions throughout the Midwest and Midsouth, a logistical strategy emerged in which groups resided at lowland base camps for some portion of the year, but deployed nut collecting parties to the uplands during the late summer and early fall in order to exploit mast. These parties lived at the temporary plant processing sites for a few days to a few weeks at a time, processing nuts into storable forms which they then brought back to the central base camp for longer term use and storage. The fact that storage disappears from sites such as Dust Cave and Modoc Rockshelter sometime after 7,000 cal. B.C. suggests that storage was occurring elsewhere (i.e., the base camp).

In sum, the climate of the Middle Archaic was significantly warmer and drier than the preceding Early Archaic. Warmer and drier conditions resulted in an increase in oak and hickory (among other nut-bearing trees), which soon spread throughout the American Midsouth. The oak-hickory forests increased the patchiness and unpredictability of plant resources while at the same time lowering the overall primary biomass in the region. Ethnographic analogy, Binford's Forager-Collector model and optimal foraging models all predict increasingly logistical behavior under such conditions. Thus, the trend seen in the Middle Tennessee River Valley of upland plant processing sites and lowland base camps during the Middle Archaic is consistent with the expectations derived from these models.

# Chapter 6

MODELING THE ROLE OF CAVES AND ROCKSHELTERS IN THE AMERICAN MIDSOUTH

The present study has developed a geoarchaeological and spatial framework for the analysis and interpretation of archaeological features in palimpsest contexts such as caves and rockshelters. Applying this methodological and theoretical construct to the site of Dust Cave demonstrates the important kinds of behavioral data contained in features. While many previous studies of feature function rely solely on morphological characteristics and/or content to determine function, this study developed a multi-disciplinary approach which integrates macromorphological, micromorphological, and geochemical analyses in order to interpret their form, function and organization. The addition of microscopic and chemical characterization of anthropogenic sediments provides a more holistic picture of the types and diversity of activities occurring at archaeological sites, as well as the many taphonomic processes that inherently obscure this record and lead to erroneous or incomplete reconstructions of past human behavior. Since modeling hunter-gatherer settlement and subsistence strategies necessarily relies on accurate interpretation at the site-level, it is vital that we correctly interpret the activities occurring at individual sites. Well designed feature analyses provide both complimentary and supplemental data to that which is traditionally derived from lithics, botanical, and faunal remains; in so doing, their study greatly enhances our understanding of Paleoindian and Archaic-period site use and settlement-subsistence strategies in the American Midsouth.

This analysis has highlighted a number of fundamental points about what archaeologists traditionally refer to as features. First, they are best studied by conceptualizing them as *anthropogenic deposits* and analyzing the sediments in terms of their source, transport agent, depositional environment, and post-depositional activity. Second, this study has emphasized the need for robust analyses of features so that the great diversity of activities they represent is not masked by a generic term such as "hearth." Instead, we must ask ourselves important questions, including whether sediments are burned *in situ* or not, and whether they have been redeposited during their history. Finally, this study highlighted the important role post-depositional and diagenetic processes have in altering the original morphology of deposits. The two processes having the greatest impact on the Dust Cave sediments, decalcification and fluvial activity, occur predominantly in the lower meter of deposits. Decalcification has resulted in the dissolution of ash and subsequent compaction of sediments, a process which ultimately decreases the size of features and artificially enriches them in charcoal. As a result, the Paleoindian and Early Archaic components appear to represent more ephemeral occupations than may actually have existed. Localized fluvial activity, in the form of dripping water through the cave ceiling and sheetwash during flood events, has similarly obscured features by washing away the light ash and obliterating feature morphology beyond recognition. Due to these destructive processes, we should never interpret feature function based on morphology alone; to do so is to risk substantial misinterpretation of human behavior.

The activities occurring at Dust Cave include cooking, burial, nut processing, refuse disposal and possibly storage. Perhaps the most important feature type identified which was previously unknown is hearths built to extract nut oil and/or parch nuts. These pit hearths look morphologically similar to the nut processing pits described for open-air sites in the Midwest (Stafford 1994; Gardner 1997). They contain large amounts of partially combusted plant material, suggesting low temperature heating. Moreover, they contain large quantities of nut charcoal and high strontium values, an element that occurs in exceptionally high concentration in nuts (Rosenthal 1981), further supporting the interpretation that these hearths functioned as nut processing pits.

This study identified numerous other feature types. Large surface hearths functioned for broiling, and also likely served as the foci around which non-cooking activities occurred, such as tool maintenance, sleeping, and/or general socializing. Shallow expedient hearths probably served as hearths for quick grilling and smoking of foods such as shellfish and fish, although they may also have been used to parch nuts. Many of these small hearths are located near the cave walls, suggesting that they may have doubled as sleeping fires that reflected light and heat off the walls. Some of the charcoal pits in the early components at the site probably functioned as expedient hearths, but it is difficult to establish this because of the dissolution of ash, though the fact that many of these pits are full of burned fish bones lends some support for this interpretation.

Another important finding is the presence of possible storage pits during the Kirk Stemmed (late Early Archaic) component. At an average of 80 cm long and 40 cm deep, these features are the largest at the site. The heterogeneous and chaotic nature of the pit fill suggests that they served as refuse; however, the straight-sided, flat-bottomed pits are characteristic of later period storage pits seen at other sites (e.g., Modoc Rockshelter). Interestingly, they only occur during the Kirk Stemmed component. Regardless of their function, their disappearance reflects a change in the use of the site.

Refuse and fireplace rake-out deposits dominate the feature assemblage during all five components. Refuse occurs both in and around hearths in the form of primary refuse deposits (scraped out coals and cooking stones), and in the rear of the cave as secondary rake-out deposits. Other refuse deposits are so thick that researchers excavated them as zones. These deposits—essentially middens—become thicker towards the rear of the cave. Concentrations of debitage, bone, and shell mirror this pattern. The overall thickness of these deposits attests to the intense burning that must have occurred in order to generate such vast quantities of combusted material. Based on the enormous quantities of ash and nut charcoal, exceptionally high strontium values, and numerous nut processing hearths occurring during the Middle Archaic, the processing of mast resources must have constituted the primary activity at the site, at least during the late Early and early Middle Archaic periods.

The organization of activities at Dust Cave appears to have been constrained largely by natural processes, namely the size of the shelter and the microtopography inside the entrance chamber. Features are tightly clustered, as one would expect given the small size of the shelter, and suggest a space conserving strategy by the occupants of the site. Feature distributions clearly reflect the importance of fluvial activity on the east side of the entrance chamber, especially early on during the Late Paleoindian and Early Side Notched occupations. By the late Early Archaic, the site dried out. Ceiling height was ample and there was little geologic constraint on feature placement. Features during the Kirk Stemmed and Eva/Morrow Mountain components are widely distributed and the site was intensively occupied. Not until the late Middle Archaic occupation—the Benton component—did use of the cave decrease. The dominant constraint during this period relates to ceiling height; indeed, by 3,600 cal. B.C., lack of headroom precluded further occupation of the site.

Despite these geologic constraints, some cultural patterns emerge which largely conform to the ethnographic use of caves and rockshelters by modern hunter-gatherers. First, hearths are located centrally, about midway between the back wall and the dripline. This is partly functional—such a location afforded the greatest ventilation—but also reflects the use of hearths as foci of social activities in addition to cooking. Fires that could have served as sleeping fires tend to occur in close proximity to cave walls, a location that would maximize heat by reflecting it off the walls. Refuse and burials were placed away from the center of domestic activity, along the periphery of the site. Finally, nut processing seems to have focused on the east side of the shelter, within the general cooking/habitation area, but still somewhat separated from this loci, in as much as space could be segmented in a small cave.

Overall, the use of Dust Cave differs in *intensity* of use over time, more so than in the *types* of activities occurring. It appears that something happened around 8,000 B.C. which prompted hunter-gatherers to use Dust Cave more intensively. The proportion of nutshell in the botanical record increases, nutting stones appear, and storage pits appear, although these disappear by the Middle Archaic. This same trend occurs at the other cave sites analyzed in this project, including Stanfield-Worley Bluff Shelter, Russell Cave, and Modoc Rockshelter. The question is, what happened during the Middle Archaic that prompted hunter-gatherers to use caves and rockshelters in this different, more intense, way?

Walthall (1998a) has argued that hunter-gatherers first exploited the habitation potential of rockshelters during the Late Paleoindian period. In his model, shelters functioned as temporary camps. But he suggests that during the Middle Archaic a major reorganization occurred, prompting groups to use shelters in very different ways than they had previously. It is during this period that Walthall notes that shelter floors become strewn with storage pits, processing pits, earth ovens, and burials. He argues that the increased use of caves and rockshelters reflects longer and more intensive use of these sites as longer-term base camps.

At Dust Cave, and the other sites considered in chapter 5, we have certainly seen evidence for such a reorganization, though it appears to have occurred towards the end of the Early Archaic, somewhat earlier than Walthall suggests. I further argue that this reorganization is not one in which caves are used as long-term base camps. Rather, central base camps were generally restricted to lowland, riverine settings, while upland sites, including caves and rockshelters, functioned as specialized extraction camps, including plant processing sites. We have seen that bulk processing of such materials can result in high pit densities and large quantities of refuse—so much in fact, that the site may take on the characteristic appearance of a long-term base camp. Thus, the prodigious pit digging and waste accumulation at such sites testifies only to the *intensity* of activity occurring there, rather than the duration it was occupied.

The exception to this trend may be Modoc Rockshelter. Styles et al. (1983) and others (Bense 1994) have suggested that during the Middle Archaic, Modoc served as a residential base camp. Based on the high diversity of features and tools, postmolds, large size of the shelter, and storage pits, the authors convincingly argue that Modoc represents a base camp. Its floodplain location nestled along a bluffline further fits the pattern of lowland base camp in Stafford's (1994) model. Rockshelter and cave sites such as Modoc have undoubtedly led some researchers to conclude that there is a shift at all caves towards longer term base camps. This study, however, has shown that some caves and rockshelters functioned as temporary extraction camps. Dust Cave, although a bluffline site like Modoc, was most likely occupied temporarily, albeit possibly during several times in the course of a year. Sites like Modoc, then, mask important variation in cave and rockshelter use, thereby giving the impression that *all* caves and rockshelters functioned as residential base camps.

The question still remains, what caused such sites to become the focus of plant processing? Munson (1986) has argued that this shift resulted from a technological change during the Middle Archaic. In particular, he argues that the adoption of stone boiling as a technique for removing hickory nutmeats from their shells transformed hickories from one of the most costly to the least costly nuts to process. In this scenario, the addition of abundant hickory nuts to the diet raised the carrying capacity of the local forests and allowed population aggregation and increased residential permanence in the river bottom habitats.

There are several problems with this interpretation, however. First, as Gardner (1997) notes, if hickory were that costly to process prior to the Middle Archaic, one would not expect them to occur in any great quantity during the Early Archaic or the Paleoindian. To the contrary, botanical studies suggest that hickory nutshell actually makes up a large proportion of the plant remains during early occupations (Stafford 1991). At Dust Cave, for example, hickory nutshell dominates the carbonized plant assemblage as early as the Late Paleoindian (Hollenbach 2009; Walker et al. 2001). Asch and Asch (1985) note that hickory is very common in Early Archaic sites in the Midwest as well. Second, if stone boiling did have such a dramatic adaptive effect, we would expect the innovation to rapidly diffuse throughout the eastern Woodlands. But looking at the relative contribution of hickory at Modoc Rockshelter versus Koster, the timing of the sharp increase in hickory use differs by nearly a millennium (Gardner 1997:175). It would seem that an adaptive technology would cause an increase in hickory exploitation at all sites within a fairly short time frame. Finally, stone boiling dates as far back as the Paleoindian (Sassaman 1993:113). It seems unlikely that a technology with such antiquity would not have been adapted to nut processing earlier than the Middle Archaic.

A more parsimonious explanation for the intensified hunter-gatherer use of caves in the Midsouth is changing vegetation communities resulting from middle Holocene warming and drying. Computer-generated climate reconstructions and pollen cores both suggest that by 8,000 B.C., annual temperatures in the Midsouth increased by more than two degrees while annual precipitation decreased by about 200 mm/year (Bryson 1999a, b; Delcourt and Delcourt 1987). These warmer and drier conditions are conducive to hickory tree growth (Thompson et al. 1999). Indeed, pollen reconstructions demonstrate that hickory trees in particular migrated into the Tennessee River Valley in significant numbers around 8,000 B.C. (Delcourt and Delcourt 1987). These vegetation changes coincide with an increase in hickory nut charcoal, appearance of pit hearths, increase in feature diversity, and intensified site use at cave and rockshelter sites beginning in the late Early Archaic. Thus, the changing use of caves and rockshelters is not necessarily one of *longer term* occupation as base camps, but rather one of intensified use as *special-purpose* sites dedicated to the collection and processing of increasingly available mast resources.

The evidence presented here suggests that the changing use of caves and rockshelters noted by Walthall reflects the changing environmental conditions of the middle Holocene. This warming and drying increased the availability of mast resources such as hickory nuts, a product very desirable to Middle Archaic hunter-gatherers in the Midsouth. Upland sites such as Dust Cave would have been ideally situated to take advantage of them. These upland sites functioned as special-purpose extraction locations dedicated to nut collecting and processing for future use at a central base camp located in lower elevation habitats. This is not to suggest that nut processing never occurred at lowland base camps; certainly nut resources grew there too. However, the low spatio-temporal predictability of mast would have necessitated exploitation from multiple sites (Stafford 1994, 1991). Logistically organized groups would therefore have been the most effective strategy for taking full advantage of these nut resources. Thus, the shift from high to low residential mobility is integrally tied to changes in climate and the concomitant shift in vegetative communities. Such an environment required a different mobility strategy in order to maximize the profit from new resources emerging as part of these broader vegetation changes. The more intense use of caves and rockshelters are just part of this complex shift. As such, caves and rockshelters represent special purpose, plant extraction and processing sites embedded within a larger logistical settlement-subsistence strategy.

Appendix A. Attributes for Dust Cave Features

Feature[1,2]	Top depth	Bottom depth	min N	max N	min W	max W	Zone	Component[3]	Shape	Field Description[4]	Mapped as:
6	135	148	60.80	61.20	66.20	66.64	D	Benton	oval	pit	
13	230	260	60.40	61.40	67.00	67.60	J3	Eva/Morrow	irregular	burial	Burial
16	225	232	59.75	60.22	67.10	67.60	J3	Eva/Morrow	circular	cc pit	Charcoal pit
23	185	215	61.80	62.25	63.45	63.85	E	Eva/Morrow	oval	cc pit	Charcoal pit
25	140	150	61.45	61.95	67.10	68.00	D	Benton	oval	burial	Burial
27	295	306	61.25	61.95	66.30	67.25	N	Eva/Morrow	oval	hearth	Surface hearth
28	225	228	61.40	61.60	66.30	66.50	K	Eva/Morrow	circular	cc pit	Charcoal pit
33	330	339	61.60	62.10	66.10	66.55	P	Kirk	oval	pit	
36	285	287	61.75	62.05	63.60	63.82	K3	Eva/Morrow	oval	ash pit	Ash pit
38	230	250	59.20	60.10	58.40	59.30	J	Eva/Morrow	circular	unknown	
40	266	274	60.40	60.62	62.40	62.66	K	Eva/Morrow	circular	cc/ash pit	Expedient hearth?
41	142	160	58.45	58.85	63.10	63.50	D	Benton	circular	Cc/ash pit	Pit hearth?
44	173	185	56.84	57.10	63.40	63.74	E9	Eva/Morrow	oval	cc pit	Charcoal pit
45	172	179	59.45	59.78	62.80	63.05	E1	Eva/Morrow	oval	cc pit	Charcoal pit
46	180	181	59.30	59.50	63.35	63.68	E1	Eva/Morrow	circular	cc smear	
47	162	184	58.30	59.20	64.00	64.28	D7	Benton	oval	hearth	Surface hearth
48	180	188	56.75	57.15	63.40	63.73	E9	Eva/Morrow	circular	cc pit	Charcoal pit
49	180	184	57.53	57.87	63.48	63.80	E9	Eva/Morrow	circular	ash pit	Ash pit
50	180	191	57.69	57.97	63.10	63.35	E9	Eva/Morrow	circular	cc pit	Charcoal pit
52	190	201	59.70	60.30	62.80	63.60	E1	Eva/Morrow	irregular	cc pit	Charcoal pit
53	190	192	58.65	58.90	63.05	63.25	E1	Eva/Morrow	oval	cc pit	Charcoal pit
54	190	204	58.04	58.50	63.00	63.45	E1	Eva/Morrow	unknown	cc pit	Charcoal pit
55	200	205	57.80	58.20	63.20	63.45	E	Eva/Morrow	oval	cc pit	Charcoal pit
56	200	208	57.73	57.95	63.45	63.75	E	Eva/Morrow	oval	cc pit	Charcoal pit

Feature[1,2]	Top depth	Bottom depth	min N	max N	min W	max W	Zone	Component[3]	Shape	Field Description[4]	Mapped as:
57	200	212	58.28	58.70	62.50	62.95	E1	Eva/Morrow	circular	cc pit	Charcoal pit
59	210	216	57.40	57.91	63.50	63.90	E	Eva/Morrow	oval	cc pit	Charcoal pit
60	210	225	57.65	58.50	63.05	63.95	E	Eva/Morrow	circular	hearth	Surface hearth
61	215	221	58.85	59.11	63.68	63.94	J	Eva/Morrow	circular	cc pit	Charcoal pit
62	215	223	59.65	60.25	62.88	63.42	J	Eva/Morrow	circular	rock pit	Rock cluster
63	212	230	59.63	59.87	63.38	63.66	J	Eva/Morrow	circular	pit	
67	222	248	59.50	60.30	61.60	62.45	J	Eva/Morrow	irregular	rock pit	Rock cluster
68	236	250	56.85	57.13	63.82	64.02	J	Eva/Morrow	irregular	cc pit	Charcoal pit
69	215	235	60.40	60.81	62.74	63.17	E	Eva/Morrow	circular	cc pit	Charcoal pit
71	248	275	56.10	58.90	63.45	63.95	K	Eva/Morrow	oval	burial	Burial
72	240	249	58.05	58.35	63.35	63.61	J	Eva/Morrow	irregular	cc pit	Charcoal pit
78	245	258	58.15	58.98	62.10	62.85	J3	Eva/Morrow	oval	hearth?	Surface hearth
79	248	260	58.80	59.21	61.97	62.46	J3	Eva/Morrow	circular	cc pit	Scrape out
82	253	267	58.70	59.10	62.44	62.80	K3	Eva/Morrow	circular	cc/ash pit	Scrape out?
83	241	260	61.50	61.84	61.80	62.20	J5	Eva/Morrow	circular	cc/ash pit	Pit hearth
88	245	251	62.80	63.18	62.50	62.96	J3	Eva/Morrow	oval	cc pit	Scrape out
92	252	257	62.25	62.65	61.55	61.95	K3	Eva/Morrow	circular	cc pit	Scrape out
93	475	480	58.48	58.71	63.50	63.75	U3	Paleo	circular	ash pit	Ash pit
95	256	268	63.15	63.60	63.12	63.60	J3	Eva/Morrow	oval	burial	Burial
97	255	261	63.70	64.20	63.20	63.75	K4	Eva/Morrow	circular	cc/ash pit	rakeout
98	283	293	58.90	59.70	63.05	63.85	N4	Eva/Morrow	oval	hearth	Surface hearth
99	452	454	63.40	63.65	62.75	63.00	U3	Paleo	irregular	cc smudge	
100	253	281	63.10	63.62	62.90	63.40	K3	Eva/Morrow	oval	burial	Burial
101	257	273	62.62	63.25	63.54	64.15	K4	Eva/Morrow	circular	cc/ash pit	Expedient hearth
102	309	316	59.20	59.70	63.30	63.80	P3	Kirk	circular	rock cluster	Surface hearth

Feature[1,2]	Top depth	Bottom depth	min N	max N	min W	max W	Zone	Component[3]	Shape	Field Description[4]	Mapped as:
103	260	270	62.65	62.95	63.20	63.45	K4	Eva/Morrow	oval	burial	Burial
104	278	294	63.26	63.60	63.04	63.36	N8	Eva/Morrow	circular	pit	
107	283	286	62.12	62.51	63.41	63.82	N8	Eva/Morrow	circular	cc/ash pit	
108	266	286	63.88	64.25	63.00	63.80	J3	Eva/Morrow	irregular	burial	Burial
111	346	388	59.63	60.60	63.96	64.16	P3e	Kirk	oval	rock pit	Rock cluster
114	356	371	62.20	63.20	62.44	63.30	Q	Kirk/ESN	oval	hearth?	
115	410	430	57.32	57.84	63.78	64.26	T2	Paleo	circular	cc pit	Charcoal pit
116	419	424	59.43	59.75	63.12	63.44	T2	Paleo	circular	cc pit	Charcoal pit
117	413	430	59.12	59.96	63.42	64.40	T5	Paleo	circular	hearth	Surface Hearth
118	455	460	59.58	59.95	63.62	64.06	U3	Paleo	oval	cc pit	Charcoal pit
119	156	160	57.80	58.25	64.42	64.71	E1	Eva/Morrow	oval	hearth	Surface hearth
120	148	167	60.25	60.70	64.70	65.40	D3	Benton	unknown	burial	Burial
121	155	169	58.35	59.25	63.65	64.65	D5	Benton	circular	hearth	Surface hearth
122	185	197	62.64	63.40	64.45	65.12	E1	Benton	oval	rock pit	Rock cluster
123	160	180	60.78	61.23	64.30	64.80	D4b	Benton	circular	Cc/ash pit	Expedient hearth
124	193	214	62.16	62.68	63.70	64.10	E1	Eva/Morrow	circular	cc/ash pit	Ash pit
127	165	171	57.86	58.18	64.02	64.25	D5	Benton	oval	cc pit	Rake out?
128	193	218	62.25	63.00	64.65	65.50	E1	Eva/Morrow	unknown	burial	Burial
129	207	215	62.06	62.60	64.12	64.65	E5	Eva/Morrow	circular	layered cc/ash pit	Expedient hearth?
133	215	228	62.83	63.26	64.16	64.53	E5	Eva/Morrow	oval	cc pit	Charcoal pit
134	170	192	58.45	59.04	64.07	65.53	D4	Benton	circular	cc pit	Scrape out?
135	170	180	58.56	58.97	64.39	64.87	D4	Benton	circular	cc/ash pit	Expedient hearth
136	174	185	58.96	59.70	64.18	65.04	D4	Benton	oval	Hearth?	Surface hearth
137	169	173	57.72	57.95	64.71	64.90	D3	Benton	circular	cc pit	Scrape out
138	175	190	59.65	60.30	64.78	65.35	D4	Benton	circular	cc/ash pit	Expedient hearth?

Feature[1,2]	Top depth	Bottom depth	min N	max N	min W	max W	Zone	Component[3]	Shape	Field Description[4]	Mapped as:
139	229	232	62.42	64.54	64.04	64.24	J1	Eva/Morrow	circular	cc pit	Charcoal pit
140	185	200	59.17	59.62	64.10	64.52	E1	Eva/Morrow	circular	hearth	Surface hearth
141	191	202	61.42	61.73	64.83	65.11	E1	Eva/Morrow	oval	cc pit	Charcoal pit
142	193	207	61.10	61.48	64.80	65.15	E1	Eva/Morrow	circular	pit	
145	190	204	58.02	58.37	64.40	64.75	E5	Eva/Morrow	circular	ash pit	Ash pit
146	171	176	59.20	59.45	61.57	62.75	D	Benton	circular	cc pit	Charcoal pit
150	189	219	58.70	59.70	64.12	64.98	E5	Eva/Morrow	oval	hearth	Surface hearth
152	205	211	59.17	59.48	61.28	61.60	E1	Eva/Morrow	circular	cc pit	Charcoal pit
154	189	205	58.38	58.68	64.73	65.13	E5	Eva/Morrow	oval	cc pit	Charcoal pit
156	197	205	59.54	59.80	64.86	65.38	E8	Eva/Morrow	circular	cc/ash pit	Expedient hearth
158	199	202	60.04	60.60	64.18	64.67	E5	Eva/Morrow	circular	cc conc	Charcoal pit
159	200	208	59.60	59.80	64.00	64.18	E5	Eva/Morrow	circular	cc conc	Scrape out
161	166	175	60.03	60.43	61.45	61.84	D	Benton	circular	cc pit	Scrape out
165	203	208	59.65	60.10	64.23	64.54	E1	Eva/Morrow	circular	cc pit	Charcoal pit
167	225	230	61.41	61.75	64.60	64.90	J1	Eva/Morrow	circular	pit	
168	180	188	60.50	60.85	61.28	61.70	D4	Benton	oval	cc pit	Expedient hearth?
169	185	205	60.25	60.53	61.50	61.78	D4	Benton	circular	ash pit	Ash pit
170	215	227	58.30	58.75	64.82	65.21	J1	Eva/Morrow	circular	rock pit	Rock cluster
171	215	223	58.32	58.77	64.64	64.92	E1	Eva/Morrow	circular	cc pit	Charcoal pit
172	215	221	59.10	59.65	64.55	65.20	J1	Eva/Morrow	circular	pit	
173	217	229	58.93	59.12	64.88	65.06	J1	Eva/Morrow	circular	cc/ash pit	Expedient hearth?
175	197	213	60.02	60.25	61.20	61.42	E1	Eva/Morrow	circular	cc pit	Charcoal pit
176	235	241	60.75	60.95	64.30	64.68	J3	Eva/Morrow	oval	burial	Burial
179	225	227	57.92	57.06	64.59	64.78	J1	Eva/Morrow	circular	cc conc	Charcoal pit
180	200	215	60.26	60.96	60.80	61.37	E1	Eva/Morrow	oval	cc/ash pit	Pit hearth?

Feature[1,2]	Top depth	Bottom depth	min N	max N	min W	max W	Zone	Component[3]	Shape	Field Description[4]	Mapped as:
182	229	254	60.06	60.70	64.15	64.56	J3	Eva/Morrow	circular	rock pit	Rock cluster
183	225	233	58.83	59.10	64.32	64.55	J3	Eva/Morrow	circular	cc pit	Charcoal pit
184	230	236	58.20	58.48	64.60	64.88	J3	Eva/Morrow	circular	cc/ash pit	Expedient hearth?
185	230	248	58.40	58.71	64.88	64.18	J1	Eva/Morrow	circular	rock pit	Rock cluster
186	228	240	58.77	59.17	64.68	64.96	J3	Eva/Morrow	oval	cc pit	Charcoal pit
188	238	245	59.96	59.41	63.72	64.25	J3	Eva/Morrow	circular	ash pit	Ash pit
189	240	250	60.08	61.02	64.00	64.70	J3	Eva/Morrow	oval	hearth	Surface hearth
190	240	247	58.10	58.71	64.58	65.09	K3	Eva/Morrow	circular	cc/ash pit	Expedient hearth?
191	234	251	59.28	59.77	64.54	65.25	J3a	Eva/Morrow	oval	cc/ash pit	Pit hearth
194	240	247	59.49	59.95	63.90	64.23	J3	Eva/Morrow	oval	cc pit	Charcoal pit
198	256	272	61.07	61.52	64.42	64.81	J3d	Eva/Morrow	circular	cc pit	Charcoal pit
199	255	270	58.50	59.15	64.45	65.25	K3	Eva/Morrow	oval	hearth	Surface hearth
200	253	265	59.25	59.70	63.90	64.25	K3	Eva/Morrow	oval	cc/ash pit	Pit hearth?
201	140	150	59.00	59.70	65.10	65.95	D4	Benton	oval	unknown	
202	165	169	61.38	61.80	65.50	65.70	D4	Benton	unknown	canine burial	
203	179	199	58.24	58.46	64.88	65.14	E1	Eva/Morrow	circular	cc conc	Charcoal pit
204	188	192	59.00	59.22	65.07	65.25	E1	Eva/Morrow	circular	cc pit	Charcoal pit
205	190	196	59.15	59.50	65.20	65.45	E1	Eva/Morrow	oval	cc pit	Charcoal pit
206	188	191	59.15	59.40	65.63	65.94	E1	Eva/Morrow	circular	cc conc	Charcoal pit
207	187	189	59.25	59.47	65.92	66.05	E1	Eva/Morrow	oval	cc stain	
211	187	189	61.10	61.26	65.32	65.48	E1	Eva/Morrow	circular	cc stain	
212	188	194	62.05	62.26	65.66	65.88	E1	Eva/Morrow	circular	gastropod conc	Expedient hearth?
213	197	206	57.92	58.20	65.78	66.10	E8	Eva/Morrow	circular	cc pit	Charcoal pit
214	195	196	59.28	59.49	65.06	65.25	E1	Eva/Morrow	circular	cc stain	
215	201	209	58.22	58.40	65.65	65.80	E8	Eva/Morrow	circular	cc pit	Charcoal pit

Feature[1,2]	Top depth	Bottom depth	min N	max N	min W	max W	Zone	Component[3]	Shape	Field Description[4]	Mapped as:
216	200	213	58.50	59.00	65.18	65.71	E8	Eva/Morrow	circular	cc pit	Pit hearth?
217	197	205	59.46	60.20	65.21	65.89	E1	Eva/Morrow	circular	unknown	
218	194	197	59.91	60.32	65.50	65.91	E1	Eva/Morrow	circular	pit	
229	210	220	58.80	59.25	65.70	66.10	E8	Eva/Morrow	circular	cc/ash pit	Ash pit
230	164	174	60.90	61.30	60.20	60.65	D4	Benton	circular	cc pit	Charcoal pit
233	209	220	59.85	60.20	65.09	65.50			unknown	unknown	
237	207	222	59.35	59.80	66.01	66.37	E8a	Eva/Morrow	circular	ash pit	Ash pit
241	238	245	61.30	61.60	65.50	65.70	J3	Eva/Morrow	oval	cc pit	Charcoal pit
243	246	250	61.20	61.40	65.25	65.50	J3	Eva/Morrow	unknown	burial	Burial
245	215	220	58.88	59.11	66.77	66.98	J1b	Eva/Morrow	oval	ash pit	Ash pit
246	233	245	59.45	59.80	66.00	66.30	J3	Eva/Morrow	oval	burial	Burial
247	253	254	61.70	61.94	64.90	65.20	K2	Eva/Morrow	circular	ash stain	
248	253	254	61.27	61.63	64.75	65.15	K2	Eva/Morrow	oval	cc stain	
249	190	214	62.26	62.98	61.05	61.70	D4	Benton	circular	cc pit	Charcoal pit
250	234	239	59.55	60.00	65.00	65.25	K1	Eva/Morrow	oval	burial	Burial
251	239	244	62.02	62.37	65.59	65.95	K1	Eva/Morrow	oval	cc pit	Charcoal pit
252	251	252	58.35	58.52	65.48	65.63	K1	Eva/Morrow	circular	cc stain	
253	197	203	60.77	61.18	59.85	60.47	D4f	Benton	oval	cc pit	Rake out?
254	206	207	59.89	60.30	60.38	60.58	E1	Eva/Morrow	oval	cc stain	
255	251	254	59.20	59.35	65.22	65.43	K1	Eva/Morrow	circular	cc conc	Charcoal pit
256	253	273	62.20	62.70	65.82	66.25	K3	Eva/Morrow	oval	cc pit	Charcoal pit
259	166	186	59.40	59.80	60.30	60.62	D4	Benton	oval	pit	Expedient hearth?
260	266	271	59.26	59.60	65.38	65.67	K3	Eva/Morrow	circular	ash pit	Ash pit
261	180	194	59.35	59.65	60.45	60.75	D4	Benton	oval	cc pit	Expedient hearth
262	195	204	59.30	59.66	60.45	60.83	E1	Eva/Morrow	circular	cc pit	Charcoal pit

Feature[1,2]	Top depth	Bottom depth	min N	max N	min W	max W	Zone	Component[3]	Shape	Field Description[4]	Mapped as:
263	273	279	59.95	60.25	68.05	68.35	K	Eva/Morrow	unknown	burial	Burial
264	215	230	61.74	62.02	61.67	61.90	E1	Eva/Morrow	circular	cc pit	Charcoal pit
265	210	219	60.94	61.40	61.60	62.02	E1	Eva/Morrow	circular	rock pit	Rock cluster
266	210	218	59.66	60.15	61.48	61.92	E1	Eva/Morrow	oval	cc pit	Charcoal pit
267	212	221	59.88	60.30	61.03	61.48	E1	Eva/Morrow	oval	cc pit	Charcoal pit
268	216	230	60.50	61.45	60.20	61.30	E1	Eva/Morrow	oval	hearth	Surface hearth
269	224	227	59.05	59.47	61.66	61.98	E1	Eva/Morrow	oval	cc conc	Charcoal pit
272	208	219	60.33	60.68	61.50	61.88	E1g	Eva/Morrow	circular	cc pit	Charcoal pit
273	228	239	61.29	61.43	61.73	61.82	J3	Eva/Morrow	circular	cc pit	Charcoal pit
274	215	235	60.80	61.45	61.30	61.95	E1g	Eva/Morrow	circular	cc/ash pit	Pit hearth?
277	223	224	60.50	60.86	60.95	61.30	E1	Eva/Morrow	circular	cc stain	
278	138	144	62.00	62.50	60.00	60.60	D3	Benton	unknown	burial	Burial
280	237	245	61.64	61.88	61.12	61.35	J3d	Eva/Morrow	circular	cc/ash pit	
282	232	234	60.20	60.36	61.33	61.57	J3	Eva/Morrow	oval	cc conc	Charcoal pit
283	230	233	59.85	60.27	60.92	61.27	J3d	Eva/Morrow	circular	cc conc	Charcoal pit
284	228	231	62.14	62.27	61.30	61.50	J3	Eva/Morrow	oval	cc conc	Charcoal pit
285	231	232	60.40	61.00	61.15	61.50	J3d	Eva/Morrow	irregular	ash stain	
286	235	250	60.15	61.78	61.45	61.98	J3	Eva/Morrow	circular	cc/ash pit	Pit hearth?
287	247	256	59.50	59.91	61.30	61.63	J3d	Eva/Morrow	oval	cc pit	Charcoal pit
289	245	253	58.87	59.34	61.50	61.93	J3	Eva/Morrow	circular	cc/ash pit	Pit hearth?
291	310	314	63.18	63.65	66.21	66.62	N1	Eva/Morrow	irregular	cc pit	Charcoal pit
292	304	329	62.50	63.00	65.50	66.10	K10	Eva/Morrow	unknown	burial	Burial
293	256	273	59.25	59.45	61.05	61.25	K10	Eva/Morrow	circular	pit	Charcoal pit
294	258	262	61.45	61.75	61.57	61.84	K10	Eva/Morrow	oval	cc pit	Charcoal pit
295	250	255	62.72	62.96	61.79	62.05	K10	Eva/Morrow	circular	cc/ash pit	Expedient hearth?

Feature[1,2]	Top depth	Bottom depth	min N	max N	min W	max W	Zone	Component[3]	Shape	Field Description[4]	Mapped as:
296	245	263	61.15	61.75	61.45	61.75	K10	Eva/Morrow	oval	rock pit	Rock cluster
297	245	255	60.82	61.28	60.85	61.35	J3d	Eva/Morrow	circular	unknown	
298	256	263	60.90	61.32	59.57	60.02	J3d	Eva/Morrow	oval	ash pit	Ash pit
300	263	267	61.85	62.21	61.52	61.80	K10b	Eva/Morrow	oval	cc pit	Charcoal pit
301	250	260	60.10	61.10	67.50	68.30	K1	Eva/Morrow	lenticular	cc pit	Rakeout
303	270	283	60.21	60.65	61.32	61.80	N2	Eva/Morrow	circular	cc/ash pit	Expedient hearth
306	212	237	59.15	59.80	60.36	61.10	E1	Eva/Morrow	circular	cc/ash pit	Pit hearth?
308	215	228	60.70	61.50	59.42	60.42	E1g	Eva/Morrow	circular	hearth	Surface hearth
309	217	230	60.60	61.10	60.65	61.10	E1	Eva/Morrow	circular	Cc/ash pit	Pit hearth
310	217	232	60.17	60.72	60.25	60.80	E1	Eva/Morrow	circular	cc/ash pit	Pit hearth
311	325	335	59.15	59.65	67.45	67.95	P5	Kirk	unknown	burial	Burial
312	215	222	61.78	62.14	60.26	60.55	E1g	Eva/Morrow	circular	cc pit	Charcoal pit
313	219	225	61.64	61.86	60.58	60.84	E1g	Eva/Morrow	circular	cc pit	Charcoal pit
314	336	351	59.90	60.50	66.10	67.12	P5	Kirk	unknown	burial	Burial
315	225	226	59.82	60.05	60.66	60.90	J3	Eva/Morrow	circular	cc stain	
316	315	318	59.50	59.80	66.47	66.69	P5	Kirk	circular	cc conc	Charcoal pit
317	223	230	61.52	61.75	60.40	60.66	E1g	Eva/Morrow	circular	cc pit	Charcoal pit
319	202	208	62.73	63.10	60.62	61.09	E1	Eva/Morrow	oval	cc pit	Charcoal pit
320	200	215	62.50	62.75	60.27	60.49	E1	Eva/Morrow	circular	cc pit	Charcoal pit
321	232	237	61.40	61.75	61.40	61.75	E1	Eva/Morrow	circular	cc pit	Charcoal pit
323	238	247	61.08	61.65	60.10	60.45	J3	Eva/Morrow	irregular	cc pit	Charcoal pit
324	241	258	60.25	60.79	60.13	60.78	J3	Eva/Morrow	circular	hearth	Surface hearth
325	250	256	59.41	59.65	60.78	61.04	K10	Eva/Morrow	circular	cc pit	Charcoal pit
326	242	248	60.28	60.85	60.68	61.03	K10b	Eva/Morrow	circular	cc pit	Charcoal pit
328	248	254	61.12	61.72	60.34	60.72	K10b	Eva/Morrow	oval	pit	

Feature[1,2]	Top depth	Bottom depth	min N	max N	min W	max W	Zone	Component[3]	Shape	Field Description[4]	Mapped as:
329	375	377	58.95	59.30	67.20	67.50	Q?	Kirk/ESN	oval	cc conc	Charcoal pit
330	382	386	58.88	59.20	67.64	67.82	Q3?	Kirk/ESN	oval	cc conc	Charcoal pit
332	267	305	59.45	60.03	64.38	64.75	K2	Eva/Morrow	oval	pit	Ash pit
333	269	275	58.87	59.40	64.14	64.66	K7	Eva/Morrow	oval	cc/ash pit	Ash pit
336	290	295	60.89	61.16	64.08	64.34	N8	Eva/Morrow	oval	cc pit	Charcoal pit
339	287	297	62.92	63.14	64.25	64.57	K5b	Eva/Morrow	oval	cc/ash pit	Ash pit
341	290	312	62.21	62.88	64.53	65.21	K7	Eva/Morrow	circular	cc/ash pit	Coals
342	297	310	60.85	61.16	64.80	65.10	N8	Eva/Morrow	circular	rock pit	Rock cluster
344	301	302	58.88	59.28	64.35	64.82	P3	Kirk	oval	ash stain	Expedient hearth
345	335	338	60.04	60.32	64.23	64.58	P3e	Kirk	oval	cc conc	
346	305	360	60.25	61.25			P8	Kirk	unknown	burial	Burial
347	325	330	61.40	61.74	65.09	65.50	P11	Kirk	oval	cc pit	Charcoal ring
348	354	358	60.00	60.21	65.55	65.88	P7	Kirk	oval	cc/ash pit	As pit
351	325	326	58.92	59.18	63.90	64.15	P3	Kirk	circular	cc stain	
352	331	337	59.21	59.44	64.81	65.08	P2a	Kirk	circular	cc/ash pit	Ash pit
354	335	338	58.96	59.22	64.14	64.22	P2	Kirk	irregular	cc conc	Charcoal pit
355	290	293	59.57	59.92	65.26	65.49	K7	Eva/Morrow	oval	cc conc	Charcoal ring
356	350	356	61.52	61.98	65.16	65.80	P14	Kirk	oval	rock pit	Rock cluster
357	299	303	59.54	60.15	65.50	66.04	N4	Eva/Morrow	oval	cc pit	?
358	341	343	62.70	63.13	65.20	65.50	P3e	Kirk	circular	cc conc	Charcoal ring
359	394	396	60.74	60.82	65.58	65.78	T2	Paleo	oval	cc stain	
360	370	376	61.05	61.41	64.55	65.02	Q4	Kirk/ESN	circular	pit	
362	315	332	59.75	60.10	65.25	65.60	P8	Kirk	circular	pit	?
363	365	374	59.02	59.39	64.75	65.05	P2a	Kirk	oval	cc pit	Charcoal ring
364	325	327	58.90	59.27	65.26	65.55	P3e	Kirk	circular	cc stain	Charcoal ring

Feature[1,2]	Top depth	Bottom depth	min N	max N	min W	max W	Zone	Component[3]	Shape	Field Description[4]	Mapped as:
365	325	330	59.24	59.45	65.05	65.30	Q4	Kirk	circular	cc pit	Expedient hearth?
367	362	368	59.10	59.38	64.20	64.44	Q4	Kirk/ESN	oval	cc pit	Charcoal pit
369	415	420	60.50	60.76	64.85	65.11	T3	Paleo	circular	cc pit	Charcoal pit
370	366	371	59.11	59.37	64.50	64.74	Q4	Kirk/ESN	circular	cc/ash pit	
371	395	396	61.55	61.71	64.44	64.70	R1d	Early Side	oval	cc conc	Charcoal stain
372	418	420	60.84	61.18	64.00	64.34	T5	Paleo	circular	cc conc	Charcoal pit
375	340	343	59.15	59.45	65.18	65.45	P5	Kirk	circular	cc conc	Charcoal ring
376	385	394	61.41	61.69	65.50	65.78	T2	Paleo	circular	pit	?
377	387	401	62.12	62.43	64.67	64.92	R1	Early Side	circular	cc pit	Charcoal pit
378	345	350	59.04	59.53	64.78	65.21	P5	Kirk	oval	cc/ash pit	Ash pit
380	395	398	62.54	62.90	63.85	64.23	R1	Early Side	circular	cc conc	Charcoal pit
382	390	395	61.50	61.79	65.18	65.51	T2	Paleo	circular	cc pit	Charcoal pit
384	395	400	60.93	61.31	65.40	65.82	T2	Paleo	circular	rock cluster	Rock basin
385	357	362	59.58	59.75	65.03	65.22	Q4	Kirk/ESN	circular	cc/ash pit	
387	417	423	61.32	61.70	64.60	64.88	T8	Paleo	oval	cc pit	Charcoal pit
388	351	362	61.95	62.36	65.65	66.00	P7b	Kirk	circular	cc/ash pit	Ash pit
389	353	358	62.30	62.59	65.04	65.36	P14	Kirk	circular	cc/ash pit	Ash pit
390	360	374	62.88	63.38	65.60	65.93	P14	Kirk	circular	hearth	rakeout
391	368	373	62.70	62.87	65.12	65.30	R1	Early Side	circular	cc pit	Charcoal pit
397	377	380	59.29	59.62	65.44	65.82	Q4	Kirk/ESN	oval	cc conc	Charcoal pit
398	375	380	59.35	59.55	64.77	64.95	Q4	Kirk/ESN	circular	cc/ash pit	
399	377	381	59.17	59.29	64.82	64.94	Q4	Kirk/ESN	circular	ash pit	Ash pit
400	375	379	59.21	59.37	64.73	64.87	Q4	Kirk/ESN	circular	ash pit	Ash pit
401	376	380	59.10	59.29	65.97	66.15	Q4	Kirk/ESN	circular	cc pit	Charcoal pit
402	379	383	59.41	59.55	64.10	64.28	R3	Early Side	irregular	cc pit	Charcoal ring

Feature[1,2]	Top depth	Bottom depth	min N	max N	min W	max W	Zone	Component[3]	Shape	Field Description[4]	Mapped as:
403	377	382	58.75	59.24	64.30	64.80	R3	Early Side	unknown	rock pit	Rock cluster
404	380	382	58.75	59.25	64.78	65.19	Q4	Kirk	unknown	clay pit	unknown
405	382	389	59.71	60.01	65.18	65.67	R6	Early Side	irregular	cc pit	Expedient hearth?
406	382	389	59.39	59.66	63.85	64.22	R3	Early Side	oval	cc pit	Charcoal pit
407	382	386	59.36	59.47	64.38	64.52	R3	Early Side	circular	cc pit	Charcoal pit
408	381	384	59.69	60.02	64.31	64.61	R3	Early Side	circular	cc conc	Charcoal pit
409	384	389	59.65	59.93	64.26	64.56	R3	Early Side	oval	cc pit	Charcoal pit
410	385	391	59.83	60.13	64.51	64.76	R3a	Early Side	circular	cc conc	Charcoal pit
411	389	391	59.65	59.98	65.46	65.75	R6	Early Side	circular	cc/ash pit	Pit hearth
412	283	311	61.40	62.11	61.68	62.28	N2	Eva/Morrow	circular	cc/ash pit	Pit hearth?
413	385	406	59.60	60.03	64.86	65.40	R6	Early Side	circular	ash conc	Ash pit
414	391	394	59.60	59.83	64.35	64.56	R3e	Early Side	circular	cc/ash pit	Expedient hearth
415	324	327	59.11	59.77	61.48	61.76	P1a	Kirk	oval	rock pit	Rock cluster
416	405	413	59.15	59.52	64.07	64.45	R3f	Paleo	oval	cc/ash pit	Pit hearth?
417	327	337	59.67	60.05	61.95	62.11	P3	Kirk	oval	pit	Pit hearth
418	285	292	60.67	61.42	61.00	61.75	N2	Eva/Morrow	irregular	cc/ash pit	Pit hearth
419	292	321	61.80	62.33	61.38	61.90	N2	Eva/Morrow	circular	cc pit	Charcoal ring
420	406	410	59.76	60.00	65.60	65.88	T3	Paleo	oval	cc stain	Rock basin
421	406	407	59.90	60.14	65.15	65.34	T3	Paleo	circular	rock pit	Charcoal pit
423	410	416	58.50	59.50	64.62	65.43	T2	Paleo	circular	cc stain	Charcoal pit
424	410	411	59.46	59.90	65.25	65.66	T3	Paleo	irregular	cc pit	Charcoal pit
425	293	300	60.71	60.89	61.65	61.85	P1a	Kirk	circular	cc pit	Charcoal pit
426	293	298	60.55	60.74	61.66	61.83	P1a	Kirk	circular	cc pit	Charcoal pit
427	292	297	59.89	60.15	61.33	61.54	P3	Kirk	circular	cc pit	Charcoal pit
428	313	316	59.38	59.52	61.93	62.16	P3	Kirk	circular	cc pit	Charcoal pit

Feature[1,2]	Top depth	Bottom depth	min N	max N	min W	max W	Zone	Component[3]	Shape	Field Description[4]	Mapped as:
429	415	417	59.73	59.98	63.97	64.23	T5	Paleo	circular	cc stain	Fireplace accessory
430	292	293	60.60	60.87	61.49	61.67	P1a	Kirk	oval	cc/ash stain	
431	300	304	61.08	61.28	61.02	61.23	P1	Kirk	circular	cc pit	Charcoal pit
432	295	299	60.09	60.37	61.33	61.64	P3	Kirk	circular	cc pit	Charcoal pit
433	430	431	59.26	59.49	64.46	64.68	U3	Paleo	irregular	cc stain	
434	318	322	55.57	59.92	61.76	62.00	P3b	Kirk	oval	cc/ash pit	Expedient hearth
435	440	442	59.68	60.00	65.86	66.15	U8	Paleo	circular	cc conc	Charcoal pit
437	306	311	61.80	62.29	61.48	62.10	P3	Kirk	oval	hearth	Surface hearth
438	445	454	59.26	59.65	65.52	66.01	U6	Paleo	oval	pit	Heath?
439	448	451	59.46	59.76	65.45	65.66	U6	Paleo	oval	cc conc	Charcoal pit
440	295	314	59.72	60.18	61.07	61.63	P3a	Kirk	circular	cc/ash pit	Pit hearth
441	449	451	59.36	59.58	63.90	64.12	U3e	Paleo	circular	cc/ash conc	Ash pit
442	290	296	59.16	59.50	6.03	61.18	P3	Kirk	irregular	cc/ash pit	Expedient hearth
443	317	332	61.14	61.73	61.30	61.88	P18	Kirk	circular	cc/ash pit	Pit hearth
444	320	325	61.62	61.90	61.01	61.16	P18	Kirk	oval	cc pit	Charcoal pit
445	306	312	60.15	60.57	61.33	61.80	P3a	Kirk	circular	cc/ash pit	Expedient hearth
446	307	313	60.53	60.91	61.50	61.89	P17	Kirk	circular	pit	Pit hearth?
448	331	334	61.79	61.92	61.05	61.21	P18	Kirk	oval	cc pit	Charcoal pit
449	315	322	60.20	60.52	61.36	61.69	P19	Kirk	circular	cc/ash pit	Expedient hearth
450	340	350	61.00	61.90	61.18	61.80	P18	Kirk	oval	hearth	Surface hearth
452	346	355	61.43	61.76	61.13	61.54	Q5	Kirk/ESN	oval	cc/ash pit	
454	360	367	61.68	62.10	61.82	62.23	P18	Kirk	circular	cc/ash pit	Expedient hearth?
455	360	367	61.29	61.58	61.00	61.32	R1	Early Side	circular	cc pit	Charcoal pit
457	364	383	59.32	60.24	60.96	61.62	Q5	Kirk	circular	rock pit	Rock cluster
458	378	382	60.60	60.74	61.35	61.59	R1	Early Side	circular	cc pit	Charcoal pit

Feature[1,2]	Top depth	Bottom depth	min N	max N	min W	max W	Zone	Component[3]	Shape	Field Description[4]	Mapped as:
460	385	395	61.12	61.49	61.23	61.69	R1	Early Side	irregular	pit	
461	381	391	59.80	60.11	61.00	61.43	R1	Early Side	oval	ash pit	Ash pit
1000	201	203	60.40	60.62	62.05	62.25	E1	Eva/Morrow	circular	cc stain	
1001	230	231	58.90	59.10	62.60	62.78	J	Eva/Morrow	circular	cc stain	
1002	233	235	58.30	58.45	62.70	62.85	J	Eva/Morrow	circular	cc stain	
1003	220	222	60.30	60.70	63.30	63.90	E8	Eva/Morrow	irregular	ash conc	
1004	252	255	62.80	63.00	61.50	61.70	K3	Eva/Morrow	circular	cc pit	Charcoal pit
1005	306	310	59.35	59.75	61.90	62.20	P	Kirk	oval	cc pit	Charcoal pit
1006	306	308	59.10	59.60	62.60	62.90	P	Kirk	irregular	cc stain	
1007	310	315	59.10	60.40	62.00	62.40	P	Kirk	irregular	ash conc	Ash pit
1008	405	410	59.60	59.85	61.80	62.10	T	Paleo	circular	cc/ash pit	Ash pit
1009	405	410	59.3	59.50	63.85	64.20	T	Paleo	oval	ash conc	Ash pit
1010	405	406	59.50	59.60	63.90	64.05	T	Paleo	oval	cc stain	
1011	245	247	60.15	69.38	63.60	63.80	K3	Eva/Morrow	circular	cc stain	
1012	345	348	59.90	60.15	63.75	63.87	P	Kirk	oval	cc conc	Charcoal pit
1013	385	388	61.80	62.15	63.70	64.10	R	Early Side	oval	cc conc	Charcoal pit
1014	413	415	60.55	60.75	62.70	62.90	U	Paleo	circular	cc/ash stain	
1015	414	416	61.10	61.20	62.10	62.20	U	Paleo	circular	cc stain	
1016	459	460	60.20	61.50	63.70	64.30	U	Paleo	oval	cc stain	
1017	453	455	60.60	60.70	62.10	62.20	U	Paleo	circular	cc stain	
1018	450	451	60.25	60.35	63.70	63.80	U	Paleo	circular	cc stain	
1019	325	326	62.40	62.80	63.60	63.95	P	Kirk	irregular	ash stain	
1020	386	389	62.40	62.60	63.15	63.27	R1	Early Side	oval	cc pit	Charcoal pit
1021	270	273	62.80	63.42	62.30	62.80	K	Eva/Morrow	oval	cc conc	Charcoal pit
1022	400	401	63.75	63.95	63.70	63.53	R1	Early Side	irregular	cc stain	

Feature[1,2]	Top depth	Bottom depth	min N	max N	min W	max W	Zone	Component[3]	Shape	Field Description[4]	Mapped as:
1023	400	408	63.23	63.53	62.88	63.25	R1	Early Side	circular	cc/ash pit	Ash pit
1024	425	426	53.20	53.40	63.78	63.95	U	Paleo	circular	cc stain	
1025	435	440	57.10	57.50	63.30	63.80	U	Paleo	circular	cc pit	Charcoal pit
1026	315	317	58.10	58.20	63.20	63.38	P	Kirk	oval	cc stain	
1027	401	407	58.22	58.35	63.55	63.75	T	Paleo	circular	cc pit	Charcoal pit
108a	271	286	64.75	64.95	63.05	63.30	J3	Eva/Morrow	oval	canine burial	
121b	155	160	59.05	59.35	64.50	64.75	D4	Benton	circular	rock pit	Scrape out
125i	190	195	60.70	61.07	65.46	65.68	E1	Eva/Morrow	oval	cc/ash pit	Scrape out
134d	180	189	58.26	58.62	64.30	64.60	D4	Benton	circular	cc pit	Charcoal pit
136d	185	187	58.84	59.16	64.38	64.68	E1	Eva/Morrow	circular	cc pit	Charcoal pit
136e	175	183	58.95	59.64	63.90	64.40	E1	Eva/Morrow	oval	unknown	
143b	195	212	58.35	58.70	64.33	64.70	E5	Eva/Morrow	circular	ash pit	Ash pit
223a	201	205	59.43	59.56	65.22	65.40	E8	Eva/Morrow	circular	cc pit	Charcoal pit
255a	250	253	59.20	59.34	65.11	65.27	K1	Eva/Morrow	circular	cc conc	Charcoal pit
456a	365	370	61.61	61.81	61.58	61.73	Q5	Kirk	circular	cc pit	Charcoal pit

[1] Bold face indicates micromorphology sample available; italics indicate chemical sample available.
[2] Gap in numerical sequence indicates features lacking the requisite data for morphologic and spatial analyses.
[3] Features from zone Q were not used in spatial analyses.
[4] Abbreviations as follows: cc = charcoal; rx = rock; conc = concentration

Appendix B. Dust Cave micromorphology samples.

Feature or Zone	Sample #	Northing	Westing	Cmbd	Field Description
41	DC-92-04	60	64	142	Charcoal/ash pit
78 & 79/zone K2	DUST-93-19	59	62	249	Hearths intruding prepared surface
81	DUST-93-27	60	64	256	Possible hearth
83	DUST-93-14	60	62	263	Charcoal/ash pit
88	DUST-93-29a	64	64	~240	Charcoal pit
88	DUST-93-29b	64	64	~240	Charcoal pit
92	DUST-93-30	64	64	~250	Charcoal pit
117	DC-00-14	60	65	413	Possible hearth
117/zone T5	DC-00-16	60	65	420	Possible hearth intruding zone T5
135	DC-96-08	59	65	170	Red lens underlying possible hearth
136b	DC-96-07	60	65	174	Red lens surrounding possible hearth
159	DC-96-12	59	64	200	Charcoal pit
160	DC-96-13	62	65	unknown	Red lens associated with feature 160
191	DC-96-16	60	65	240	Charcoal/ash pit
301	DC-00-26	60	69	250	Lenticular charcoal pit
341	DC-99-04	63	66	300	Charcoal and ash pit
342	DC-99-02	62	65	305	Unknown
350	DC-99-05	61	65	355	Rock concentration
355	DC-99-13	60	66	290	Charcoal ring
356	DC-99-14	62	66	345	Rock concentration
356a	DC-99-19	62	66	355	Charcoal ring
357	DC-99-15	60	66	300	Unknown
358	DC-99-17	63	66	340	Charcoal ring
362	DC-99-18	60	66	315	Unknown
363	DC-99-20	60	65	355	Charcoal ring
363a/370	DC-99-24	60	65	365	Charcoal ring
364	DC-99-21	60	66	325	Charcoal ring
366	DC-99-32	62	65	405	Ash lens
368	DC-99-25	60	66	335	Charcoal/ash pit
369	DC-99-23	61	65	415	Charcoal ring
371	DC-99-22	62	65	395	Charcoal concentration
374	DC-99-28	60	66	340	Charcoal ring
376	DC-99-27	62	66	385	Unknown
377	DC-99-26	63	65	390	Charcoal pit
380	DC-99-29	63	65	395	Charcoal concentration
381/T2	DC-99-31	61	65	425	Charcoal stain intruding zone T2
382/T2	DC-99-30a	62	66	390	Charcoal pit intruding zone T2
384	DC-99-33	62	66	395	Rock concentration
387	DC-99-34	62	65	415	Charcoal pit

Feature or Zone	Sample #	Northing	Westing	Cmbd	Field Description
389	DC-99-37	63	66	350	Ash pit
395	DC-00-01	60	66	370	Charcoal ring
397	DC-00-02	60	66	375	Charcoal pit
398	DC-00-03	60	65	375	Charcoal pit
402	DC-00-05	60	65	380	Charcoal ring
404	DC-00-06	60	66	380	Clay pit
410	DC-00-08	60	65	385	Charcoal pit
412	DC-00-100	62	62	285	Limestone from feature fill
412/419	DC-00-12a	62	62	285	Charcoal/ash pits intrusive to each other
412/419	DC-00-12b	62	62	285	Charcoal/ash pits intrusive to each other
412/419	DC-00-12c	62	62	285	Charcoal/ash pits intrusive to each other
417	DC-00-10a	60	62	327	Charcoal/ash pit
417	DC-00-10b	60	62	327	Charcoal/ash pit
420	DC-00-11	60	66	406	Charcoal ring
423/T2c	DC-00-13	60	66	410	Possible hearth/charcoal stringer
423	DC-00-101	60	66	410	Limestone surrounding feature
429	DC-00-15	60	65	415	Charcoal pit
438	DC-00-17	60	66	445	Unknown
440	DC-00-102	--	--	--	Limestone from feature fill
443	DC-00-18	62	62	317	Charcoal/ash pit
445	DC-00-19	61	62	306	Charcoal/ash pit
449	DC-00-21	61	62	315	Charcoal/ash pit
450	DC-00-103	--	--	--	Limestone surrounding feature
450	DC-00-104	--	--	--	Limestone surrounding feature
D4d	DC-96-56	61	62	170	Stacked red clay and ash
J3	DC-98-63	63	62	223	Zone fill along northwest wall
J3b	DC-96-28	62	65	224	Ash lens
K2/F.79	DUST-93-17	59	62	249	Prepared surface
K3c	DC-02-003	59	67	255	Prepared surface
P11	DC-99-03	61	65	325	Unknown
P14/P7/P7B	DC-99-35	62	66	365	Stacked charcoal, ash, and red clay
P3	DC-98-57	59	64	362	Zone fill along northwest wall
R3g	DC-99-36	62	66	390	Stacked charcoal, ash, and red clay
R6/Q4	**DC-00-04**	60	66	375	Ash concentration
R6b	DC-00-25	60	66	390	Prepared surface
U8/U6	DC-00-24	60	66	460	Charcoal stringer

Feature or Zone	Sample #	Northing	Westing	Cmbd	Field Description
Bedding in pit	DC-98-77	60	68	270	Unknown pit identified in profile
Intrusive pit, N4	DC-98-87	60	66	290	Unknown pit identified in profile
Residual cave clay	BClay	--	--	--	Residual clay from Basket Cave
Experimental surface	DC-02-004	--	--	--	Experimental prepared surface
Experimental surface	DC-02-005	--	--	--	Experimental prepared surface
Trampled hearth	Trampled	--	--	--	Trampled half of experimental hearth
Untrampled hearth	Untrampled	--	--	--	Untrampled half of experimental hearth

Appendix C. Descriptions for common materials, microartifacts, and structures identified in Dust Cave thin Sections. Plates refer to images in Homsey 2004:Appendix D.

Material	Plate(s)	Description
Accessories		Refers to mineral grains other than quartz that comprise the distinctive mineralogy of Tennessee River alluvium. Usually dominated by muscovite, but also includes other minerals in minor amounts: feldspar, biotite, hornblende, and pyroxene. Accessories usually comprise between 2 and 5% of alluvial grains.
Aggregates		Soil aggregates, identified and described by Sherwood (2001) come in four types: red brown, dark brown, light brown, and yellow brown. Red brown aggregates have a probable autochthonous origin derived from the cave's interior. The other three aggregates have a probable allochthonous origin derived from colluvial material originating in soil horizons on top of the bluff above the cave.
Chert	4.7, 4.8	Refers to the relatively coarse microcrystalline fossiliferous chert derived from the Tuscumbia Formation. In thin section, it exhibits extensive weathering compared to the finer grained, angular, and relatively unweathered blue/gray Fort Payne chert used to manufacture lithics at Dust Cave. Frequently occur as rounded sand to gravels with highly birefringent iron-rich residual clays and compound quartz grains weathering out.
Limestone		General category referring to all highly birefringent, fossiliferous carbonate based rock comprising the Tuscumbia Formation.
Mica	4.10	Includes both muscovite and biotite in thin, rod-shaped, weathered grains. In thin section, muscovite is noted by its high birefringence in cross polarized light and biotite is noted by its pleochroic appearance in plane polarized light. Muscovite is far more abundant than biotite, and may comprise anywhere between 2 and 5% of alluvial sediments.
Papules	4.11	Dense deep red, non-calcareous, layered high-relief clay. Appears as rounded aggregates, or (less often) angular fragments. Derived from insoluble clay residues and most likely introduced into the cave from the weathering of the cave ceiling (Courty et al. 1989). May also be introduced by the movement of clay by people.
Quartz	4.13	Anisotropic white to gray. Subangular sand and silt grains dominate the Dust Cave sediments. Typically poorly sorted. Microcrystalline quartz grains may appear weathering from cherts associated with the Tuscumbia Limestone.
Roof spall (i.e., ceiling rain)	4.16	Refers to rounded sand or silt sized micritic fragments of limestone associated with the Tuscumbia Formation. Usually appears as single grains, often a single fossil representing grain by grain attrition of the ceiling.
Microartifacts		
Ash	4.1, 4.2, 4.3, 4.4	Ash crystals may appear as (1) silt sized single yellow to gray highly birefringent calcium carbonate crystals in three shapes (lozenge, rhomboid, and spherulite) and (2) aggregates representing the structure of the original burned material (i.e., calcitic pseudomorphs). Lozenge crystals have been associated with deciduous species, rhomboid with conifers, and spherulites with leaves and the reproductive organs of angiosperms (Courty et al. 1989, Wattez and Courty 1987).
Bone	4.5	Calcium phosphate fragments and whole bones of fish and microfauna which appear in both burned and unburned contexts. Bone is identified primarily by its low birefringence and "ropy" texture, appearing pale yellow to brown in PPL and blue-gray in XPL (Courty et al. 1989). In general, the more burned the darker brown under PPL. Degree of decalcification varies.
Charcoal	4.6	Black to opaque, often with distinct cellular structure visible. The degree of combustion varies widely from only partially combusted to nearly complete conversion to ash crystals. Nut charcoal is differentiated from wood charcoal as being denser and lacking the fine cellular structure seen in wood charcoal.

Material	Plate(s)	Description
Lithic debitage	4.9	Refers to the blue-gray chert of the Fort Payne Formation used to manufacture lithics at Dust Cave. Identified by its microcrystalline texture, angularity, and relative absence of weathering compared to the chert weathering out from the Tuscumbia Formation.
Partially combusted organics	4.12	Generally brown to dark brown opaque material, often with cellular structure still visible. Degree of combustion varies widely.
Shell	4.14 4.15	Composed of highly birefringent fibrous calcium carbonate in elongated thin fragments of original shell shape. Occasionally larger fragments are preserved. When possible, identified as mussel, gastropod, or terrestrial snail. When burned, has a darker brown to gray, dull appearance.
Sedimentary Structures		
Calcitic coatings		Occur as highly birefringent microcrystalline deposits coating the outer surfaces of grains and aggregates and the inner surfaces of voids (Stoops 2003). Usually result from the biochemical activity of roots (Bullock et al. 1985) or the percolation of calcium-rich waters through sediment (Sherwood 2001). Decalcification is the loss of calcium carbonate via dissolution in weak acids (e.g., carbonic acid).
Cross Bedding		Characterized by the arrangement of sediments at an angle to the main stratification. Originate in bedforms such as ripples and dunes by the motion of sediment due to a flowing fluid such as water or wind.
Gradded Bedding		Characterized by distinct vertical gradation in grain size which fine upwards (Boggs 1995). Occurs in response to a decrease in current velocity, such as during floods
Slacking Crusts		Form from the splash effects of water drops. As the drop hits, surface grains are eroded; eroded materials accumulate in small depressions forming a crust consisting of fining upward sequences of silt and clay (Courty et al. 1989). Occur on the scale of millimeters or smaller.
Voids		Refers to empty spaces within a deposit which appear as black when resin-impregnated samples are viewed petrographically. Types include packing, channel, vesicular, vugh, chamber, plane, and sponge (Bullock et al 1985; Courty et al. 1989). Channel voids can result from extensive root activity (Courty et al 1989). Vesicles may form as a result of extensive puddling of water (Courty 1989), causing inside edge of vesicles to fill in with dusty clays or become coated with charcoal. Compaction due to heavy machinery has been known to create planar voids (Courty et al 1989).

References Cited

Adams, Jonathan (compiler)
2001 *North America During the Last 150,000 Years.* URL:www.esd.ornl.gov/projects/qen/nercNORTHAMERICA.html.

Adams, Jonathan and H. Faure
1997 Paleovegetation Maps of the Earth during the Last Glacial Maximum and the Early and Mid Holocene: An Aid to Archaeological Research. *Journal of Archaeological Science* 24:623-647.

Ahler, Steven R.
1984 Archaic Settlement Strategies in the Modoc Locality, Southwest Illinois. Unpublished Ph.D. Dissertation, Department of Anthropology, University of Wisconsin, Milwaukee.
1993 Stratigraphy and Radiocarbon Chronology of Modoc Shelter, Illinois. *American Antiquity* 58:462-489.
2004 Synopsis of Modoc Main Shelter Features and Feature Types. Manuscript on file with the author.

Akoshima, K.
1993 *Site Structure Analyses of the Abri Dufaure and Mill Iron Sites.* Ph.D. Dissertation. Department of Anthropology, University of New Mexico, Albuquerque.

Aldenderfer, Mark S.
1998 *Montane Foragers: Asana and the South-Central Andean Archaic.* University of Iowa Press, Iowa City.

Anderson, David G.
1994 The Excavations at Dust Cave to Date: A Commentary. *Journal of Alabama Archaeology* 40:237-246.
1995 Recent Advances in Paleoindian and Archaic Period Research in the Southeastern United States. *Archaeology of Eastern North America* 23:145-176.
1996 Models of Paleoindian and Early Archaic Settlement in the Lower Southeast. In *The Paleoindian and Early Archaic Southeast*, edited by David G. Anderson and Kenneth E. Sassaman, pp. 29-57. University of Alabama Press, Tuscaloosa.
2001 Climate and Culture Change in Prehistoric and Early Historic Eastern North America: *Archaeology of Eastern North America* 29:143-186.

Anderson, David G. and J.C. Gillam
2000 Paleoindian Colonization of the Americas: Implications from an Examination of Physiography, Demography, and Artifact Distribution. *American Antiquity* 65:43-66.

Anderson, David G. and Glen T. Hanson
1988 Early Archaic Settlement in the Southeastern United States: A Case Study from the Savannah River Valley. *American Antiquity* 53:262-286.

Anderson, David G., Lisa D. O'Steen, and Kenneth E. Sassaman
1996 Environmental and Chronological Considerations. In *The Paleoindian and Early Archaic Southeast*, edited by David G. Anderson and Kenneth E. Sassaman, pp. 3-15. University of Alabama Press, Tuscaloosa.

Anderson, David G. and Kenneth E. Sassaman
1996 Modeling Paleoindian and Early Archaic Settlement in the Southeast: A Historical Perspective. In *The Paleoindian and Early Archaic Southeast*, edited by David G. Anderson and Kenneth E. Sassaman, pp. 16-28. University of Alabama Press, Tuscaloosa.

Anderson, David G. ad Joseph Schuldenrein
1983 Early Archaic Settlement on the Southeastern Atlantic Slope: A View from the Ruckers's Bottom Site, Elbert County, Georgia. *North American Archaeologist* 4(3):177-210.

Arrhenius, O.
1931 Die Bodenanalyse im Dienst der Archäologie. Zeitschrift für Pflanzenernährung, Düngung und Bodenkunde, Teil B, 10, 427-439.

Asch, David L. and Nancy B. Asch
1987 Archaeobotany of Buckshaw Bridge: An Archaic Site in Brown County, Illinois. Center for American Archaeology, Archaeobotanical Laboratory Report 77.

Asch, David L., Richard I. Ford, and Nancy B. Asch
1972 *Paleoethnobotany of the Koster Site: The Archaic Horizons.* Report of Investigations No. 24. Illinois State Museum, Springfield.

Baden, W.W.
1985 Evidence of Changing Settlement Patterns in the Little Tennessee River Valley of East Tennessee. In Exploring *Tennessee Prehistory: A Dedication to Alfred K. Guthe.* Report of Investigations No. 42. University of Tennessee, Department of Anthropology, Knoxville.

Bahn, Paul G.
1997 Dancing in the Dark: Probing the Phenomenon of Pleistocene Cave Art. In *The Human Use of Caves*, edited by Clive Bonall and Christopher Tolan-Smith, pp. 35-37. BAR International Series 667, Oxford.

Bar-Yosef, O. B. Vandermeersch, B. Arensburg, A. Belfer-Cohen, P. Goldberg, H. Laville, L. Meignen, Y. Rak, J.D. Speth, E. Tchernov, A.M. Tillier, and S. Weiner
1992 Excavations in Kebara Cave, Mountain Carmel. *Current Anthropology* 33:497-550.

Bellomo, Randy V.
1993 A Methodological Approach of Identifying Archaeological Evidence of Fire Resulting from Human Activities. *Journal of Archaeological Science* 20:525-553.

Bense, Judith A.
1994 *Archaeology of the Southeastern United States.* Academic Press, San Diego.

Bettinger, Robert L.
1991 *Hunter-Gatherers: Archaeological and Evolutionary Theory.* Plenum Press, New York.

Beynon, Diane E.
1981 The Geoarchaeology of Meadowcroft Rockshelter. Unpublished Ph.D. Dissertation, Department of Geology and Planetary Science, University of Pittsburgh, Pittsburgh.

Binford, Lewis L.
1979 Organization and Formation Processes: Looking at Curated Technologies. *Journal of Anthropological Research* 35:255-273.
1980 Willow Smoke and Dogs' Tails: Hunter-Gatherer Settlement Systems and Archaeological Site Formation. *American Antiquity* 45:4-20.
1982 The Archaeology of Place. *Journal of Anthropological Archaeology* 5:1-37.
1983 In *pursuit of the Past: Decoding the Archaeological Record*. Thames and Hudson, New York.

Blatt, Harvey
1982 *Sedimentary Petrology*. W.H. Freeman and Company, San Francisco.

Boffa, J.M., Yameogo, G., Nikiema, P., and Kundson, D.M.
1996 Shea nut (*vitellaria paradoxa*) Production and Collection in Agroforestry Parklands of Burkina Faso. In *Domestication and Commercialization of Non-timber Forest Products in Agroforestry Systems*. Food and Agriculture Organization, Rome.

Boggs, Sam Jr.
1995 *Principles of Sedimentology and Stratigraphy*. Prentice Hall, Upper Saddle River, New Jersey.

Bordes, Frances
1972 *A Tale of Two Caves*. Harper and Row, New York.

Braun, D.D.
1989 Glacial and Periglacial Erosion of the Appalachians. *Geomorphology* 2:233-256.

Branigan, Keith
1997 Working in the Dark? Caves as Workshops in Roman Britain. In *The Human Use of Caves*, edited by Clive Bonsall and Christopher Tolan-Smith, pp. 114-121. BAR International Series 667, Oxford.

Brown, James A. and Robert K. Vierra
1985 What Happened in the Middle Archaic? Introduction to an Ecological Approach to Koster Site Archaeology. In *Archaic Hunters and Gatherers in the American Midwest*, edited by James L. Phillips and James A. Brown, pp. 165-196. Academic Press, New York.

Bryson, Reid A.
1999a Modeled Temperature History: Muscle Shoals, Alabama. Manuscript on file, Center for Climatic Research, University of Wisconsin, Madison.
1999b Modeled Precipitation History: Muscle Shoals, Alabama. Manuscript on file, Center for Climatic Research, University of Wisconsin, Madison.

Bryson, Reid A. and R.U. Bryson
1997 High Resolution Simulation of Iowa Holocene Climates. *Journal of the Iowa Archaeological Society* 44:121-128.

Bullock P., N. Federoff, A. Johgerius, G.J. Stoops, and T. Tursina
1985 *Handbook for Soil Thin Section Description*. Waine Research Publications, Wolverhampton.

Butzer, K.W.
1981 *Archaeology as Human Ecology*. Cambridge University Press, New York.
1982 Cave Sediments, Upper Pleistocene Stratigraphy and Mousterian Facies in Cantabria. *Journal of Archaeological Science* 8:133-183.

Boffa, J.M., Yameogo, G., Nikiema, P., and Kundson, D.M.
1996 Shea nut (*vitellaria paradoxa*) Production and Collection in Agroforestry Parklands of Burkina Faso. In *Domestication and Commercialization of Non-timber Forest Products in Agroforestry Systems*. Food and Agriculture Organization, Rome.

Cable, John S.
1996 Haw River Revisited: Implications for Modeling Terminal Late Glacial and Early Holocene Hunter-Gatherer Settlement Systems in the Southeast. In *The Paleoindian and Early Archaic Southeast*, edited by David G. Anderson and Kenneth E. Sassaman, pp. 107-148. University of Alabama Press, Tuscaloosa.

Carr, Christopher
1991 Left in the Dust: Contextual Information in Model-Focused Archaeology. In *The Interpretation of Archaeological Spatial Patterning*, edited by Ellen M. Kroll and T. Douglas Price, pp. 221-256. Plenum Press, New York.

Carney, Judith and Marlene Elias
2007 Revealing Gendered Landscapes: Indigenous Female Knowledge and Agroforestry of African Shea. *Canadian Journal of African Studies* 40:235-267.

Casey, Joanna
2004 *Shea Butter and the Gendered Economy in Northern Ghana*. Paper presented at the 37th annual Chacmool Conference, Calgary.

Chalfin, Brenda.
2007 *Shea Butter Republic: State Power, Global Markets, and the Making of an Indigenous Community*. Taylor and Francis.

Chapman, Jefferson
1973 *The Icehouse Bottom Site (40MR23)*. Report of Investigations 13, Department of Anthropology, University of Tennessee, Knoxville.
1975 The Rose Island Site and the Bifurcate Point Tradition. Report of Investigations 14, Department of Anthropology, University of Tennessee, Knoxville.
1976 Early Archaic Site Location and Excavation in the Little Tennessee River Valley: Backhoes and Trowels. *Southeastern Archaeology Conference Bulletin* 19:31-36.

1977 *Archaic Period Research in the Lower Little Tennessee River Valley, 1975: Icehouse Bottom, Harrison Branch, Thirty Acre Island, Calloway Island*. Report of Investigations 18, Department of Anthropology, University of Tennessee, Knoxville.

1978 *The Bacon Farm Site and a Buried Site Reconnaissance*. Report of Investigations 23, Department of Anthropology, University of Tennessee, Knoxville.

1985 *Tellico Archaeology*. University of Tennessee Press, Knoxville.

Chapman, J. and A.B. Shea
1981 The Archaeobotanical Record: Early Archaic Period to Contact in the Lower Little Tennessee River Valley. *Tennessee Anthropologist* 6:61-84.

Claassen, Cheryl
1991 Gender, Shellfishing, and the Shell Mound Archaic. In *Engendering Archaeology: Women and Prehistory*, edited by J.M. Gero and M.W. Conkey, pp. 276-300. Basil Blackwell, Oxford.

1996 A Consideration of the Social Organization of the Shell Mound Archaic. In *Archaeology of the Mid-Holocene Southeast*, edited by Kenneth E. Sassaman and David G. Anderson, pp. 235-258. University of Florida Press, Gainesville.

Clagget, Stephen R. and John S. Cable
1982 *The Haw River Sites: Archaeological Investigations at Two Stratified Sites in the North Carolina Piedmont*. Report R-2386, Commonwealth Associates, Jackson, Michigan.

Cobb, Richard M.
1987 A Speleoarchaeological Reconnaissance of the Pickwick Basin in Colbert and Lauderdale Counties of Alabama. Report submitted to the University of Alabama, Alabama State Museum of Natural History, Division of Archaeology, Tuscaloosa, Al.

Cobb, Richard M., Boyce Driskell, and Scott Meeks
1995 Speleological Reconnaissance and Test Excavation in the Pickwick Basin. In *Cultural Resources in the Pickwick Reservoir*, edited by Catherine C. Meyer, pp. 219-262. Report of Investigations 75. Division of Archaeology, University of Alabama, Tuscaloosa.

Coe, Joffre L.
1964 *The Formative Cultures of the Carolina Piedmont*. Transactions of the American Philosophical Society 54(5). Philadelphia.

Collins, Michael B.
1990 Rockshelters and the Early Archaeological Record in the Americas. In *The First Americans: Search and Research*, edited by T.D. Dillehay and D.J. Meltzer, pp. 157-182. CRC Press, Boston.

Collins, Michael B., Wulf A Gose, and Scott Shaw
1994 Preliminary Geomorphological Findings at Dust Cave. In *The Journal of Alabama Archaeology* 40:35-56.

COMAP members
2002 Climate Changes of the Last 18,000 Years: Observations and Model Simulations. *Science* 241:1043-1052.

Cook, Thomas
1976 *Koster: An Artifact Analysis of Two Archaic Phases in West-Central Illinois*. Northwestern University Archaeological Program, Prehistoric Records 1, Koster Research Reports 3.

Cook, S.F. and R.F. Heizer
1965 *Studies in the Chemical Analysis of Archaeological Sites*. University of California Publications in Anthropology 2, Berkley.

Courty, Marie Agnes, Paul Goldberg, and Richard MacPhail
1989 *Soils and Micromorphology in Archaeology*. Cambridge University Press, Cambridge.

Daniel, I. Randolph
1998 *Hardaway Revisited: Early Archaic Settlement in the Southeast*. University of Alabama Press, Tuscaloosa.

2001 Stone Raw Material Availability and Early Archaic Settlement in the Southeastern United States. *American Antiquity* 66:237-266.

DeJarnette, David L., E.B. Kurjack, and J.W. Cambron
1962 Excavations at the Stanfield-Worley Bluff Shelter. *Journal of Alabama Archaeology* 8:1-124.

1963 Unpublished field notes of the Stanfield-Worley Bluff Shelter Excavations, 1962-1963. On file at the Moundville Archaeological Park, Office of Archaeological Research, Moundville, Alabama.

Delcourt, Paul A.
1980 Goshen Springs: Late-Quaternary Vegetation Record for Southern Alabama. *Ecology* 61:371-386.

Delcourt, Paul A. and Hazel R. Delcourt
1987 *Long-Term Forest Dynamics of the Temperate Zone: A Case Study of Late-Quaternary Forests in Eastern North America*. Springer-Verlag, New York.

Delcourt, Hazel R. and Paul A. Delcourt
1991 *Quaternary Ecology: A Paleoecological Perspective*. Chapman and Hall, London.

Delcourt, P.A., H.R. Delcourt, P.A. Cridlebaugh, and J. Chapman
1986 Holocene Ethnobotanical and Paleoecological Record of Human Impact on Vegetation in the Little Tennessee River Valley, Tennessee, U.S.A. *Quaternary Research* 25:330-349.

Delcourt, H.R., P.A. Delcourt, and E.C. Spiker
1983 A 12,000-Year Record of Forest History from Cahaba Pond, St. Clair County, Alabama. *Ecology* 64:874-887.

Dering, Paul
1999 Earth Oven Plant Processing in Archaic Period Economies: An Example from a Semi-Arid Savannah in South-Central North America. *American Antiquity* 64:659-674.

Detwiler, Kandace R.
2001 Plant Use During the Late Paleoindian and Early Side Notched Transition at Dust Cave. Paper presented at the 58th annual meeting of the

Detwiler-Hollenbach, Kandace
2003 Nuts and More Nuts: Archaic Plant Use at Dust Cave. Paper presented at the 60th annual meeting of the Southeastern Archaeology Conference, Charlotte.

Dickens, Roy S., Jr.
1985 The Form, Function, and Formation of Garbage-filled Pits on Southeastern Aboriginal Sites: An Archaeobotanical Analysis. In *Structure and Process in Southeastern Archaeology*, edited by Roy S. Dickens, Jr. and H. Tarwick Ward, pp. 11-33. University of Alabama Press, Tuscaloosa.

Donahue, Jack and James Adovasio
1990 Evolution of Sandstone Rockshelters in Eastern North America: a Geoarchaeological Perspective. In *Archaeological Geology of North America*, edited by Norman Lasca and Jack Donahue, pp. 231-51. Geological Society of America, Boulder.

Driskell, Boyce N.
1994 Stratigraphy and Chronology at Dust Cave. *Journal of Alabama Archaeology* 40:17-34.
1996 Stratified Late Pleistocene and Early Holocene Deposits at Dust Cave, Northwestern Alabama. In *The Paleoindian and Early Archaic Southeast*, edited by David G. Anderson and Kenneth E. Sassaman, pp. 315-330. University of Alabama Press, Tuscaloosa.
2001 Field Investigations at Dust Cave, Northwest Alabama, 1989-2000. Paper presented at the 58th Annual Meeting of the Southeastern Archaeological Conference, Chattanooga.

Dwyer, Peter D. and Monica Minnegal
1985 Andaman Islanders, Pygmies, and an Extension of Horn's Model. *Human Ecology* 13:111-119.

Dye, David D.
1977 A Model for Late Archaic Subsistence Systems in the Western Middle Tennessee Valley During the Bluff Creek Phase. *Tennessee Anthropologist* 2:63-80.
1996 Riverine Adaptations in the Midsouth. In *Of Caves and Shell Mounds*, edited by Kenneth C. Carstens and Patty Jo Watson, pp. 140-159. University of Alabama Press, Tuscaloosa.

Eidt, Robert
1973 A Rapid Chemical Field Test for Archaeological Site Surveying. *American Antiquity* 38:206-210.
1985 Theoretical and Practical Considerations in the Analysis of Anthrosols, In *Archaeological Geology*, edited b G. Rapp, Jr., G. Gifford, & J.A. Gifford, pp. 155-190. Yale University Press, New Haven.

Eilas, Marlene and Judith Carney
2007 African Shea Butter: A Feminized Subsidy from Nature. *Africa* 77:37-62.

Ellis, Christopher, A.C. Goodyear, D.F. Morse, K.B. Tankersley
1998 Archaeology of the Pleistocene-Holocene Transition in Eastern North America. *Quaternary International* 49-50:151-166.

Emerson, T.E., D.L. McElrath, and J.A. Williams
1986 Patterns of Hunter-Gatherer Mobility and Sedentism During the Archaic Period in the American Bottom. In *Foraging, Collecting, and Harvesting: Archaic Period Subsistence and Settlement in the Eastern Woodlands*, edited by S. Neusius, pp. 247-274. Occasional Paper No. 6. Center for Archaeological Investigations, Southern Illinois University, Carbondale.

Farrand, William R.
1985 Rockshelter and Cave Sediments. In *Sediments in Archaeological Context*. edited by Julie K. Stein and William R. Farrand, pp. 21-38. Center for the Study of Early Man, Oronco, Maine.
2001 Sediments and Stratigraphy in Rockshelters and Caves: A Personal Perspective on Principles and Pragmatics. *Geoarchaeology* 16:537-557

Ferris, R.S.B., Collinson, C., Wanda, K., Jagwe, J., and Wright, P.
2001 *Evaluating the Marketing Opportunities for Shea Nut and Shea Nut Processed Products in Uganda*. University of Greenwich, National Resources Institute. Kent.

FitzPatrick, E.A.
1990 Roots in Thin Sections of Soils. In *Soil Micromorphology: A Basic and Applied Science*, edited by L. A. Douglas, pp. 9-19. Elsevier, Amsterdam.
1993 *Soil Microscopy and Micromorphology*. John Wiley and Sons, Great Britain.

Freeman, Sharon
2003 Prepared Surfaces: A First Impression. Paper presented at the 60th annual meeting of the Southeastern Archaeology Conference, Charlotte.

Fortier, Andrew C.
1983 Settlement and Subsistence at the Go-Kart North Site: A Late Archaic Titterington Occupation in the American Bottom, Illinois. In *Archaic Hunters and Gatherers in the American Midwest*, edited by James L. Phillips and James A. Brown, pp. 243-260. Academic Press, New York.

Fowler, Melvin
1959 Summary Report of Modoc Rock Shelter: 1952, 1953, 1955, 1956. Report of Investigations No. 8. Department of Registration and Education. Springfield, Ill.

Funk, Robert E.
1989 Some Contributions of Archaeology to the Study of Cave and Rockshelter Sediments: Examples from Eastern New York. *Man in the Northeast* 37:35-112.

Futato, Eugene
1980 An Overview of Wheeler Basin Prehistory. *Journal of Alabama Archaeology* 26:110-135.
1983 *Archaeological Investigations in the Cedar Creek and Upper Bear Creek Reservoirs*. Report of Investigations 29. Report submitted to the Tennessee Valley Authority, Norris, by the University of Alabama, Office of Archaeological Research, Tuscaloosa.

1982 Some Notes on the Distribution of Fluted Points in Alabama. *Archaeology of Eastern North America* 10:30-33.

Gamble, Clive
1991 An Introduction to the Living Spaces of Mobile Peoples. In *Ethnoarchaeological Approaches to Mobile Campsites: Hunter/Gatherer and Pastoralist Case Studies*, edited by C.S. Gamble and W.A. Boismer, pp. 1-23, International Monographs in Prehistory, Ethnoarchaeological Series 1, Ann Arbor, Michigan.

Galanidou, Nena
1997 *'Home is Where the Hearth is': The Spatial Organisation of the Upper Palaeolithic Rockshelter Occupations at Klithi and Kastristsa in Northwest Greece*. BAR International Series 687, Oxford.
2000 Patterns in Caves: Foragers, Horticulturalists, and the Use of Space. *Journal of Anthropological Archaeology* 19:243-275.

Gardner, Paul S.
1997 The Ecological Structure and Behavioral Implications of Mast Exploitation Strategies. In *People, Plants, and Landscapes: Studies in Paleoethnobotany*, edited by Kristen J. Gremillion, pp. 161-178. University of Alabama Press, Tuscaloosa.

Gé, T. M.A. Courty, W. Matthews, and J. Wattez
1993 Sedimentary Formation Processes of Occupation Surfaces. In *Formation Processes in Archaeological Context*, edited by P. Goldberg, D.T. Nash, and M.D. Petraglia, pp. 149-164. Prehistory Press, Madison.

Gebhardt, A.
1993 Micromorphological Evidence of Soil Determination Since the Mid-Holocene at Archaeological Sites in Brittany, France. *The Holocene* 3:333-341.
1992 Micromorphological Analysis of Soil Structural Modification Caused by Different Cultivation Implements. In *Actes de la Table Ronde DNRS: Préhistorie de L'agriculture: Nouvelles Approches Expérimentales et Ethnographiques*, edited by P. Anderson, pp. 373-383. Valbonne: Monographie du CRA 6, CNRS.

Gebhardt, A. and R. Langohr
1999 Micromorphological Study of Construction Materials and Living Floors in the Medieval Motte of Werken (West Flanders, Belgium). *Geoarchaeology* 4:595-620.

Gerhardt, Klaus O., Scott Searles, and William R. Biers
1990 Corinthian Figure Vases: Non-Destructive Extraction and Gas Chromatography-Mass Spectrometry. In *Organic Contents of Ancient Vessels: Materials Analysis and Archaeological Investigation*, edited by W.R. Biers and P.E. McGovern, pp. 41-50. MASCA Research Papers in Science and Archaeology, University of Pennsylvania, Philadelphia.

Gillieson, D.
1996 *Caves: Processes, Development, and Management*. Blackwell Publishers, Oxford.

Goldberg, Paul A.
1979a Micromorphology of Pech-de-L'Aze II Sediments. *Journal of Archaeological Science* 6:1-31.
1979b Micromorphology of Sediments from Hayonim Cave, Israel *CATENA* 6:60-67.
1980 Micromorphology in Archaeology and Prehistory. *Paleorient* 6:159-165.
2000 Micromorphology and Site Formation at Die Kelders Cave 1, South Africa. *Journal of Human Evolution* 38:43-90.

Goldberg, P. and T. Arpin
2000 Micromorphological Analysis of Sediments from Meadowcroft Rockshelter, Pennsylvania: Implications for Radiocarbon Dating. *Journal of Field Archaeology* 26:325-342.

Goldberg, P. and O. Bar-Yosef
1998 Site Formation Processes in Kebara and Hayonim Caves and Their Significance in Levantine Prehistoric Caves. In *Neanderthals and Modern Humans in Western Asia*, edited by T. Akazawa, K. Aoki, and O.Bar-Yosef, pp. 107-123. Plenum Press, New York.

Goldberg, Paul A. and Sarah C. Sherwood
1994 Micromorphology of Dust Cave Sediments: Preliminary Results. *Journal of Alabama Archaeology* 40:57-65.
2006 Deciphering Human Prehistory through the Geoarchaeological Study of Cave Sediments. *Evolutionary Anthropology* 15:20-36.

Goldberg, P. and Whitbread, I.
1993 Micromorphological Study of a Bedouin Tent Floor. In *Formation Processes in Archaeological Context*, edited by P. Goldberg, D.T. Nash, and M.D. Petraglia, pp. 165-188. Prehistory Press, Madison.

Goldman-Finn, Nurit S.
1994 Dust Cave in Regional Context. *Journal of Alabama Archaeology* 40:208-226.
1995a *Archaeological Survey in the Middle Tennessee River Uplands, Colbert and Lauderdale Counties, Alabama*. University of Alabama Office of Archaeological Services, Report of Investigations 74.
1995b The Natural and Cultural Setting. In *Cultural Resources in the Pickwick Reservoir*, edited by Catherine C. Meyer, pp. 11-44. University of Alabama Division of Archaeology, Report of Investigations 75.
1997 *Analysis of Collections from Stanfield-Worley Bluff Shelter, Northwest Alabama*. Unpublished report of investigations filed with the Office of Archaeological Research, University of Alabama Museums, Moundville, Alabama.

Goldman-Finn, N. and B.N. Driskell
1994 Introduction to Archaeological Research at Dust Cave. *Journal of Alabama Archaeology* 40:1-16.

Goldman-Finn, Nurit S. and Renee B. Walker
1994 The Dust Cave Bone Tool Assemblage. *Journal of Alabama Archaeology* 40:107-115.

Goodyear, Albert

1974 *The Brand Site: A Techno-Functional Study of a Dalton Site in Northeast Arkansas.* Research Series 7, Arkansas Archaeological Survey, Fayetteville.

1982 The Chronological Position of the Dalton Horizon in the Southeastern United States. *American Antiquity* 47:382-395.

1989 A Hypothesis for the Use of Cryptocrystalline Raw Materials among Paleoindian Groups of North America. In *Eastern Paleoindian Lithic Resource Use*, edited by Christopher Ellis and J.C. Lothrop, pp. 1-9. Westview Press, Boulder.

Gorecki, P.P

1988 Hunters and Shelters—the Need for Ethnoarchaeological Data. In *Archaeology with Ethnography: an Australian Perspective*, edited by B. Meehan and R. Jones, pp. 159-170. Australian National University, Research School of Pacific Studies, Canberra.

1991 Horticulturists as Hunter-Gatherers: Rockshelter Usage in Papua New Guinea. In *Ethnoarchaeological Approaches to Mobile Campsites*, edited by C.S. Gamble and W.A. Broismier, pp. 237-262. International Monographs in Prehistory, Ann Arbor, Michigan.

Graham, Alan

1998 Quaternary North American Vegetational History. In *Late Cretaceous and Cenozoic History of North American Vegetation*, pp. 274-317. Oxford University Press, New York.

Gregg, Susan A., Keith W. Kintigh, and Robert Whallon

1991 Linking Ethnoarchaeological Interpretation and Archaeological Data: The Sensitivity of Spatial Analytical Methods to Postdepositional Disturbance. In *The Interpretation of Archaeological Spatial Patterning*, edited by Ellen M. Kroll and T. Douglas Price, pp. 149-196. Plenum Press, New York.

Gremillion, Kristen J.

1996 Diffusion and Adoption of Crops in Evolutionary Perspective. *Journal of Archaeology* 15:183-204.

1998 Changing Roles of Wild and Cultivated Plant Resources among Early Farmers of Eastern Kentucky. *Southeastern Archaeology* 17:140-157.

2002 Foraging Theory and Hypothesis Testing in Archaeology: An Exploration of Methodological Problems and Solutions. *Journal of Anthropological Archaeology* 21: 142-164.

Griffen, John W.

1962 Field Notes of the Russell Cave Archaeological Project, 1961-1962. Accession no. 342, vol. 4. On file at the Southeastern Archaeological Center, Tallahassee, Fl.

1974 *Investigations In Russell Cave.* Publications in Archaeology 13, National Park Service, U.S. Department of the Interior, Washington D.C.

Hall, Charles

1985 *The Role of Rockshelter Sites in Prehistoric Settlement Systems: An Example from Middle Tennessee.* Masters Thesis. Department of Anthropology, University of Tennessee, Knoxville.

Harpending, Henry and H. Davis

1977 Some Implications for Hunter-Gatherer Ecology Derived from the Spatial Structure of Resources. *World Archaeology* 8:275-286.

Hawkes, Kristen

1996 Foraging Difference Between Men and Women: Behavioral Ecology of the Sexual Division of Labor. In *The Archaeology of Human Ancestry: Power, Sex, and Tradition*, edited by James Steele and Stephen Shennan, pp. 283-305. Routledge, New York.

Hertz, Norman and E. Garrison

1998 *Geological Methods for Archaeology.* Oxford University Press, New York.

Hogue, Homes S.

1994 Human Skeletal Remains from Dust Cave. *Journal of Alabama Archaeology* 40:173-191.

2003 Bioarchaeology at Dust Cave, 1 Lu 496. Paper presented at the 60th annual meeting of the Southeastern Archaeology Conference, Charlotte, NC, November 12-15, 2003.

Hollenbach, Kandace D.

2005 Gathering in the Late Paleoindian and Early Archaic Periods in the Middle Tennessee River Valley, Northwest Alabama. Unpublished Ph.D. dissertation, Department of Anthropology, University of North Carolina, Chapel Hill.

2007 Gathering in the Late Paleoindian: Archaeobotanical Remains from Dust Cave, Alabama. In *Foragers of the Terminal Pleistocene*, edited by Renee B. Walker and Boyce N. Driskell, pp. 132-147. University of Nebraska Press, Lincoln.

2009 *Foraging in the Tennessee River Valley: 12,500 to 8,000 Years Ago.* University of Alabama Press, Tuscaloosa.

Holliday, Vance T. and William G. Gartner

2007 Methods of Soil P analysis in Archaeology. *Journal of Archaeological Science* 34:301-333.

Hollingsworth, Caryen Yeager

1991 Archaeology of Sheeps Bluff Shelter (1 Fr 324), Franklin Co., Alabama. *Journal of Alabama Archaeology* 37:1-155.

Homsey, Lara K.

2001 *Feature Variability in the Late Paleoindian and Early Archaic Components at Dust Cave, Al.* Paper presented at the 58th annual meeting of the Southeastern Archaeology Conference, Chattanooga.

2003a *Geochemical Characterization of Archaeological Sediments at Dust Cave, Alabama.* Master's Thesis. Department of Geology and Planetary Sciences, University of Pittsburgh, Pittsburgh.

2003b *Feature Function and Variability in the Early and Middle Archaic Components at Dust Cave.* Paper presented at the 60th annual meeting of the Southeastern Archaeology Conference, Charlotte.

2003c *The Spatial Organization of Dust Cave, Al.* Paper presented at the 68th Annual Meeting of the Society for American Archaeology, Milwaukee.
2004 The Form, Function and Organization of Anthropogenic Deposits at Dust Cave, Alabama. Unpublished Ph.D. dissertation, Department of Anthropology, University of Pittsburgh, Pittsburgh.
2009 The Identification and Prehistoric Selection Criteria of Fire-Cracked Rock: An Example from Dust Cave, Alabama. *Southeastern Archaeology* 28: 99-114.
2010 The Identification and Description of Prepared Clay Surfaces at Stanfield-Worley Bluff Shelter, Northwest Alabama. Manuscript on file, Department of Geosciences, Murray State University, Murray, Kentucky.

Homsey, Lara K. and Rosemary C. Capo
2006 Integrating Geochemistry and Micromorphology to Identify Feature Use at Dust Cave, a Paleoindian through Middle Archaic Site in Northwest Alabama. *Geoarchaeology* 21:237-269

Homsey, Lara K. and Sarah C. Sherwood
2010 The Role of Actualistic Studies and the Interpretation of Prepared Clay Surfaces. *Ethnoarchaeology: Journal of Archaeological, Ethnographic, and Experimental Studies* 2:73-98.

Homsey, Lara K., Renee B. Walker, and Kandace D. Hollenbach
2010 What's for Dinner? Investigating Food Processing Technologies at Dust Cave, Alabama. *Southeastern Archaeology* 29(1):in press.

Horn, H.S.
1968 The Adaptive Significance of Colonial Nesting in the Brewers Blackbird (Euhagus Cyanocephalus). *Ecology* 49:682:694.

Hudecek-Cuffe, Caroline R.
1998 *Engendering Northern Plains Paleoindian Archaeology: Decision Making and Gender Roles in Subsistence and Settlement Strategies.* BAR International Series 699, Oxford.

Hudson, Charles
1976 *The Southeastern Indians.* University of Tennessee Press, Knoxville.

Ingbar, Eric
1985a Analysis of Hidden Cave Feature Morphology. In *The Archaeology of Hidden Cave*, edited by David Hurst Thomas, pp. 307-321. Anthropological Papers of the American Museum of Natural History, vol. 61: Part I. New York.
1985b Spatial Analysis of Hidden Cave. In *The Archaeology of Hidden Cave*, edited by David Hurst Thomas, pp. 322-331. Anthropological Papers of the American Museum of Natural History, vol. 61: Part I. New York.

Jahren, A.H., Gabel, M.L., & Amundson, R.
1998 Biomineralization in Seeds; Developmental Trends in Isotopic Signatures of Hackberry. *Palaeogeography, Palaeoclimatology, Palaeoecology* 138: 259-269.

Jefferies, Richard W.
1982 The Black Earth Site. In *The Carrier Mills Archaeological Project: Human Adaptation in the Saline Valley, Illinois*, edited by Richard W. Jefferies and Brian M. Butler, pp. 77-451, Center for Archaeological Investigations, Research Paper 33, Southern Illinois University at Carbondale, Carbondale, Ill.
1987 *Carrier Mills*. Southern Illinois University Press, Carbondale.
1996 The Emergence of Long-Distance Exchange Networks in the Southeastern United States. In *The Paleoindian and Early Archaic Southeast*, edited by David G. Anderson and Kenneth E. Sassaman, pp. 222-234. University of Alabama Press, Tuscaloosa.
2008 *Holocene Hunter-Gatherers of the Lower Ohio River Valley*. University of Alabama Press, Tuscaloosa.

Jefferies, Richard W. and Brian M. Butler (editors)
1982 *The Carrier Mills Archaeological Project: Human Adaptation in the Saline Valley, Illinois*. Southern Illinois University at Carbondale, Center for Archaeological Investigations, Research Paper 33.

Jefferies, Richard W. and B. Mark Lynch
1985 Dimensions of Middle Archaic Cultural Adaptation at the Black Earth Site, Saline County, Illinois. In *Archaic Hunters and Gatherers in the American Midwest*, edited by James L. Phillips and James A. Brown, pp. 299-322. Academic Press, New York.

Jenkins, N.L.
1974 Subsistence and Settlement Patterns in the Western Middle Tennessee Valley During the Transitional Archaic-Woodland Period. *Journal of Alabama Archaeology* 20:183-193.

Johnson, Hunter B. and Scott C. Meeks
1994 Source Areas and Prehistoric Use of Fort Payne Chert. *Journal of Alabama Archaeology* 40:79-106.

Karkansas, P., M. Koumouzelis, J. Kozlowski, V. Sitlivy, K. Sobczyk, F. Berna, and S. Weiner
2004 The Earliest Evidence for Clay Hearths: Aurignacian Features in Klisoura Cave 1, Southern Greece. *Antiquity* 78:513-525.

Karkansas, Panagiotis, Ofer Bar Yosef, Paul Goldberg, and Steve Weiner
2000 Diagenesis in Prehistoric Caves: the Use of Minerals that Form In Situ to Assess the Completeness of the Archaeological Record. *Journal of Archaeological Science* 27:915-929.

Keeley, Lawrence
1980 *Experimental Determination of Stone Tool Use*. University of Chicago Press, Chicago.

Kelly, Robert L.
1983 Hunter-Gatherer Mobility Strategies. *Journal of Anthropological Research* 39: 277-306.

1995 *The Foraging Spectrum: Diversity in Hunter-Gatherer Lifeways.* Smithsonian Institution Press, Washington D.C.

Kelly, Robert L. and Lawrence C. Todd
1988 Coming into the Country: Early Paleoindian Hunting and Mobility. *American Antiquity* 53:231-244.

Kent, Susan
1984 *Analyzing Activity Areas: An Ethnoarchaeological Study of the Use of Space.* University of New Mexico Press, Albuquerque.
1987 Understanding the Use of Space: An Ethnoarchaeological Approach. In *Method and Theory for Activity Area Research*, edited by S. Kent, pp. 1-60. Columbia University Press, New York.
1991 The Relationship between Mobility Strategies and Site Structure. In *The Interpretation of Archaeological Spatial Patterning*, edited by Ellen M. Kroll and T. Douglas Price, pp. 33-60. Plenum Press, New York.
1999 The Archaeological Visibility of Storage: Delineating Storage from Trash Areas. *American Antiquity* 64:79-94.

Kintigh, K.W.
1990 Intrasite Spatial Analysis: A Commentary on Major Methods. In *Mathematics and Information Science in Archaeology: a Flexible Framework*, edited by A. Voorips, pp. 165-200. Studies in Modern Archaeology 3. Holos, Bonn.

Kintigh, K.W. and A.J. Ammerman
1982 Heuristic Approaches to Spatial Analysis in Archaeology. *American Antiquity* 47:31-63.

Nicholas, David and Carol Kramer
2001 *Ethnoarchaeology in Action.* Cambridge University Press, New York.

Lambert, Joseph B.
1997 *Traces of the Past*. Helix Books. Reading, Massachusetts.

Leitch, Roger and Christopher Tolan-Smith
1997 Archaeology and Ethnohistory of Cave Dwelling in Scotland. In *The Human Use of Caves*, edited by Clive Bonsall and Christopher Tolan-Smith, pp. 122-126. BAR International Series 667, Oxford.

Lewis, Barry R.
1983 Archaic Adaptations in the Illinois Prairie: The Salt Creek Region. In *Archaic Hunters and Gatherers in the American Midwest*, edited by James L. Phillips and James A. Brown, pp. 99-116. Academic Press, New York.

Leroi-Gourhan, A.
1976 Les Structures d'habitat au Paléolithique Supérieur. In *La Préhistoire Française*, edited by H. de Lumley, pp. 656-663. Tome 1. CNRS, Paris.

Lippi, R.D.
1988 Paleotopography and Phosphate Analysis of a Buried Jungle Site in Ecuador. *Journal of Field Archaeology* 15:85-97.

Logan, Wilfred D.
1952 *Graham Cave: An Archaic Site in Montgomery County, Missouri.* Missouri Archaeological Society Memoir No. 2, Columbia.

Lopinot, Neal H.
1984 *Archaeobotanical Formation Processes and Late Middle Archaic Human-Plant Interrelationships in the Midcontinental U.S.A.* Ph.D. dissertation, Southern Illinois University, Carbondale. University Microfilms, Ann Arbor.

Lowell, Julia C.
1999 The Fires of Grasshopper: Enlightening Transformations in Subsistence Practices through Fire-Feature Analysis. *Journal of Anthropological Archaeology* 18:441-470.

Malainey, Mary
2007 Analysis of the Fatty Acid Compositions of Residues form Archaeological Cave Features and Natural Cave Deposits and Experimental Residues. Unpublished MS, Department of Geosciences, Murray State University.

McMillian, Katherine E., Kandace D. Hollenbach, Renee B. Walker and Lara K. Homsey
2008 Gendered Perspectives on the Late Paleoindian at Dust Cave, Alabama. Manuscript on file, Department of Anthropology, University of Tennessee.

Macphail, R.I. and J. Cruise
2001 The Soil Micromorphologist as Team Player: A Multianalytical Approach to the Study of European Microstratigraphy. In *Earth Science and Archaeology*, edited by P. Goldberg, V.T. Holliday, and C. Reid Ferring, pp. 241-268. Kluwer Academic/Plenum Publishers, New York.

Macphail, R.I. and P. Goldberg
1995 Recent Advances in Micromorphological Interpretations of Soils and Sediments from Archeological Sites. In *Archaeological Sediments and Soils: Analysis, Interpretation and Management*, edited by A.J. Barham and R.I. Macphail, pp. 1-24. Institute of Archaeology, University College, London.

Macphail, R.I., J.C.C. Romans, and L. Roberson
1997 The Application of Micromorphology to the Understanding of Holocene Soil Development in the British Isles, with Special Reference to Holocene Cultivation. In *Proceedings of the International Working Meeting in Soil Micromorphology*, 7, edited by N. Fedoroff, L.M. Bresson, and M.A. Courty, pp. 647-656. Paris.

Manzanilla, Linda and Luis Barba
1990 The Study of Activities in Classic Households: Two Case Studies from Coba and Teotihuacán. *Ancient Mesoamerica*, 1:41-49.

Matthews, W.
1995 Micromorphological Characterization and Interpretation of Occupation Deposits and Microstratigraphic Sequences at Abu Salabikh, Southern Iraq. In *Archaeological Sediments and Soils: Analysis, Interpretation, and Management*, edited by A.J. Barham and R.I.

Macphail, pp. 41-74. Institute of Archaeology, London.

Matthews, W., C.A.I. French, T. Lawrence, D.F. Cutler, and M.K. Jones
1997 Microstratigraphic Traces of Site Formation Processes and Human Activities. *World Archaeology* 29:281-308.

Meeks, Scott C.
1994 Lithic Artifacts from Dust Cave. *Journal of Alabama Archaeology* 40:79-106.
1998 The Use and Function of Late Middle Archaic Projectile Points in the Midsouth. Masters Thesis. Department of Anthropology, University of Alabama, Tuscaloosa.
2001 Wandering Around Dust Cave: An Overview of Late Paleoindian and Early Archaic Settlement Patterns in the Middle Tennessee River Valley. Paper presented at the 58th annual meeting of the Southeastern Archaeology Conference, Chattanooga.
2003 Environmental Change and Cultural Process during the Middle Holocene: Middle Archaic Land-use in the Highland Rim of Northern Alabama. Paper presented at the 60th annual meeting of the Southeastern Archaeology Conference, Charlotte.

Meltzer, D.J. and B.D. Smith
1986 Paleo-Indian and Early Archaic Subsistence Strategies in Eastern North America. In *Foraging, Collecting, and Harvesting: Archaic Period Subsistence and Settlement in the Eastern Woodlands*, edited by S. Neusius, pp. 1-30. Center for Archaeological Investigations, Southern Illinois University, Carbondale.

Mickelson, Andrew M.
2002 Changes in Prehistoric Settlement Patterns as a Result of Shifts in Subsistence Practices of Eastern Kentucky. Unpublished Ph.D. Dissertation. Department of Anthropology, Ohio State University, Columbus.

Middleton, William D. and T. Douglas Price
1996 Identification of Activity Areas by Multi-element Characterization of Sediments form Modern and Archaeological House Floors Using Inductively Coupled Plasma-Atomic Emission Spectroscopy. *Journal of Archaeological Science* 23: 673-687.

Moeller, Roger W.
1992 *Analyzing and Interpreting Late Woodland Features*. Occasional Publications in Northeastern Anthropology, No. 12. Archaeological Services, Bethlehem, CT.

Morse, Dan F.
1973 Dalton Culture in Northeast Arkansas. *Florida Anthropologist* 26:23-38.
1975 Reply to Schiffer. In *The Cache River Archaeological Project: An Experiment in Contract Archaeology*, edited by B. Schiffer and J.J. House, pp. 113-120. Research Series 8, Arkansas Archaeological Survey, Fayetteville.
1997 An Overview of the Dalton Period in Northeastern Arkansas and in the Southeastern United States. In *Sloan: A Paleoindian Dalton Cemetery in Arkansas*, edited by Dan F. Morse, pp. 123-139. Smithsonian Institution Press, Washington, D.C.

Morse, Dan F., and Phyllis A. Morse
1983 *Archaeology of the Central Mississippi Valley*. Academic Press, New York.

Movius, H.L., Jr.
1975 *Excavation of the Abri Pataud, Les Eyzies (Dordogne)*, American School of Prehistoric Research, Bulletin 31. Harvard University, Cambridge, Ma.

Munson, Patrick J.
1986 What Happened in the Archaic in the Midwestern United States? *Reviews in Anthropology* 13:276-282.

Munson, Cheryl A. (editor)
1980 *Archaeological Salvage Excavations at Patoka Lake, Indiana: Prehistoric Occupations of the Upper Patoka River Valley*. Glenn Black Laboratory of Archaeology, Research Reports 6.

Neusius, Sarah W.
1982 *Early-Middle Archaic Subsistence Strategies: Changes in Faunal Exploitations at the Koster Site*. Ph.D. dissertation, Department of Anthropology, Northwestern Unviersity.

Newland, H. Osman
1919 *The Planting, Cultivation and Expression of Coconuts, Kernels, Cacao and Edible Vegetable Oils and Seeds of Commerce*. Charles Griffin & Company, London.

Nicholson, Annie and Scott Cane
1991 Desert Camps: Analysis of Australian Aboriginal Proto-historic Campsites. In *Ethnoarchaeological Approaches to Mobile Campsites*, edited by C.S. Gamble and W.A. Broismier, pp. 263-253. International Monographs in Prehistory, Ann Arbor, Michigan.

Panter-Brick, Catherine
2002 Sexual Division of Labor: Energetic and Evolutionary Scenarios. *American Journal of Human Biology* 14:627-640.

Parmalee, Paul W.
1994 Freshwater Mussels from Dust and Smith Bottom Caves, Alabama. *Journal of Alabama Archaeology* 40:135-162.

Parnell, J.J., Terry, R.E., & Golden, C.
2001 Using in-field phosphate testing to rapidly identify middens at Piedras Negras, Guatemala. *Geoarchaeology* 16:855-873.

Pearsall, Deborah M.
2000 *Paleoethnobotany: a Handbook of Procedures*. San Diego: Academic Press.

Pétrequin, A.M. and P. Pétrequin
1988 Ethnoarchaéologie de l'Habitat en Grotte de Nouvelle-Guinée: une Transposition de l'Espace Social et Economique. Bulletin du Centre Genevois d'Anthropologie 1, 61-82.

Pierce, Christopher, K.R. Adams, and J.D. Steward

1998 Determining the Fuel Constituents of Ancient Hearth Ash Via ICP-AES Analysis. *Journal Archaeological Science* 25:493-503.

Pike, Meta G.
2003 Comparing Feature Types from a Middle Archaic Component at Dust Cave. Paper presented at the 60th annual meeting of the Southeastern Archaeology Conference, Charlotte.

Pike, Meta G., Kandace D. Hollenbach, and Lara K. Homsey
2005 Changing Patterns in Plant Use and Processing Technologies at Dust Cave, Alabama. Poster presented at the 70th Annual Meeting of the Society for American Archaeology, Salt Lake City.

Pollard, Mark A. and Carl Heron
1996 *Archaeological Chemistry*. The Royal Society of Chemistry, Cambridge.

Quine, T.A.
1995 Soil Analysis and Archaeological Site Formation. In *Archaeological Sediments and Soils: Analysis, Interpretation and Management*, edited by A.J. Barham and R.I. Macphail, pp. 77-98. Institute of Archaeology, University College, London.

Randall, Asa R.
2001 Untangling Late Paleoindian and Early Side Notched Stone Tool Assemblages at Dust Cave, Alabama. Paper presented at the 58th annual meeting of the Southeastern Archaeology Conference, Chattanooga.

2002 Technofuntional Variation in Early Side-Notched Stone Hafted Bifaces: A View from the Middle Tennessee River Valley in Northwest Alabama. Unpublished Masters Thesis, Department of Anthropology, University of Florida, Gainesville.

2003 Archaic Technological Practice at Dust Cave. Paper presented at the 60th annual meeting of the Southeastern Archaeology Conference, Charlotte.

Randall, Asa R. and Kandace R. Detwiler
2002 Reinvestigating Stanfield-Worley Bluff Shelter. Paper presented at the 60th Annual Meeting of the Southeastern Archaeological Conference, Charlotte.

Raymond, D.E., Osborne, W.E., Copeland, C.W., & Neathery, T.L.
1988 *Alabama Stratigraphy*, Circular 140. Geological Survey of Alabama Tuscaloosa.

Redfield, Alden and John H. Moselage
1970 The Lace Place, a Dalton Project Site in the Western Lowlands in Eastern Arkansas. *Arkansas Archaeologist* 11:21-44.

Rigaud, J.
1982 *Le Paléolithique en Périgord*. Ph.D. Dissertation, Université de Bordeaux I, Bordeaux.

Rigaud, Jean Philippe and Jan F. Simek
1991 Interpreting Spatial Patterns at the Grotte XV: A Multiple-Method Approach. In *The Interpretation of Archaeological Spatial Patterning*, edited by Ellen M. Kroll and T. Douglas Price, pp. 199-220. Plenum Press, New York.

Rosenthal, Harold L.
1981 Content of Stable Strontium in Man and Animal Biota. In *The Handbook of Stable Strontium*, edited by S. Skornya, pp. 503-513. Plenum Press, New York.

Russo, Michael
1996 Southeastern Archaic Mounds. In *Archaeology of the Mid-Holocene Southeast*, edited by Kenneth E. Sassaman and David G. Anderson, pp. 259-287. University of Florida Press, Gainesville.

Sánchez, A., & Cañabate, M.L.
1999 Identification of Activity Areas by Soil Phosphorus and Organic Matter Analysis in Two Rooms of the Iberian Sanctuary "Cerro El Pajarillo." *Geoarchaeology* 14:47-62.

Sandor, Jonathan A.
1992 Long-term Effects of Prehistoric Agriculture on Soils. In *Soils in Archaeology*, pp. 217-246, edited by Vance Holliday. Smithsonian Institution Press, Washington D.C.

Saraydar, Stephen C.
2008 Replicating the Past: The Art and Science of the Archaeological Experiment. Waveland Press, Long Grove, Il.

Sassaman, Kenneth E.
1993 *Early Pottery in the Southeast*. University of Alabama Press, Tuscaloosa.

Sassaman, K.E. and D.A. Anderson
1996 *The Paleoindian and Early Archaic Southeast*. University of Alabama Press, Tuscaloosa.

Schuldenrein, Joseph
1995 *Geochemistry, Phosphate Fractionation, and the Detection of Activity Areas at Prehistoric North American Sites*. In Pedological Perspectives in Archaeological Research, edited by Mary E. Collins and others, pp. 107-132, Soil Science Society of America special publication, v. 44.

2001 Stratigraphy, Sedimentology, and Site Formation at Konispol Cave, Southwest Albania. *Geoarchaeology* 16:559-602.

Schiegl, Sloveig, Paul Goldberg, Ofer Bar-Yosef, and Steve Weiner
1996 Ash Deposits in Hayonim and Kebara Caves, Israel: Macroscopic, Microscopic and Mineralogical Observations, and Their Archaeological Interpretations. *Journal of Archaeological Science* 23:763-781.

Schiffer, Michael B.
1975 Some Further Comments on the Dalton Settlement Pattern Hypothesis. In *The Cache River Archaeological Project: an Experiment in Contract Archaeology*, edited by B. Schiffer and J.J. House, pp. 103-112. Research Series 8. Arkansas Archaeological Survey, Fayetteville.

1987 *Formation Processes of the Archaeological Record*. University of Utah Press, Salt Lake City.

Schroedl, Gerald F.
1986 *Overhill Cherokee Archaeology at Chota-Tanasee*. University of Tennessee Department of Anthropology Report of Investigations 38. Knoxville.

Semenov, S.A.
1964 *Prehistoric Technology*. Barnes and Nobel, New York.

Sherard, H.
1977 *Soil Survey of Lauderdale County, Alabama*. United States Department of Agriculture, Soil Conservation Service, Washington D.C.

Sherwood, Sarah C.
2001 The Geoarchaeology of Dust Cave: A Late Paleoindian Through Middle Archaic Site in the Western Middle Tennessee River Valley. Unpublished Ph.D. Dissertation. Department of Anthropology, University of Tennessee, Knoxville.

Sherwood, Sarah C. and Jefferson Chapman
2003 Prepared Clay Surfaces at Dust Cave and Icehouse Bottom. Poster Presented at the 68th Annual Meeting of the Society for American Archaeology, Milwaukee.

Sherwood, Sarah C. and Paul Goldberg
2001 A Geoarchaeological Framework for the Study of Karst Cave Sites in North America. *Midcontinental Journal of Archaeology* 26:145-168.

Sherwood, Sarah C. and Jefferson Chapman
2005 The Identification and Potential Significance of Early Holocene Prepared Clay Surfaces: Examples from Dust Cave and Icehouse Bottom. *Southeastern Archaeology* 24: 70-82.

Sherwood, Sarah C., Boyce N. Driskell, Asa R. Randall, and Scott C. Meeks
2004 Chronology and Stratigraphy at Dust Cave, Alabama. *American Antiquity* 69: 533-554.

Simek, Jan.
1984 *A K-Means Approach to the Analysis of Spatial Structure in Upper Paleolithic Habitation Sites: Le Flageolet and Pincevent 36*. British Archaeological Reports, Oxford.

Skibo, James M.
2009 Archaeological Theory and Snake-Oil Peddling: The Role of Ethnoarchaeology in Archaeology. *Ethnoarchaeology* 1:27-56.

Smith, Craig S. and L.M. McNees
1999 Facilities and Hunter-Gatherer Long-Term Land Use Patterns: An Example from Southwest Wyoming. *American Antiquity* 64:117-136.

Stafford, C. Russell
1991 Archaic Period Logistical Foraging Strategies in West-Central Illinois. *Midcontinental Journal of Archaeology* 16:212-245.

1994 Structural Changes in Archaic Landscape Use in Dissected Uplands of Southwestern Indiana. *American Antiquity* 59:219-237.

Stein, Julie K.
1987 *Deposits for Archaeologists. Advances in Archaeological Method and Theory* 1:337-395.

1985 Interpreting sediments in Cultural Settings. In *Archaeological Sediments in Context*, edited by J.K. Stein and W.R. Farrand, pp. 5-19. Centre for the Study of Early Man, Orono, Me.

Stevenson, Marc G.
1991 Beyond the Formation of Hearth-Associated Artifact Assemblages. In *The Interpretation of Archaeological Spatial Patterning*, edited by Ellen M. Kroll and T. Douglas Price, pp. 269-300. Plenum Press, New York.

Stoops, Georges
2003 *Guidelines for Analysis and Description of Soil and Regolith Thin Sections*. Soil Science Society of America, Madison, Wisconsin.

Straus, Lawrence Guy
1997 Convenient Cavities: Some Human Uses of Caves and Rockshelters. In *The Human Use of Caves*, edited by Clive Bonsall and Christopher Tolan-Smith pp. 1-8. BAR International Series 667, Oxford.

1991 Underground Archaeology: Perspectives on Caves and Rockshelters. In *Archaeological Method and Theory*, edited by M.B. Schiffer, vol. 2, pp. 255-304. University of Arizona Press, Tucson.

Straus, L. and G. Clark
1986 *La Riera Cave*. Anthropological Research Papers No 36. Arizona State University, Tempe, Az.

Straus, L.G., B.V. Eriksn, J.M. Erlandson and D.R. Yesner
1996 *Humans at the End of the Ice Age: The Archaeology of the Pleistocene-Holocene Transition*. Plenum Press, New York.

Struever, Stuart and F.A. Holton
1979 *Koster: Americans in Search of Their Prehistoric Past*. Doubleday, New York.

Styles, Bonnie W., Steven R. Ahler, and Melvin L. Fowler
1983 Modoc Rock Shelter Revisited. In *Archaic Hunters and Gatherers in the American Midwest*, edited by James L. Phillips and James A. Brown, pp. 261-297. Academic Press, New York.

Talalay, L. D.R. Keller and P.J. Munson
1984 Hickory Nuts, Walnuts, Butternuts, and Hazelnuts: Observations and Experiments Relevant to Aboriginal Exploitation. In *Experiments and Observations on Aboriginal Wild Plant Utilization in Eastern North America*, edited by P.J. Munson, pp. 338-359. Indiana Historical Society Prehistory Research Series, vol. 6, no. 2. Indianapolis.

Teller, James T., David W. Leverington, and Jason D. Mann
2002 Freshwater Outbursts to the Oceans from Glacial Lake Agassiz and Their Role in Climate Change during the last Deglaciation. *Quaternary Science Reviews* 21:879-887.

Terry, R.E., P. Hardin, S. Houston, S. Nelson, M. Jackson, J. Carr, and J. Parnell.

1999 Quantitative Phosphorus Measurement: a Field Test Procedure for Archaeological Site Analysis at Piedras Negras Guatemala. *Geoarchaeology* 15:151-166.

Thomas, David Hurst
1985 *The Archaeology of Hidden Cave*. Anthropological Papers of the American Museum of Natural History, vol. 61: Part I. New York.
1988 *The Archaeology of Monitor Valley: 3. Survey and Additional Excavations*. Anthropological Papers of the American Museum of Natural History, Volume 66: Part 2, New York.

Thomas, William.
1972 *Mississippian Stratigraphy of Alabama*. Monograph 12, University of Alabama, Tuscaloosa.

Thompson, R.S., K.H. Anderson, and P.J. Bartlein
1999 *Atlas of Relations Between Climatic Parameters and Distributions of Important Trees and Shrubs in North America*. United States Geologic Survey, Reston, Virginia.

Tykot, R.H. and S.M.M. Young
1996 Archaeological Applications of Inductively Coupled Plasma-Mass Spectrometry. In *Archaeological Chemistry: Organic, Inorganic, and Biochemical Analysis*, edited by Mary Virginia Orna, pp. 116-130. American Chemical Society, Washington D.C.

Vento, Frank J.
1985 *The Geology and Geoarchaeology of the Bay Springs Rockshelters, Tishomingo County, Mississippi*. Ph.D. Dissertation, Department of Geology and Planetary Science, University of Pittsburgh, Pittsburgh.

Wadley, Lynn
2000 The Use of Space in a Gender Study of two South African Stone Age Sites. In *Gender and Material Culture in Archaeological Perspective*, edited by W. Donald and L. Huncambe, pp. 153-168. St. Martins Press, New York.

Walker, Renee B.
1998 The Late Paleoindian through Middle Archaic Faunal Remains from Dust Cave, Alabama. Unpublished Ph.D. Dissertation. Department of Anthropology, University of Tennessee, Knoxville.
2000 Subsistence Strategies at Dust Cave: Changes from the Late Paleoindian through Middle Archaic Occupations. Report of Investigations 78. Office of Archaeological Research, University of Alabama Museums, Moundville, Al.
2001 Refining Our Understanding of Subsistence Strategies at Dust Cave: An Analysis of a Recently Excavated Late Paleoindian Faunal Sample. Paper presented at the 58th Annual Meeting of the Southeastern Archaeological Conference, Chattanooga.
2007 Hunting in the Late Paleoindian Period: Faunal Remains from Dust Cave. In *Foragers of the Terminal Pleistocene in North America*, edited by Renee B. Walker and Boyce N. Driskell, pp. 99-115. University of Nebraska Press, Lincoln.

Walker, Renee B., Kandace R. Detwiler, Scott C. Meeks, and Boyce N. Driskell
2001 Berries, Bones, and Blades: Reconstructing Late Paleoindian Subsistence Economy at Dust Cave, Alabama. *Midcontinental Journal of Archaeology* 26:169-195.

Walker, Renee B., Lara K. Homsey, and Kandace D. Hollenbach
2007 Investigation Archaeological Correlates for Food Processing at Dust Cave Alabama. Paper presented at the 64th Annual Meeting of the Southeastern Archaeological Conference, Knoxville.

Walker Renee B, Darcy F. Morey and John H. Relethford
2005 Early and Mid-Holocene Dogs in Southeastern North America: Examples from Dust Cave. *Southeastern Archeology* 24:83-92.

Walker, Renee B. and Paul W. Parmalee
2004 A Noteworthy Cache of Goose Humeri from Late Paleoindian Levels at Dust Cave, Northwestern Alabama. *Journal of Alabama Archaeology* 50:18-35.

Walthall, John A.
1980 *Prehistoric Indians of the Southeast: Archaeology of Alabama and the Middle South*. University of Alabama Press, Tuscaloosa.
1998a Rockshelters and Hunter-Gatherer Adaptation to the Pleistocene/Holocene Transition. *American Antiquity* 63:223-238.
1998b Overwinter Strategy and Early Holocene Hunter-Gatherer Mobility in Temperate Forests. *Midcontinental Journal of Archaeology* 23:1-22

Wandsnider, LuAnn
1997 The Roasted and the Boiled: Food Consumption and Heating with Special Emphasis on Pit-Hearth Cooking. *Journal of Anthropological Archaeology* 16:1-48.

Wandsnider, LuAnn and Fateh Singh Sodha
1997 *Pit Hearth Heat Transfer*. Paper presented at the 62nd annual meeting of the Society for American Archaeology, Nashville.

Ward, H. Tarwick
1985 Social Implications of Storage and Disposal Patterns. In *Structure and Process in Southeastern Archaeology*, edited by Roy S. Dickens, Jr. and H. Tarwick Ward, pp. 60-81. University of Alabama Press, Tuscaloosa.

Wattez, J. and M.A. Courty
1987 Morphology of Plant Materials. In *Soil Micromorphology*, edited by N. Fedoroff, L.M. Bresson and M.A. Courty, pp. 677-683. AFES, Plaisir, France.

Webb, W.S
1974 *Indian Knoll*. University of Tennessee Press, Knoxville.

Webb, Thompson, III, Patrick J. Bartlein, Sandy P. Harrison, and Katherine H. Anderson
1993 Vegetation, Lake Levels, and Climate in Eastern North America for the Past 18,000 Years. In *Global Climates since the Last Glacial Maximum*, edited by

H.E. Wright, Jr., J.E. Kutzbach, T. Webb, III, W.F. Ruddiman, F.A. Street-Perrott, and P.J. Bartlein, pp. 415-467. University of Minnesota Press, Minneapolis.

Wells, E.C., Terry, R.E., Parnell, J.J., Hardin, P.J., Jackson, M.W., & Houston, S.D.
2000   Chemical Analyses of Ancient Anthrosols in Residential Areas at Piedras Negras, Guatemala. *Journal of Archaeological Science* 27:449-462.

Whallon, Robert E.
1973   Spatial Analysis of Occupation Floors: the Application of Dimensional Analysis of Variance. *American Antiquity* 38:266-278.
1984   Unconstrained Clustering for the Analysis of Spatial Distribution in Archaeology. In *Intrasite Spatial Analysis in Archaeology*, edited by H. Hietala, pp. 242-277. Cambridge University Press, Cambridge.

Wilmsen, E.N.
1973   Interaction, Spacing Behavior, and the Organization of Hunting Bands. *Journal of Anthropological Research* 29:1-31.

Wilson, Jack H., Jr.
1985   Feature Zones and Feature Fill: More than Trash. In *Structure and Process in Southeastern Archaeology*, edited by Roy S. Dickens, Jr. and H. Tarwick Ward, pp. 34-59. University of Alabama Press, Tuscaloosa.

Wolynec, Renata Bohdanna
1977   The Systematic Analysis of Features from the Koster Site, a Stratified Archaic Site. Unpublished Ph.D. Dissertation. Department of Anthropology, Northwestern University, Evanston, Illinois.

Wood, W. Raymond and R. Bruce McMillan
1976   *Prehistoric Man and His Environments: A Case Study in the Ozark Highland*. Academic Press, New York.

www.ingramcontent.com/pod-product-compliance
Lightning Source LLC
Chambersburg PA
CBHW041708290426
44108CB00027B/2894